"Hannah is one of those food voices (in a world of countless food voices) that stops you in your tracks. That's exactly what happened to me a couple of years ago when I first stumbled upon her cooking videos, which showcase not just her affinity for true Southern comfort food but also her warm, endearing personality and her genuine home cook point of view. Hannah's recipes are simple but refined, familiar but fresh, and this book is an open window into her creative mind, Southern soul, and generous heart. If you're looking for recipes that not only work but also wow, you will absolutely love this cookbook!"

—REE DRUMMOND, the Pioneer Woman

"Hannah's videos make the world a better place, and that's how I felt after reading this gorgeous book. It's like having a favorite family member or old friend right there in the kitchen with you. She has such a fresh voice, and her take on cooking and life is encouraging, uplifting, funny, honest, and comforting. I promise that you are going to want to make everything in this book. I know I do, and I can't wait to cook my way through it. I hope I get to spend time with Hannah in her kitchen someday. Maybe I can even snag an invite to the holiday tequila thing at Aunt Teisha's!"

—MARTINA McBRIDE, country music icon and cookbook author

MEASURE *with* YOUR HEART

MEASURE with YOUR HEART

Southern Home Cooking to
Feed Your Family & Soul

HANNAH TAYLOR

Photographs by Rinne Allen

Clarkson Potter/Publishers
New York

To my beautiful children, who always inspire me to be the best version of myself, and give me the courage to pursue my dreams to inspire them.

Contents

INTRODUCTION . . . 9
HOW TO MEASURE WITH YOUR HEART . . . 18
KITCHEN CONFIDENCE ('Cause Confidence Is Sexy) . . . 21

❖ Homemade Kitchen Staples

Vanilla Extract 33

B & B Twofer:
Butter & Buttermilk 34

Start Me Up Lazy
Sourdough Starter 37

All-Purpose Seasoning 38

Apple Cider Vinegar 41

Never Go Back to
Store-Bought Mayonnaise 42

Zesty Mustard 45

Dill Me a Pickle Relish 46

Homemade Fresh Cheese 49

Pasta Dough & Noodles 50

Beef Bone Broth 53

Chicken Bone Broth 54

❖ Kids & Pups

Cinnamon Toasted
Cereal Squares 58

Let's Get Saucy
Cranberry Applesauce 61

Fruity Roll 'em Ups 62

Bluegurt Ice Pops 65

Buck's Poppin' Tarts 66

Lil's Chick Nuggs 71

Luke the Duke's Corn Dogs . . . 72

Rookie's Cookies
(Homemade Dog Treats) 75

❖ Breakfast

Savory

Baked Cheesy
Garlic Grits 79

Sweet Meets Spicy
Supreme Omelet 80

Hahira Breakfast Cups 83

Sunrise Quiche 85

Breakfast Hash
Croissant Sandwiches 90

Chicken & Waffles 93

Sweet

Soufflé French Toast
Casserole 97

Mixed Berry Scones 98

Hoe Cakes with
Cranberry Jam &
Powdered Sugar 101

Sour Cream Vanilla
Coffee Cake 102

Cranberry-Orange
Cinnamon Rolls with
Lemon Glaze 104

Apple Cinnamon
Strudels 107

Whipped Chocolate
Ganache Donuts 109

❖ Snacks, Apps & Sides

Aunt Teisha's Cowboy Caviar . . 114

Smoked Salmon Dip 117

Mama's Classic
Fried Deviled Eggs 118

Fry Me a River,
Corny Fritters! 121

Loaded-Up Potato Skins 122

Hot, Sweet & Sexy Wings . . . 125

Spring Creek Boat Rolls 126

Mini Pizza Pies 129

Bebop's Sweet Bacon
Collard Greens 131

Smokin' Honey Bacon
Green Beans 132

The Absolute Best
Sweet Potatoes 135

Ultimate Mashed Potatoes . . 136

❖ Mains

Meat & Seafood

Mama's Chicken Pot Pie 141

Butter-Roasted Chicken 145

Good Ole Fish Tacos 146

Jazzy Jambalaya 149

Sloppy James 150

Finger Lickin' Fried Chicken . . 153

Chicken Fried Steak
with Gravy. 157

Mary's Meatloaf 158

Slow Cooker BBQ Ribs 161

My Go-To Pot Roast 162

James's Smash Burgers 165

Casseroles & Pastas

You Butter Believe
Butternut Squash Casserole . . 167

BBQ Pineapple
Chicken Bake 168

Chicken & Rice Casserole. . . 171

Crispy Creamy
Mac 'n' Cheese 172

Sauced Up
Shrimp Linguine 175

Scalloped Potatoes
& Ham Casserole 176

Lover's Lasagna 178

Soups & Stews

Knock-Out Ham Hock
Lima Bean Soup 183

Nice & Creamy Crab Bisque . . 184

Won't Make You Cry
Onion Soup 187

Cream of Mushroom Soup . . 188

Chicken & Dumplings
for My Dumplin' 191

First Night Chili 193

Damn Good
Chicken Gumbo 197

Slow Cooker
Brunswick Stew. 198

❖ Biscuits, Breads & Rolls

Classic Biscuits &
Milk Sausage Gravy 204

Cinnamon Raisin Biscuits . . . 208

Southern Sweet Cornbread
with Honey Butter 213

Butter My Rolls. 214

Cheddar Jalapeño Bagels . . . 217

Flaky & Fluffy Croissants . . . 219

Homemade Sandwich Bread . . 222

My Favorite
Sourdough Loaf. 224

Cheesy & Herby
Dutch Oven Bread 228

❖ Drinks

Homebrewed
Blueberry Wine 232

Strawberry Sip 'n' Spritz. . . . 234

Bushwacker. 237

Sweetie's Sweet Iced Tea . . . 238

Twang, Tang & Tart
Lemonade 241

Fizzy Cranberry Punch. 242

Hannah's Famous
Hot Chocolate 245

❖ Desserts

Cookies, Candies & More

Classic Peanut Brittle 248

Divinity "Kiss Me" Candy . . . 251

Mama's Oatmeal Raisin
Cookies 252

Chocolate Date Caramel
Brownies 255

Apple Cinnamon
Bread Pudding 256

Cobblers & Cakes

Midnight's Blackberry
Dumplings 259

Sexy 'n' Spicy Peach
Pecan Cobbler 260

Lily's Poppy Stems 263

Blue Ridge S'more
Cupcakes 266

Pineapple Upside-Down
Cake 269

Citrus Pound Cake 271

Georgia Peach Cheesecake . . 275

Indie Lou's Blueberry Cake . . 277

ACKNOWLEDGMENTS **281**
INDEX **282**

Introduction

I didn't grow up in the kitchen. Food was not my community's love language. But my "off the land," free-spirited childhood in the Georgia woods shaped the homey person and cook I've become, and the person my new community has gotten to know over the last few years.

I come from working-class people, factory workers, and avid Pizza Hut–goers. My Mama, dad, brother, and me had our mobile home parked behind my grandpa's (Papa's) log cabin, and when he and my dad went into mechanics together, part of the property slowly turned into a junkyard—and a playground for me. If my fingernails didn't have dirt under them at the end of the day, I had to have been sick in bed.

When I wasn't messing around near those cars, I was frolicking all over my grandparents' property in southeast Georgia, in a little town nicknamed "Nash Vegas" (because everyone there acts like me—can you even imagine??). It was a little farm built by my dad and Papa. They had chickens, goats, dogs, pigs. Papa and my Granny Mary loved to garden. But despite being surrounded by beautiful greens, homegrown fruits, and farm animals, the people in my life didn't cook much. All the adults were working long hours, so convenience and thrift for our meals were everything. My Mama swore by her Crock-Pot for dinners. Most of my days consisted of someone throwing peanut butter and jelly on bread and sending me on my merry way until the evening. I was raised on processed, packaged, chemical products we bought from the grocery store. But at times, Granny did surprise me with her biscuits. And when she did, taking a flaky, buttery bite filled my whole body with warmth. I could feel her love in all her baking.

I remember watching Granny cook on sunny mornings when she wasn't at work, the house smelling of wood, and mechanic's grease on every surface (even the kitchen counter). When I could finally pull myself up onto my Granny's high barstools, I would go into a trance, completely enamored with the wrinkles on her hands rolling around as she worked the biscuit dough. Her motions, how she played with the dough, felt very old and fragile. There was something almost nostalgic about it. Like even at my young age I knew she had watched her mother do it the same way. I was mesmerized by her elegance and the dance she did with the ingredients. How it all went from just flour, butter, and buttermilk to something as complex and full of different textures as a biscuit. When she'd find me staring intently, we would laugh as if I got caught doing something sneaky. The memory makes me feel so much love today, and it's no wonder biscuits were one of the first recipes I made myself.

I was a wild child in that I always had my own way of doing things regardless of what I was told I was "supposed" to do; the outdoors helped satisfy that desire to learn hands on. I hated the curriculum and structure at school, but I loved band and dancing (surprise, surprise). I enjoyed the arts and things that weren't taught so much as *experienced.* I loved that aspect about myself and I feel proud that I've always stayed true to that trait.

Years later, I got out of my first, abusive marriage and I needed to support me and my daughter, Lily, but I didn't want a career that would take away from my free-spiritedness and love for myself. I wanted my baby to grow up watching her mom do what she enjoyed, no matter the circumstances. I owned a good professional camera and decided to take it seriously; I was mentored by local photographers in all sorts of genres: portraits, weddings, nature—you name it. For many years, photography was my main source of income and inspiration. Eventually I would become a mentor to others and launch my own wedding and elopement photography business. It made me realize that it's possible to support yourself, have structure, *and* find purpose and beauty in what you do. I'm so grateful Lily got to see that, too.

After I left my first marriage, I was single for a *long* time. I had pretty much given up on dating. I dabbled a bit in my early 30s, but let me tell you, it was some nonsense out there. But on Thanksgiving in 2019, I was over at my Aunt Teisha's, doing our holiday tequila thing, and her son suggested I try Tinder. I had a couple more tequilas (and an edible) and later that evening I thought, "Screw it, I'll try it." James was one of the first profiles I saw that night. We texted for one week straight. I didn't want Lily to know I was dating yet, so we kept it quiet. I was so into him, though, and I had to make sure he wasn't a complete weirdo before I got in too deep. So I FaceTimed him and told him we were just going to stare into each other's eyes and he's not allowed to say anything to me. I swear we both fell in love on that video call. James came over to my house for our first date a few days later, and he never left. A week later we were engaged. Three weeks later we were married, in early 2020. Lily got new siblings when we had two beautiful children together, Buck and Indie Lou.

Before I became a mother, I had been known to make a slow-cooker meal or two (I love a Brunswick stew), but I wasn't all that interested in getting into the kitchen. I was still eating all the food I had grown up on, like boxed macaroni and cheese, store-bought bread, and jarred mayonnaise. But as a mother I began cooking for necessity. My kids' well-being and health means everything to me, and I started to get curious about what I was feeding them. Let me tell you, I was not happy with the information I was finding: ingredients twenty letters long I couldn't even begin to pronounce. Bread made with two dozen chemicals when really it should just be wheat, salt, and yeast. And if it felt scary putting that stuff into my adult body, I got even more freaked out about those preservatives going into their tiny, growing bodies.

I decided we should all be eating better and cleaner—which doesn't always have to mean the food is "healthy." (I love my desserts and carbs, and if I had my way, we'd eat fried chicken five times a week.) But our food should be made from scratch, so I know exactly what's in it. And with that decision, I went from cooking just once in a while to being the main source of my family's nutrition. I was now making my own sandwich bread, the macaroni and cheese from scratch, and my own mayonnaise, as well as all the classics I grew up on, like chicken pot pie, and some new dishes of my own invention.

As I spent more time in the kitchen, I started to feel more joy. I wanted to grow as a cook and flex my creativity. So I dabbled with homemade projects like freshly baked biscuits, and I sent photos to my friends showing off my little creations. Eventually, my dear friend Preston suggested I stop sending them to him and instead share what I was doing with more people on a platform everyone had just started using, called TikTok. So just for fun, James and I hopped on that train. Since it started with my need to feed my kids better, I chose the name "LilyLouTay," combining my girls into my handle. (Sorry, Buck! "LilyLouBuck" just didn't sound quite right, but the Tay is all you, baby.) With my background in photography and videography, using a camera was second nature for me.

I started uploading videos documenting the process of cooking recipes I'd made before and some new ones that were pure experimentation (which, frankly, most of my recipes are). The response to the videos was overwhelmingly positive. Within a year, I had over a million followers. I moved over to Instagram, started my website, a newsletter, and my online family just kept growing and growing. I'm not sure if it's the Southern hospitality, my wild personality, or the chaotic cooking, but people were rushing to see what I was sharing. The response was, and still is, mind-blowing to me. But it also made me realize how many people I was affecting and teaching, all while doing what I love and being inspired every day. I think seeing my mistakes in the kitchen was such a relief to people. It gave them permission to get in there, too. I am truly so blessed to get to do what I do, and to help people find their creativity.

I think my cooking style stems from growing up in a place where holidays were more about coming together for the drinks than for the cuisine. It was about the experience rather than the food, about gathering and having a fun time *around* food, despite eating whatever was thrown in a pot to fill our bellies (and soak up the booze). There was no pressure to make perfect meals, and that contributed to my free-spiritedness in the kitchen. The videos where you see me trying things out, using my intuition, and getting my hands dirty are the ones my viewers love the most. And I get it. When I see a recipe with "¾ teaspoon of this" and "1 tablespoon plus 1 teaspoon of that," I just kind of shut down. That's intimidating! It's certainly not welcoming. Give me "a pinch of this" and "add that till you're happy" any day. I know what I like, you know what you like, and all we can do is feel our way to deliciousness in the kitchen.

I live my life just like I cook in the kitchen. I trust my judgment, do what feels good, and try things out. That's what I wanted to collect in one place, in this book. *Measure with Your Heart* means trusting your internal voice and intuition to craft in the chaos. I learn as I go, and that's the main message I want to leave you with as you read my cookbook. It's not about being perfect and making something to show off; rather, it's about the fun and playfulness of creating something from a few raw ingredients, and nourishing the ones you love. Go ahead and mess up! Who cares? Every time you get in the kitchen you'll learn more and get a little better, I promise. And a meal is never *really* inedible (unless your chicken is raw, but that's an easy fix—just throw it back on the stove).

In being unapologetically unpolished and eye-balling a lot of recipes, I hope to bring a sense of comfort and acceptance to readers, especially now in a world where so much of what you see is fabricated and negative—or even worse, perfect. I've tried to make my videos and writing a place for more than just recipes; it's also a place that brings people together. It's nice to be reminded to stop and enjoy the sweets if they make you feel good and warm your soul. If you've had a bad day and want some extra sugar, throw it in there! Feeling confident and bold? Add that extra seasoning. You are sexy and amazing just as you are, and don't let any hang-ups stop you from being your best self—in the kitchen and in all of your life.

I want to encourage people to see cooking as a way of appreciating themselves and embracing what feels good. It took me a very long time to learn to love myself, and I'm here to help every single person join me there. It's okay to sing and dance, to feel confident in your skin. When you read my cookbook, I want you to feel like you're getting a big bear hug from me. It's a nice change of pace—to be reminded that not being perfect *is* perfect, that trying things out based on intuition rather than a rigid guideline is freeing, and that being true to your inner child feeds a confidence and beauty we all have within ourselves. That's why I've thrown the measurements out where I can, and I share with you my favorite experiments and my unapologetic taste. I like my cake more like a brownie, my seasonings to be extremely generous, and my butter to always be salted. These recipes are exactly who *I* am.

And these 100 recipes—oooooh, I just know you're going to love them. They're what I cook every day, for every meal. My style of cooking is a mix of the Southern standards I grew up on and the new, quicker dishes me and James have come up with that satisfy all five of us. In between breakfast and dinner, I got you covered with my favorite snacks and drinks. For more wholesome cooking, I also include all the homemade ingredients and versions of our store-bought favorites we use daily. I've got pantry staples from condiments like Zesty Mustard (page 45) to the Beef Bone Broth (page 53) I use in, well, everything. There are breads for all your carby needs, including My Favorite Sourdough Loaf (page 224). I've got treats for kids and dogs alike—don't sleep on Rookie's Cookies on page 75— the whole family's nourished in my book! And of course, you know I saved the best for last and have given you a big ole chapter on desserts. Life's too short to not savor Indie Lou's Blueberry Cake (page 277) or my Sexy 'n' Spicy Peach Pecan Cobbler (page 260). These recipes are all so special to me, and I hope they become just as special for you.

I want cooking from this book to feel just like you're dropping by my house for a meal. So depending on the day, I might be making classics like Finger Lickin' Fried Chicken (page 153) with Bebop's Sweet Bacon Collard Greens (page 131). These are the recipes the women in my family have been cooking for generations, and I've continued the tradition, with my own Hannah touches. Or, maybe you'd catch me on a day when I'm feeling experimental, and I'll make you one of my own inventions. Dinners like BBQ Pineapple Chicken Bake (page 168) started with just throwing what I had into a skillet and seeing how it turned out. (Delicious.) Or, if you're stopping by for breakfast, well, that's going to be a real treat. Breakfast is my favorite meal to cook, and I can whip you up anything from Chicken & Waffles (page 93) to Cranberry-Orange Cinnamon Rolls with Lemon Glaze (page 104). You're going to be eating good, and then afterwards we're all going to need a nap. Maybe we'll head on out to the porch and sip on a Fizzy Cranberry Punch (page 242) or some Homebrewed Blueberry Wine (page 232) while we digest. Doesn't that just sound like a perfect day?

I hope these recipes feel like you got a friend by your side, and they help you find your way in the kitchen. I want you to open my cookbook and feel ready to have fun at the playground, not fit into a box. I hope that through the recipes and ideas here, I can guide you through my Georgia cooking—like the big ole hug from the Georgia woods I got growing up. Then I can teach you how to measure with your own heart, follow your own intuition, and create your own unique and delicious recipes. I want to show you that nature provides us with so many tools to make simple, delicious food. And most important, I want to remove the fear about "play." These recipes are easy, made with love, and a great introduction to some of my favorite Southern foods for those who haven't experienced them. And for those who have, I hope they encourage you to put your own spin on what you know.

So, have fun with it, embrace the mess, and accept that nothing is perfect— but that's also why it is.

Big Hugs,

How to Measure with Your Heart

I know this is scary to some people. But this is the best part of cooking! Following recipes to the letter is no way to feel empowered, sexy, or confident. It's not going to call you back into the kitchen, day in and day out. The only way to get comfortable with cooking is to *get going* and make mistakes, mess up, and figure out what you love.

❖ *First, You Got to Remove the Fear*

To find joy in the kitchen, you have to completely change how you've been thinking about it. Cooking is not intimidating; it's fun, and I don't want you to ever forget that. When you see my videos, even when I drop a cake on the floor, or something turns out all lopsided and raw in the center, you see pure joy in my eyes. That's because the kitchen is my playground, and I want it to be yours, too. You have to let go of the fear you have about messing up and the need to be perfect. I'm not perfect. You're not perfect. Your dinner isn't perfect. And I wouldn't want life to be any other way. Everyone you're cooking for can feel the love in what you make, and I don't know a single person who would turn their nose up at a hot, homemade meal filling their belly. But you have to accept that you're going to mess up—that's all part of the process. That's also why I got a whole list on page 25 of ways to fix your

messes. Dust yourself off and cook again, my friend.

❖ *Then, You Got to Feel Good*

There's a good chance you're here because you heard my "two if you're sexy" at some point on your feed. That phrase came about early in my filming days. I was just messing around, and I figured, *Who doesn't need a little extra vanilla in their cake?* And now it's one of the things I think my online family connects most with. Y'all, I don't want to start my cookbook off with a load of tears, but this idea is so important to me. I've worked very hard, for a long time, on learning to love myself, and I've finally gotten to a place where I truly do accept me for who I am. I want everyone to feel that way! I try to spread the message in whatever I do: YOU are sexy and wonderful, and when you're feeling yourself, I swear your food tastes better. So, when I'm baking, I throw an extra splash of vanilla into my batter

because I know it will make me happy; I add an extra spoonful of sugar to everything because I got a sweet tooth; and I go heavy on the seasoning if the spirit moves me (and it always does). Be your best self in the kitchen, and always add a little more of what you love. Your food will be better for it.

❖ *Follow Your Heart and Your Taste Buds*

A big part of feeling confident in the kitchen is knowing what you like and how to use what you got. Take my Slow Cooker Brunswick Stew (page 198): It's a classic Southern dish I grew up eating, and my Mama made it with only beef. I love the way she made it, but I also love chicken (and always have a freezer full of it). So, I get to thinking: *This would be good with chicken, too.* And you know what? I like it even better. Make experimenting fun! You already know what you like, and you gotta play around a bit to figure out what can be added, subtracted, and swapped for each other. One meat can often go in place of another. Switch up your beans, your fruit, your greens. Try to stick to similar textures if you can, but if you can't, that's okay, too. It's rarely going to ruin anything! If you see a recipe that calls for just a little bit of cheese, but you know you love cheese, go ahead and add another handful. Then another. If it calls for Colby jack, but you love sharp Cheddar, use that! When you experiment, you may make something that's not a home run, but I guarantee it will mean the dish will be even better the next time. You know what you like and what you've got stocked, so listen to that inner voice.

❖ *Never Accept Bland Food*

I like my food big, bold, and making all my senses sing. That's why you've got to remember to taste, and taste some more, at every step you can. Every time you can taste your food—as long as there's nothing raw in there you're not supposed to be tasting yet—get in there and make sure you're on your way to happiness. Add some more spice if it needs it, more butter if it's not rich enough for you, or another pinch of salt if it's not popping yet. Don't move on to the next step of cooking until

you're satisfied with how your food is tasting. If you take a bite and you *don't* shimmy your shoulders and want to flip ya' hair, then you probably need another pinch of some all-purpose seasoning, garlic salt, or just straight salt. If you're baking, I'd bet a little extra sugar will fix what ails your batter.

❖ *Measurements Are the Bumpers*

I want you to think of these recipes like bumper bowling, and once you feel good and ready (or maybe when it feels the most intimidating), remove those bumpers and get rolling. Just like with bowling, I absolutely do not want you to rely on the bumpers forever. Hell, if you never used them, I'd be even happier. But I understand that some people do need them when they start out. It's not how I like to cook, but I know they can provide a sense of safety and comfort. Plus, I want you to at least have a sense of what *my* food is like. Because it's damn good, I can tell you that much. Try it once, and then follow your heart to make it your own the next time.

Now, of course I know that with baking it's a little harder to throw the measurements out the window (and that some people

prefer their weights; don't worry; I got you covered), but even those recipes have plenty of room to play. For example, I can tell you one thing you will never find in my cookbook: a dry-ass cake. I make adjustments to all my recipes so they're moist, rich, and the first ones gone at the cookout. My cake batters might have a bit more dairy than you're used to, and that's all a result of my experiments. If you need to use the bumpers a few times, that's what they're there for. And each time you make a recipe, you figure out what you like and grow from there. Maybe the next time you make one of my cakes, you scale back a bit on the dairy. Trust yourself! And if it doesn't work out, I got a fix for you on page 25.

When you watch me cooking, it's a hell of a lot easier to get at least some ideas of the measurements than it is just reading a recipe on the page. I measure by feel, not by spoons. Yes, I use spoons sometimes, but more often than not, they're out of sight. You gotta replace those spoons with some confidence. So, we're feeling our way to delicious food with pinches and palmfuls and love. And *that's* how you measure with your heart.

Kitchen Confidence

('Cause Confidence Is Sexy)

To be happy and at ease in the kitchen, you don't need much. First, you have to know in your heart what you like (more on that on page 18). Then, you need a couple of tools and some pantry ingredients. And whether you're just starting out or you've been cooking for years, we could all use a little bit of advice on fixing mistakes (because they will happen!).

❖ My Kitchen Necessities

There's really no special equipment needed to make the recipes in this book; maybe a stand mixer, but it's not required (though I couldn't live without mine!). Here's what I've got at home and what I use in this book. You probably don't even need all this; I could do just about everything in my favorite cast-iron and my Bundt pan.

Pots and Pans

• One 9-inch cast-iron skillet (just for cornbread)

• One 10-inch cast-iron skillet

• One 12-inch cast-iron skillet

• One 10-inch ceramic nonstick skillet

• A large Dutch oven (5- or 6-quart is good)

• Handful of some random pots: as long as you got a "small," a "medium," and a "large," you're good

• A big ole iron griddle

Baking Equipment

• One 9 × 5-inch loaf pan

• One 8-inch square baking dish

• A couple 8-inch round cake pans

• One 9-inch glass pie plate

• A couple of rimmed baking sheets

• One standard 12-cup Bundt pan

• One or two 12-cup muffin tins

• One 9 × 13-inch glass baking dish

• One 10-inch springform (cheesecake) pan

• A stand mixer or handheld mixer

• Some glass liquid measuring cups and a set of dry measuring cups and spoons

Utensils

• A set of wooden spoons and spatulas (I don't use metal on my cast-iron)

• At least one good, sharp knife

• One carving knife (I butcher a hell of a lot of chicken; you may not)

• Tongs or a spider strainer (for removing things out of pots)

• A whisk

The Other Kind of Seasoning

Y'all know I do just about everything in my beloved cast-irons, but it takes some tender loving care to keep them slick. When one of my pans is getting a little grippy, I have James sand it down for me with his power sander and 220 grit paper until it's so shiny I could do my hair in it. Then I oil it up with olive oil, put it upside down in a 400°F oven for 30 minutes, and let it sit until cool, which takes a couple hours. If it's slightly tacky, I repeat the oiling and baking again, until it's not. If you're in the market for a cast-iron, my best advice is to find a used one, because they sure don't make them like they used to.

Storage and More

- Lots of 8-ounce (1-cup), 16-ounce (1-pint), and 32-ounce (1-quart) mason jars, regular and wide-mouth
- Parchment paper
- Reusable bowl covers and/or beeswax wrap (I don't use plastic wrap in my kitchen)
- Glass storage containers
- One big ole cutting board
- Mixing bowls of all sizes
- A bunch of cheesecloth
- Big stack of kitchen towels
- Some colanders and strainers
- A cheese grater
- An instant-read thermometer
- A stand blender or handheld blender, or both
- A food processor
- A mortar and pestle or spice grinder
- A slow cooker (mine is 6-quart)

❖ Stock Ya Pantry

Since we're cooking all the time in this house, our dry goods are pretty well stocked to make the foods we love the most. Make sure you have fresh ingredients, plus everything in the Homemade Kitchen Staples chapter, and you don't need to have too much more on hand to make my recipes. And if your spice jars are full—then your heart will be, too.

For Baking

- King Arthur unbleached all-purpose flour
- White Lily self-rising flour
- Yellow cornmeal (I don't pay attention to the grind; any will work)
- Active dry yeast (you can also use instant)
- Baking powder
- Baking soda
- Granulated sugar (I like pure cane sugar)
- Light or dark brown sugar (doesn't matter which)
- Powdered sugar
- Light corn syrup
- Whole vanilla beans ('cause we fancy)
- Unsweetened cocoa powder

For Seasoning

- Fine sea salt (I like Redmond's)
- Flaky sea salt
- Black peppercorns (and a good pepper mill)
- Everglades All-Purpose Seasoning
- Slap Ya Mama Cajun Seasoning
- Chef Paul Prudhomme's Blackened Redfish Magic (or your favorite seafood seasoning)
- Ranch seasoning
- Cayenne pepper
- Red pepper flakes
- Sweet paprika
- Ground cinnamon
- Ground nutmeg

- Ground cumin
- Onion powder
- Garlic powder
- Garlic salt
- Chili powder
- Some dried herbs (I like oregano, basil, thyme, and rosemary, but you do you)

For All the Rest

- Any vegetable oil, for frying
- Avocado oil, for dressings and such
- Olive oil
- Bacon grease or the fat of your choice (for greasing pans and cooking)
- Tabasco
- Barbecue sauce (I like Sweet Baby Ray's)
- Worcestershire sauce
- A.1. Sauce
- Dale's Seasoning (James's secret for mind-blowing burgers)
- Yellow mustard
- Dijon (if I'm out of my homemade mustard)
- Tomato paste
- Canned tomatoes
- Honey
- Maple syrup
- Distilled white vinegar
- Yellow rice or white rice
- And a stash of booze

❖ Life Happens

Look, we're all going to mess up something in the kitchen. But we're not throwing our precious ingredients away. We bought or made them with hard-earned money and time! So, we're fixing our mistakes, and then we're sitting down at the table to enjoy what we cooked.

Too Much Salt

How to recover will really depend on what you're cooking. Sugar will balance out salt, so if it's a sauce you could stir some sugar into, or a baked good you could sprinkle some on top of, go for that. We were notorious for oversalting our meats in this house, but when that happens, just flush it out. Rinse your meat, if you need to. If it's all in the slow cooker, scoop out some of the liquid and add water. If it's a soup, add some water or chicken stock. You want to dilute the salt.

If you find you're often oversalting, try cooking with garlic salt for your savory foods. I love garlic salt because it adds more than just a pure salt flavor, and it makes oversalting harder to do. Don't worry; you'll get it down. I don't oversalt anything anymore.

Too Little Salt

This one's easy: Add a pinch more salt, mix, taste, and repeat until you're happy. If it's already done and you can't mix anything in, sprinkle some salt on top. And remember for next time how much you added.

Too Spicy

I swear cayenne pepper should come with a warning label on it. That stuff is *hot.* Fat and sugar will temper it. Butter, sour cream, or milk will do the trick, depending on what will complement what you're cooking. Something sweet, like brown sugar, honey, maple syrup, even ketchup, will also tame the heat. You can trust us; it's happened more than once and James has fact-checked all this information here.

Your Food Is Bland

Add pinches of all-purpose seasoning, garlic salt, salt, and/or cayenne pepper until you're happy. If it's something like a meatloaf and you can't mix in more seasonings, douse it in a barbecue sauce or gravy, or sprinkle on some cheese. And always remember: Taste as you go if you can, so you don't get to the end of cooking and say "Well, damn, that doesn't taste very good."

You Got Dry Cake

I have strong feelings about dry cake! I *hate* it! If yours comes out dry, turn it into cake pops (see page 263) by crumbling it and mixing it with frosting. Then for next time, try upping your fat, or just use the recipes in this book, which will never have this issue.

Your Cake Is Raw in the Middle

Stick it back in the oven! Or, just serve it. I have been known to serve a slightly—shall we say, gooey—cake. Just go with it and say you did it on purpose. Or, cut around the middle so no one is none the wiser.

The Bottom (of Anything) Is Burnt

Go ahead and cut that burnt part right off. If it's a soup or a stew, scoop it into a new pot, making sure to leave the burnt bits on the bottom behind. Then call it "smoked," and wait for the compliments to roll in.

Overcooked Meat

This is where sauce is your new best friend. Drench that overcooked meat in ketchup, barbecue sauce, ranch dressing, or gravy. I once badly overcooked chicken wings, but as soon as I tossed them in something delicious, nobody could even tell. Next time, just check it a little earlier.

Undercooked Meat

Put it in a pan on the stove and sear it until it's where you want it. When James messes up the steaks, that's what he does. If it's already seared enough on the outside, stick the meat in a low oven (300°F or so) and keep checking until the meat is cooked through. If that takes too long, break out the potato chips and call it cocktail hour.

Flat Bread

There's no coming back for this loaf, so turn it into bread crumbs or chop it up for bread pudding. For the next loaf, try letting it proof longer, until it's doubled in size and you can poke it and it bounces back. Also, replace your yeast, as it may be old. No matter what kind of yeast you're using, let it foam a bit in some water first so you know it's good. And don't forget to give it a little food when you do—yeast needs some sugar or honey. Then, let it sit until you smell the alluring aroma of rotten beer (just kidding, I love that smell).

Overbaked Pie Crust

If your pot pie is overdone, make some gravy and pour it on. If your fruit pie is baked too much, vanilla ice cream is your best friend. Next time, cover it with foil if it starts browning before your filling is finished.

Soggy Pie Crust

Well, for starters, you must not have been using my recipe! (James says mine is the best.) Soggy crust usually means you haven't baked it long enough. If you're using your cast-iron, be sure to preheat it. Or, use a glass pie plate so you can check the bottom. And if you over-correct, see my point above.

Gravy's Not Right

You're looking for something thick and delicious and creamy that you can drizzle over your favorite foods. What you're not looking for is something watery, clumpy, or—and I swear this has happened to me—unsalted. If your gravy has been simmering for a bit but it's too thin, add a spoonful of flour or cornstarch and give it a few more minutes. Or, if a spoon could stand up straight in it, add a splash of water or milk, whatever the liquid in it is. And for the love of God, taste it before you serve it.

You Dropped It

Follow the five-second rule and blow on it real hard. I'm just messing. (Maybe.) Pick up what you can; there's always at least some worth saving.

HOMEMADE KITCHEN STAPLES

—◆—

You gotta start with the basics, y'all.

Vanilla Extract

GETS YOU 1 CUP (THEN AN UNLIMITED AMOUNT) ❖ TAKES 6 MONTHS

I *always* want more vanilla in my batter—it's one of my favorite flavors. After I'd been baking regularly, I got curious about making my own. In my Granny's old recipe book, I found a handwritten recipe and took that as a sign. I used some of the Jim Beam that me and James like to keep on hand (you know, for company), but you can use vodka, or any whisky or bourbon. It may take months, but once it's ready, homemade vanilla lasts forever. Keep topping it up with fresh booze as you use it, and if it ever loses its robust flavor, just stick a fresh vanilla bean or two in there. Making vanilla is kind of like love: Give it time, always replenish your stash, and don't be stingy with it.

❖ *Gather Up*

11 whole vanilla beans

8 ounces (1 cup) Jim Beam Bourbon (or the booze of your choice, like vodka or whisky), plus more for upkeep

❖ *Don't Forget*

A 16-ounce (1-pint) mason jar

❖ *Let's Make My Favorite Ingredient*

Sterilize your mason jar by washing it really good with dish soap and hot water. Let it air-dry. (All that Jim Beam is gonna kill any germs, but let's not risk it.)

Place **11 whole vanilla beans** on your cutting board. Get a sharp knife to cut each in half crosswise, then cut each open longways, but keeping it attached at the end and leaving all the vanilla seeds inside.

Put the sliced beans in the mason jar and add **8 ounces (1 cup) Jim Beam Bourbon.** Make sure the vanilla beans are completely covered; you may need to push them down a bit. Seal the jar and let the extract do its thing in a cool, dark spot in the pantry for 6 months before using.

Store the vanilla in the pantry forever, topping it up with fresh Jim Beam (plus a splash for yourself) when needed to keep the jar full.

B & B Twofer
Butter & Buttermilk

GETS YOU 1 CUP BUTTER PLUS ⅓ CUP BUTTERMILK ❖
TAKES 15 MINUTES (30 MINUTES BY HAND)

Butter is truly a miracle ingredient, and I love making my own. About once a month or so, usually when I'm making biscuits since I know I'm about to use up my reserves, I'll start another batch at the same time. Since I'm already in the kitchen, letting the machine run for 5 to 10 minutes while I'm doing other things is no sweat off my back. It's like the butter practically makes itself. When I'm feeling particularly spicy, I add some dried herbs or some all-purpose seasoning in there, too. Use what you got, and what you love, in yours. The fresh old-fashioned buttermilk is a delicious bonus. I add it to the biscuits I'm usually making at the moment, or I save it for pancakes or a chocolate cake.

❖ *Gather Up*

2 cups heavy whipping cream, cold

Fine sea salt, if you want

Herbs like dried rosemary or basil, all-purpose seasoning (see page 38), or any other seasoning you like, if you want

Ice water

❖ *Don't Forget*

Your food processor or blender (or see my Note)

❖ *Let's "Churn" Some Butter*

Grab your food processor (or blender) and add **2 cups heavy whipping cream** (make sure it's *cold*). Blend for 5 to 10 minutes, until you see the butter solids come together in one big chunk and separate from the liquid.

Once the butter forms, grab your strainer and place it over a measuring cup or jar. Pour the butter mixture through to separate the solid butter and the liquid buttermilk. Your homemade buttermilk is ready! Get a spoon and use the back to press the butter in the strainer to form it into a ball and squeeze out any remaining buttermilk.

If you want to make salted butter or flavored butter: Put the butter in a small bowl and sprinkle on some **fine sea salt (**I sprinkle in about a palmful; if you don't love it as much as I do, start with a few pinches and keep tasting until you're happy) and/or **a few pinches any other seasoning you like** on top. Get in there with your hands and knead the butter until the salt or flavorings are evenly distributed. Taste a little bit and add more seasonings if you like.

Now, shape the butter into a smooth ball with your hands.

Fill a medium bowl with **ice water.** Put the butter ball into the water for 15 to 30 seconds to chill it and firm up its shape.

Wrap the butter tightly in parchment or beeswax wrap and refrigerate for up to 1 month. The buttermilk will keep in a sealed jar in the fridge for about 1 month, too. Congrats, you just made two delicious ingredients!

Instant Buttermilk

If you want to make only buttermilk from scratch, mix **1 cup whole milk** and **1 tablespoon distilled white vinegar** in a measuring cup. Stir the ingredients together and let it sit for 5 minutes, then it's ready to use.

Note: *If you don't have a blender or food processor, or you're trying to tone your arms, you can also make butter by hand. Put the cream in a large mason jar and shake it. You'll have to constantly shake your mason jar for about 25 minutes, until the butter solids form one big lump—I KNOW, but don't give up! Hand it off to your kids, wife, husband, friends if you need to. Then follow the directions from the second step.*

Lazy Sourdough Starter

GETS YOU 2 CUPS STARTER ❖ TAKES 1 DAY

I have one husband, three kids, three dogs, seven cats, one turkey, and seventy chickens. I do not have twelve days to wait for wild yeast to ferment my flour into a starter, nor do I have time to feed a starter to keep it going for years. This was my solution when I was getting into sourdough bread baking, but on *my* schedule. This starter is ready to use within 24 hours, which puts fresh baked sourdough bread on our table almost two weeks faster than the loaf I made with a from-scratch starter (maybe making a starter takes less time where you live, but for me, it was sloooow). I use it to make My Favorite Sourdough Loaf (page 224), and put any left into my waffles, pancakes, cookies, and brownies for extra flavor and nutrition. I've grown to prefer the taste of sourdough bread over plain bread and I think you will, too. Especially when you can get that sourdough flavor on your own time.

❖ *Gather Up*

1½ cups (340 grams to be exact) warm water

1 (¼-ounce) packet instant or active dry yeast (2¼ teaspoons)

1 cup (120 grams) all-purpose flour

¼ cup (28 grams) whole wheat flour

❖ *Let's Start This Starter*

Grab a small bowl and add **1½ cups (340 grams to be exact) warm water** (a little warmer than body temperature, 100° to 110°F) and **1 (¼-ounce) packet instant or active dry yeast (2¼ teaspoons)**. Do not stir. Let sit for 10 minutes in a warm place until it's frothy. Add **1 cup (120 grams) all-purpose flour** and **¼ cup (28 grams) whole wheat flour** and mix well with a whisk or fork. Make sure there's no lumps or dry pockets of flour.

Move the mixture over to a small, clean bowl, cover with a kitchen towel, and let sit for 24 hours in a warm place. After 1 day it should be very bubbly and have a slight sour smell, which means it's ready to use. Now it's time to get baking. (Once it's made, I use it all up, and just make a fresh batch next time I want to bake. You could probably keep it going with regular feedings, if you wanted.)

All-Purpose Seasoning

GETS YOU ABOUT ¼ CUP ❖ TAKES 5 MINUTES

Stick with me now—have you ever grown something yourself, like a potato, or eaten a scallop you pulled right out of the water? For me, those foods that don't come from a grocery store have a deeper, earthier flavor. I swear, Everglades All-Purpose Seasoning was the first seasoning I ever tried that I thought put that earthiness *back* into food. I don't know if it's the MSG, or maybe it's the celery salt, but it's so good I use this on everything. If you've watched my videos, you know it by name. Everglades is from Sebring, Florida (close to where James is from), and you can order it online. If that's not in the cards for you, here's how to make something pretty damn close yourself.

❖ *Gather Up*

2 teaspoons fine sea salt

1½ teaspoons garlic salt

1½ teaspoons Accent Flavor Enhancer or MSG

1 teaspoon ground black pepper

1 teaspoon celery salt

1 teaspoon onion salt

1 teaspoon sugar

½ teaspoon cayenne pepper

½ teaspoon ground cumin

½ teaspoon garlic powder

½ teaspoon ground turmeric

❖ *This Is the Only Time You're Gonna See Exact Seasoning Measurements in My Book!*

Grab your small bowl and pour in **2 teaspoons fine sea salt, 1½ teaspoons garlic salt, 1½ teaspoons Accent Flavor Enhancer, 1 teaspoon ground black pepper, 1 teaspoon celery salt, 1 teaspoon onion salt, 1 teaspoon sugar, ½ teaspoon cayenne pepper, ½ teaspoon ground cumin, ½ teaspoon garlic powder,** and **½ teaspoon ground turmeric.** Stir it all together and keep it in a glass jar or shaker in the pantry for many weeks or until it's gone.

Apple Cider Vinegar

GETS YOU 2 CUPS ❖ TAKES 4 WEEKS

I suppose I could have called this the No Waste chapter, but that doesn't have as nice a ring to it, does it? My kids love apples and I have an enormous amount of apples in my house at any given moment. And because I peel them for their snacks, I have all these apple cores and peels left over. I thought to myself, *What on earth could I do with the scraps when even the chickens are sick of them?* Then it hit me: apple cider vinegar. I always got a batch going because it takes a few weeks, and I collect the apple scraps in the freezer until I have enough to start a new one. That's really all there is to that; couldn't be easier.

❖ *Gather Up*

6 apples

¼ cup sugar

2 cups warm water

❖ *Don't Forget*

A 32-ounce (1-quart) mason jar

❖ *Let's Brew Some Vinegar*

Sterilize your mason jar by washing it thoroughly with dish soap and hot water. Let it air-dry.

Peel the skins and take out the cores from **6 apples** and add the skins and cores to the jar (snack on the rest of it). Sprinkle in ¼ **cup sugar,** then top with **2 cups warm water.** Give everything a stir. Place a square of cheesecloth over the top, then add the ring from the lid loosely just to hold the cloth in place. Set the jar in a warm, dark spot in your pantry for 2 weeks.

After 2 weeks, fish out and compost the solids. Return the cheesecloth and ring to the jar and ferment for up to 2 more weeks, tasting it every week. The vinegar is ready when it is tangy to your liking. Cooking's magic, ain't it? Always make sure you're using a clean utensil in the jar, and if at any point you see blue or black mold around the top of the jar, throw out the whole batch immediately.

Store the vinegar in a sealed jar in the pantry for many weeks.

Never Go Back to Store-Bought
Mayonnaise

GETS YOU 1¼ CUPS ❖ TAKES 5 MINUTES

James and I come from picky people. There ain't nothing wrong with that: They like what they like and stick to the classics they know in a box or jar. When I started making our favorite foods from scratch, mayonnaise was definitely on my list. But let me tell you, making it threw me for a loop. My first few tries tasted *disgusting.* Turns out oil and egg on their own are gross. But I kept adding lemon juice and mustard, and seasoning it up real well with salt, and soon this mayo was tasting divine. Our friends wouldn't touch that stuff with a ten-foot pole, though. It took them coming over for James's famous burgers (see page 165) and all I had to offer them was my own mayo, so they caved. Now, of course, they prefer my recipe, which I think I deserve a gold star for! One taste will change your mind, too. If you're worried about raw egg, try using pasteurized eggs from the store.

❖ *Gather Up*

1 large egg, room temperature

1 cup avocado oil

½ lemon

1 teaspoon mustard, homemade if you want (see page 45) or Dijon

Fine sea salt and ground black pepper

❖ *Don't Forget*

A 16-ounce (1-pint) wide-mouth mason jar

Your handheld blender

❖ *Let's Whip Up Some Mayonnaise*

Crack **1 room-temperature large egg** into the mason jar. Add **1 cup avocado oil** and squeeze in the juice from ½ **lemon.** Grab your handheld blender and put it down into the bottom of the jar, making sure the blade is fully covered in the oil. Start to blend, keeping the blade submerged throughout the process. Blend for about a minute, until you start to see a thick and creamy mayonnaise form.

When the mayo fully comes together, add about **1 teaspoon mustard, a couple pinches of fine sea salt,** and **a pinch of ground black pepper.** Blend again for 15 to 30 more seconds, keeping the blade under the surface, until the mustard is well mixed in. Taste it to enjoy your hard work and see if it needs more of anything; keep seasoning until you're happy.

Use the mayo right away or refrigerate it in the sealed jar for up to 1 week.

Flavored Mayo

You can add any seasoning you like to this recipe—the sky's the limit for flavored mayo. When you add the mustard, salt, and pepper, try a grated garlic clove, a few roasted garlic cloves, some grated lemon zest, a few dashes of jalapeño hot sauce, or whatever else your imagination dreams up. Start with a small amount and you can always add more when you taste it!

Zesty Mustard

GETS YOU 1 CUP ❖ TAKES 15 MINUTES

We use this mustard on our sandwiches, of course, but it's so dang tasty it finds its way into all sorts of other dishes, too. When me and James are frying up fish, instead of an egg coating with our dredge, we'll just baste the fish with this mustard, adding that mouth-puckering flavor to every bite. I think it's perfect as is, but if you're in the mood to add a little more pep to your step and your meal, you could mix it with herbs or all-purpose seasoning. I add my vinegar a splash at a time because I don't like a heavy vinegar taste, but if you do you, keep tasting and adding until it's as zesty as you are.

❖ *Gather Up*

¼ cup yellow mustard seeds

2 tablespoons brown mustard seeds

2 tablespoons apple cider vinegar, homemade if you want (see page 41)

1 tablespoon honey

Fine sea salt

❖ *Don't Forget*

Your mortar and pestle or spice grinder

An 8-ounce (1-cup) mason jar

❖ *You're Not Gonna Believe How Easy This Is*

In a mortar and pestle or spice grinder, coarsely grind ¼ **cup yellow mustard seeds** and **2 tablespoons brown mustard seeds.**

Put the ground mustard in the mason jar and add ¼ **cup water, 2 tablespoons apple cider vinegar** (start with half if you don't love vinegar and keep tasting), **1 tablespoon honey,** and **a couple pinches of fine sea salt.** Stir well until everything comes together. Taste it and see if it needs any more of the seasonings. Take another taste because it's just so damn good.

Refrigerate in the sealed jar for months and months.

Dill Me a Pickle
Relish

GETS YOU 4 CUPS ❖ TAKES AT LEAST 7 HOURS

One summer we had so many cucumbers in the garden I couldn't keep up, so I learned how to pickle them. My pickles are heavy on the dill. I love anything with a lot of dill, and if I could make a relish entirely of dill I would, but then I wouldn't be using up the cucumbers I needed to. It's especially good stirred into an egg salad, or mixed in with sour cream and ranch seasoning to make a dip for chips. Save this in your back pocket when it's time to harvest that cucumber vine, or you got a taste for dill.

❖ *Gather Up*

1 **to 1½ pounds cucumbers (3 or 4 medium)**

1 **medium Vidalia onion**

4 **garlic cloves**

1 **tablespoon pickling salt**

A big handful of fresh dill

1 **cup distilled white vinegar**

1 **tablespoon mustard seeds (yellow or brown; it doesn't matter)**

1 **tablespoon black peppercorns**

❖ *Don't Forget*

A 32-ounce (1-quart) wide-mouth mason jar

❖ *Let's Pickle These Cucumbers*

Sterilize your mason jar by washing it thoroughly with dish soap and hot water. Let it air-dry.

Chop **1 to 1½ pounds cucumbers** (peels, seeds, and all) nice and small, then peel and chop **1 medium Vidalia onion** the same way. Chop **4 garlic cloves.** Add it all to your large bowl. Sprinkle with **1 tablespoon pickling salt** and stir it really good. Put the bowl to the side. Now, get in there and chop up **a big handful of fresh dill** nice and small, until you get to about ¼ cup and set that aside, too.

In a small pot over medium-high, bring **1 cup water, 1 cup distilled white vinegar, 1 tablespoon mustard seeds, 1 tablespoon black peppercorns,** and the chopped dill to a boil. As soon as that pot starts boiling, take it off the heat.

Add your chopped cucumber mixture to the mason jar. Pour in the hot brine, leaving about a ½ inch of space at the top. Seal the mason jar, shake the contents to blend, and let it cool down to room temperature, around 2 hours. Move it to the fridge for at least 4 hours (overnight is best) before you dig in.

Store in the sealed jar in the fridge for up to 2 weeks.

Homemade Fresh Cheese

GETS YOU ABOUT 1¼ POUNDS ❖ TAKES 1 HOUR

My cheese tastes like ricotta and cream cheese got together one night and did the thing. It looks a little bit like ricotta, a little bit like burrata, and has the creamy goodness of mozzarella. Sorry to brag, but this cheese is so good. I use it to make my lasagna (see page 178), and I love it spread on sourdough bread with tomato and avocado. Once I even fried it up into the most delicious, but messy, cheese sticks I've ever made.

❖ Gather Up

- **1 gallon whole milk**
- **1 to 1¼ cups distilled white vinegar, as you need it**
- **Ice water**
- **Fine sea salt, if you want**

❖ Let's Get Cheesy

Grab a large pot and pour **1 gallon whole milk** into it. Put the milk over medium-high and let it warm, not messing with it, until it's 110°F, 10 minutes or so. (If you don't have a thermometer, it should be a little warmer than body temperature.)

Move the pot off the heat and start stirring. Keep stirring while you slowly pour in **1 cup distilled white vinegar** bit by bit—don't stop stirring! You should start to see the liquid curding up and looking like cottage cheese. Cover your pot and let sit for 10 minutes.

After 10 minutes, if it still looks milky, add **another good splash of vinegar** (call it ¼ cup), cover, and let it sit another 5 minutes or so. At this point, you should see the curd and liquid separated (which will look kind of like cloudy water and not like milk).

Get your handheld strainer, line it with cheesecloth, and put it over a large bowl. Using your slotted spoon, scoop all the cheese curds from the pot and place in the cheesecloth. Bring together all the ends of the cheesecloth so it covers the cheese, then lift it out of the strainer and give it a gentle squeeze over the bowl to get the rest of the liquid out.

Keep your cheese in the cheesecloth and let it rest in the strainer over the bowl. Give gravity 30 minutes to do any additional draining. Toss the whey (the liquid) when the cheese is done draining.

Now, divide the cheese into 3 equal pieces. Roll each into a ball between your hands. If your cheese is too crumbly to roll, that's okay; just gently pat it into balls. Put them aside.

Fill a clean large bowl with **ice water.** Dunk the cheese balls in the cold water for 5 minutes, until they form a skin to help keep them together. Move them to a plate. At this point I sprinkle some **fine sea salt** on the surface for flavor, but you don't have to.

Pop the cheese in the fridge for about 10 minutes to harden some more, until the balls hold together. Move them to an airtight container to refrigerate for up to 1 week. You now officially have homemade cheese!

Pasta Dough & Noodles

GETS YOU 1 POUND ❖ TAKES 2 HOURS

James and Indie Lou are my big pasta eaters—you should see the way their eyes light up when they find out it's a pasta night. Every week or so, I make this homemade dough because I love the way those noodles taste when they're made with eggs from our chickens. I know it seems intimidating, but making your own pasta really is not that hard. (I don't even own a pasta machine!) You just need flour, salt, eggs, and patience. The trick is not taking it too seriously—this is basically adult playdough. You can always roll the dough back up into a big ball if you need to start over. Your family will taste the love in every noodle.

❖ *Gather Up*

2 cups (240 grams to be exact) all-purpose flour, plus more for rolling

3 large eggs

1 teaspoon fine sea salt, plus more for cooking

❖ *I'll Take Homemade over Pretty Any Day*

On your counter, mound up your **2 cups (240 grams to be exact) all-purpose flour** into a small pile. Take your measuring cup and make a crater in the middle that will hold the eggs without spilling out everywhere. Crack **3 large eggs** into the crater and add **1 teaspoon fine sea salt.**

With your fingers, mix the eggs and salt until they're mostly smooth. Then, gradually by hand, fold the flour into your egg mix, trying to preserve the crater walls for as long as you can. If the eggs spill, that's no problem—just quickly mix them into the flour. Keep mixing until you've worked in most of the flour, and then start kneading until it comes together into a tacky dough (it should feel a little bit sticky but won't come off on your hands). If it's too dry, sprinkle on a few drops of water and keep kneading. If it's too wet and sticky, sprinkle with a little flour, knead again, and repeat until it's dry enough.

Pat the dough into a ball. Wrap it tightly in parchment paper or beeswax wrap and place in the fridge for 1 hour so the dough hydrates and relaxes. You can do the same now.

After an hour, lightly flour your counter. Uncover the dough and roll it around to coat it in the flour. Use your hands or a rolling pin to flatten your ball to about one finger's width or so, then cut the dough into 4 pieces. Cover them all with a kitchen towel for now.

Using your rolling pin, roll out one piece at a time into a long, thin rectangle. The dimensions don't matter except for getting it real thin (like 1/16 to 1/8 inch; if you're eyeballing it, that means *thin*). Sprinkle the dough with a little more flour and flip it over as you're rolling it if it starts to stick. Set the finished sheet aside, dust with flour to keep it from sticking, and cover with another kitchen towel while you roll out the rest.

(recipe continues)

If you're making lasagna: Trim the rough and rounded edges from the sheets, then cut the sheets to fit the size of your lasagna pan.

If you're making noodles: Cut the sheets of pasta into however long you like your noodles. Use a sharp knife to cut across to make noodles, and flour them again in case they're sticking to each other. You can cover them and let sit out for an hour or two before cooking, or put them in a sealed container in the fridge for up to 12 hours.

To cook the noodles: Bring a large pot of water to a boil over medium-high. Add **a few good pinches of salt**—don't be shy—to season the noodles. Line a baking sheet or two with clean towels if you're making lasagna. Put the pasta in the boiling water and cook, swishing gently around so nothing clumps, until it's tender, 2 to 4 minutes. Get your slotted spoon or a spider strainer to scoop the lasagna sheets out of the boiling water and set them on the lined pans to cool—without touching, so they don't stick. If you made noodles, scoop 'em out and sauce 'em up!

Beef Bone Broth

I started drinking bone broth in the mornings because I was teaching myself how to use up a whole animal. Making this rich broth was my way of getting every last drop of goodness out of the beef we were cooking. Plus, I swear my whole body is happier when I drink it.

❖ *Gather Up*

10 **beef marrow bones (about 3 pounds total)**

2 **medium Vidalia onions**

1 **head of garlic**

 Distilled white vinegar

❖ *Don't Forget*

 Your slow cooker

 A few large mason jars

❖ *Let's Make the Good Stuff*

Preheat your oven to 450°F.

Get a large baking dish and put **10 beef marrow bones** in it in one layer. Roast, without messing with it, until the bones are browned and there are some juices in the bottom of the pan, around 1 hour.

While the bones roast, cut **2 medium Vidalia onions** in half (you can peel them if your heart desires) and cut **1 head of garlic** crosswise through the middle. Get your slow cooker ready, too.

When the bones are done, grab your tongs and move the bones to your slow cooker. Then carefully pour the juices from your baking dish in there, too. Throw in your onion halves, the split garlic head, and **a splash of distilled white vinegar** (call it 1 tablespoon). Fill the pot with **enough water to cover everything.** Put the lid on the cooker and set the cooker to high. Cook for 12 hours.

Set a strainer over whatever storage containers you choose and pour the broth through the strainer into your containers. (I like to use a couple big (1-quart) mason jars and a large spouted measuring cup, but you do you.) You can either drink the broth right away or let it cool for 30 minutes or so, then close up the containers and put it in the fridge to fully cool.

Refrigerate the broth for up to 4 days. It's normal to see a layer of fat form at the top once the broth is refrigerated. You can also freeze it for up to 3 months (but I like mine best fresh). Enjoy all that goodness; you deserve it.

Chicken Bone Broth

This stuff is liquid gold. I use it as a soup base whenever me or anyone else is feeling the ick, or even when my dogs need some extra nutrients. Any time I cook a whole chicken, I save the carcass to get started on my next batch. If we're running low on bone broth and don't have any leftover chicken, I'll get a fresh chicken just for this purpose (that's how much we use it; see my Note). I carve off all the meat first so we can use it in another meal, then I set that baby in a slow cooker and don't think about it for a whole day.

Now, you know how much I love salt, but I don't add any here so I can have some flexibility when I use the broth.

❖ *Gather Up*

1 **garlic clove**

1 **medium to large Vidalia onion**

1 **carcass from a cooked (4- to 5-pound) chicken, meat picked off and saved for something else**

❖ *Don't Forget*

Your slow cooker

Some large mason jars

❖ *Let's Simmer Some Broth*

First, make sure your slow cooker is set up. Smash **1 garlic clove** with the side of your knife, peel it, and add it to your cooker. Peel and roughly chop **1 medium to large Vidalia onion** and throw it in there, too.

Place the **carcass from 1 (4- to 5-pound) cooked chicken** right into the cooker. Fill your slow cooker with **enough water to cover your chicken.** Put on the lid, turn the slow cooker on low, and let it cook for 24 hours.

Set a strainer over whatever storage containers you choose and pour the broth through the strainer into your containers. (I like to use 1-quart mason jars and a large spouted measuring cup, but you do you.) Use the broth right away, or let it cool on the counter for 30 minutes or so, then close up the containers and put them in the fridge to fully cool.

The broth keeps in the fridge for up to 4 days. It's normal to see a layer of fat form at the top once the broth is refrigerated. You can also freeze the broth for up to 3 months (but I like mine best fresh). Drink up, friend!

Note: If you're using a 4- to 5-pound fresh chicken and want to have the meat for another meal (you don't have to; you can also throw the whole chicken in there), use your carving knife to separate the meat, limb by limb, by carving off the meat around the bones. The goal is to get all the meat off the chicken carcass so get right next to the bones with the knife. Place the meat in a large bowl as you work and save it for your next chicken dinner. It's optional, but you can leave the organs in for more flavor. Then place the carcass in the slow cooker and get on with it.

KIDS
&
PUPS

———◇———

My best recipes for the
most important
members of the family.

Cinnamon Toasted Cereal Squares

GETS YOU 3 CUPS OR SO ❖ TAKES 45 MINUTES

We're not a big cereal family, but I noticed a lot of interesting cereal recipes popping up online, and so I decided to make a healthy flax recipe. Now, it was delicious, but not something the kids would be into, you know? So, I turned it into a slightly sweeter, more fun cereal I knew they'd go crazy for. And they do. When we feel like having cereal, I'm okay with them having a second bowl if they want, since I know exactly what went into their cereal: a boatload of maple syrup and cinnamon (there's *a lot* of cinnamon, start with less if you don't love it as much as me!).

❖ *Gather Up*

For the Cereal

1 cup (120 grams to be exact) all-purpose flour

4 tablespoons (½ stick/ 57 grams) salted butter, homemade if you want (see page 34), room temperature, plus more if you need it

1 tablespoon ground cinnamon

1 teaspoon fine sea salt

¼ cup (78 grams) maple syrup

1 tablespoon vanilla extract, homemade if you want (see page 33)

For the Cinnamon Topping

2 tablespoons salted butter

¼ cup sugar

Ground cinnamon

Cold milk, for serving

❖ *Don't Forget*

Your food processor

A large mason jar for storage

❖ *Yes, We're Gonna Make Some Cereal*

Preheat your oven to 350°F.

Start with the cereal: Get out your food processor and add **1 cup (120 grams to be exact) all-purpose flour, 4 tablespoons (½ stick/57 grams) softened salted butter, 1 tablespoon ground cinnamon,** and **1 teaspoon fine sea salt** and pulse it until the mixture looks like fine sand. Add in **¼ cup (78 grams) maple syrup** and **1 tablespoon vanilla extract,** and mix until it comes together to form a tacky dough ball. If it's really dry and there's loose flour, add another 1 tablespoon salted butter and mix. Keep adding butter until it's tacky (meaning it's sticky but doesn't come off on your hands).

Cut 2 pieces of parchment paper the size of your baking sheet and turn the dough out onto one of them. Cover the dough with the other sheet and start rolling with a rolling pin. Keep going until the dough is as thin as cereal but still fits on the parchment.

Now, make the topping: In a small saucepan over low heat, or in a small bowl in the microwave, melt **2 tablespoons salted butter.** In a small bowl, combine the melted butter and **¼ cup sugar,** and sprinkle in **a palmful of ground cinnamon,** then go right ahead and sprinkle in another palmful because you know that's the good stuff. Mix with a spoon until you've worked the butter and cinnamon into the sugar. Taste and make sure there's enough cinnamon.

Peel off just the top layer of parchment and spread the topping all over the dough with your fingers, then cut the dough into little squares (up to you what size and just cut, don't move 'em yet). Slide that parchment paper onto the baking sheet. Bake until the squares are golden brown, 10 minutes or so. Let the cereal cool for a few minutes on the pan until it's room temperature, before breaking up the squares and adding some to bowls to serve with **cold milk.**

I hope you love this cereal as much as we do! Store any extra in a mason jar on the counter for a few days.

Let's Get Saucy
Cranberry Applesauce

GETS YOU 2 CUPS ❖ TAKES 1 HOUR

All my kids' vitamins need to come from fruit, which they love, because they sure as hell do not love vegetables. I love tart cranberries (for my punches, like the one on page 242, and my baked goods, like the one on page 104), and they love any and all apples, so this is a combination that makes us all happy. I can make it to order since I always have both ingredients in the house at any given moment.

❖ *Gather Up*

2 **large tart apples (I like Honeycrisp)**

1 **cup sugar**

Ground cinnamon

Fine sea salt

Cayenne pepper

1 **cup fresh or frozen cranberries**

Vanilla extract, homemade if you want (see page 33)

❖ *Don't Forget*

Your handheld blender (or regular blender)

❖ *It's About to Get (Apple)saucy in Here*

Peel and chop **2 large tart apples** and measure out 2 cups (save the rest for snacks).

In a medium pot over medium-high, bring **1 cup sugar, a couple pinches each of ground cinnamon** and **fine sea salt, a pinch of cayenne pepper,** and ½ **cup water** to a boil, stirring every so often to dissolve the sugar.

Stir in **1 cup cranberries** and the chopped apples. Simmer, stirring regularly, until slightly thickened and the berries begin to pop, which should take about 10 minutes. Move the pan off the heat and cool to room temperature. Add **a splash of vanilla extract,** and using a handheld blender right in the pot (or pour it into a regular blender), blend until nice and smooth and creamy. Taste it and make sure you're happy with the seasonings. It will keep in the fridge for at least a week.

Fruity Roll 'em Ups

This is just fruit leather, but when you make it seem like Fruit Roll-Ups, it's a lot more appealing to kids. They're excited for a sweet treat, and I'm excited to give them pure fruit and honey. This is my favorite mix of berries, but you are welcome to use more of what you've got and skip what you don't. As long as you've got 3 cups total, you're good—and so are these.

❖ *Gather Up*

 1 **cup fresh cherries**

 ½ **cup fresh strawberries**

 ½ **lemon**

 ½ **cup fresh blueberries**

 ½ **cup fresh raspberries**

 ½ **cup fresh blackberries**

 2 **tablespoons honey**

❖ *Don't Forget*

 Your food processor

 A large mason jar for storage

❖ *Let's Roll Up Some Fruit*

Preheat your oven to 150°F or as low as it will go. Go ahead and line your baking sheet with parchment paper.

First, pit **1 cup fresh cherries** and trim the tops off ½ **cup fresh strawberries.** Juice ½ **lemon** to get you about 1 tablespoon juice.

Get out your food processor and add the cherries, strawberries, lemon juice, ½ **cup fresh blueberries,** ½ **cup fresh raspberries,** ½ **cup fresh blackberries,** and **2 tablespoons honey.** Blend until it's smooth.

Pour the puree onto the baking sheet, spread it into a very thin rectangle, maybe ⅛ inch thick, and make sure it's as even as you can get it so it sets nicely.

Bake until the fruit is no longer sticky when you press it lightly—4 to 6 hours, depending on your oven. Let it cool and set on the baking sheet in the oven for about 30 minutes, or until it's room temperature, then remove from the sheet. Use scissors to cut the parchment and fruit leather together into 6 strips. Get the kids in to help you roll 'em up! Keep them in a mason jar in the fridge for a week or so.

Bluegurt Ice Pops

GETS YOU 6 ICE POPS ❖ TAKES AT LEAST 4¼ HOURS

When it's hot here, we're tired of punch, and are hungry in the afternoon, an ice pop is our go-to snack. I like a creamy pop, but I'm not about to give the kids ice cream all the time, so yogurt is a nice compromise. Use whatever fruit you like, honestly. I do blueberries because they're Buck's favorite, but any berry, peaches, or even mango would be delicious here.

❖ *Gather Up*

2 **cups fresh or frozen blueberries**

4 **tablespoons honey**

Vanilla extract, homemade if you want (see page 33)

3 **cups plain yogurt**

❖ *Don't Forget*

Your ice pop molds (any shape will do)

❖ *Let's Make Some Frozen Treats*

In a medium pot, combine **2 cups blueberries** and **2 tablespoons honey** and put it over medium. Cook, stirring all the while, until the berries are nice and soft and there's lots of juices to make them all saucy, 5 minutes or so. Move the pot off the heat and stir in **a splash of vanilla extract** (2 if you're sexy). Let the mixture cool to room temperature, 30 minutes or so. Taste it and see if it needs more vanilla.

In a medium bowl, combine **3 cups plain yogurt,** your last **2 tablespoons honey,** and start adding **vanilla** a splash at a time and tasting until it's as vanilla-y as you like.

Now, alternate spooning the yogurt and the blueberry mix into the molds, one spoonful at a time, so you get nice layers. Once you've used up all the yogurt and blueberry mix, put them babies in the freezer and freeze until solid, at least 4 hours. Eat them on a scorching day. They'll keep for a couple months in the freezer.

Buck's Poppin' Tarts

Sometimes I like to have something sweet for the kids' breakfast, or for when we're on the go, since these tarts travel well (minus all the flaky crumbs that get everywhere, but that's just a sign of quality). My tarts taste fresh, are full of vanilla, and have none of the chemicals or processed ingredients you'll find in the store-bought ones. I adapted my trusty pie dough recipe to make these, and it's so much better than the weird chalky texture of the crust on the other ones. They're filled with fresh strawberry goodness because those are my favorite.

❖ *Gather Up*

For the Crust

8 tablespoons (1 stick/ 113 grams to be exact) cold salted butter, homemade if you want (see page 34)

2 cups (240 grams) all-purpose flour, plus more for rolling

1 tablespoon granulated sugar

1 teaspoon fine sea salt

½ cup (114 grams) plus 1 tablespoon cold water

1 large egg

For the Filling

1 pint fresh strawberries

½ lemon

½ cup granulated sugar

Vanilla extract, homemade if you want (see page 33)

❖ *Good Choice—These Tarts Are Poppin'*

Start with the crust: Cube **8 tablespoons (1 stick/113 grams to be exact) cold salted butter.** (Make sure it's *cold.* Stick it back in the fridge or freezer if you need to.)

Grab your food processor and add **2 cups (240 grams) all-purpose flour, 1 tablespoon granulated sugar,** and **1 teaspoon fine sea salt** and pulse it to mix. Add your cubed butter and **½ cup (114 grams) cold water** and pulse until you have a shaggy dough—so it's all mixed but not smooth or dry—just a few pulses. Divide the dough into 2 disks, wrap each in parchment or beeswax wrap, and let rest in the fridge for at least 1 hour (it can go up to 8 hours).

Meanwhile, make your filling: Cut off the tops from **1 pint fresh strawberries,** and chop them so you got about 2 cups (save any extra for snacking). Juice **½ lemon** to get 1 tablespoon of juice or so.

In a small pot, combine the strawberries, lemon juice, and **½ cup granulated sugar.** Put it over medium-high and let it come to a boil, mashing the strawberries with a fork so they break down and turn into jam. When the strawberries have cooked down to half their amount, no more than 10 minutes after you started, move the pan off the heat and add **a splash of vanilla extract.** Cover the pot and put the whole thing in the fridge to chill while you go back to your dough, at least 1 hour. When it's chilled, make sure it's as thick as jam and has enough vanilla for you.

Preheat your oven to 425°F. Go ahead and line a baking sheet with parchment paper.

Now, get back to your crust: Lightly flour your counter. Unwrap 1 dough disk and start rolling it into a square. Keep flouring it and turning the dough if you need to so it doesn't stick as you roll.

For the Glaze

1 **cup powdered sugar,
   plus more if you need**

2 **tablespoons whole milk,
   plus more if you need**

   Vanilla extract

   **Pretty sprinkles, for
   sprinkling, of course**

❖ *Don't Forget*

   Your food processor

It needs to be ⅛ inch thick and I roll mine out to be about 9 inches to make cutting easier. Ideally, the sides should be straight but if your tarts are a little wonky, no one's gonna care.

Now, cut that dough into 9 squares, 2 to 3 inches on each side. Drop a tablespoon of strawberry filling into the center of each, then spread it out, leaving a ½-inch border all around.

Roll out the second disk the same way, and cut it the same way, too. Top each piece of the dough with the filling with a piece of plain dough. Use a fork to crimp the sides and seal them all. Move them over to your baking sheet.

Break **1 large egg** into a small bowl, add the remaining **1 tablespoon water,** and whisk until it's completely smooth. Brush the tops of the tarts with the egg wash and poke a few holes in the surface with a fork so the steam can escape.

Bake until the tops are nice and golden, 20 minutes or so. When your tarts are done, move them over to a rack and allow them to cool completely so they won't melt the glaze, at least 30 minutes.

Make your glaze: In a medium bowl, combine **1 cup powdered sugar, 2 tablespoons whole milk,** and **a splash of vanilla extract** and mix well so there are no more lumps in there and you can drizzle it. If it's really thick, add just a tiny bit more milk and mix. If it's too thin, sprinkle in some more powdered sugar until it thickens up.

Now that the tarts have cooled a bit, drizzle the glaze over them in whatever pattern you desire. I like to drizzle it with a spoon and make a crisscross pattern, but they're your tarts, so do what you like. Shower them with **pretty sprinkles** and enjoy! Any extras you can keep in a container in the fridge for a few days.

Lil's Chick Nuggs

FEEDS 4 (GETS YOU ABOUT 32 NUGGETS) ❖ TAKES 1 HOUR

The closest one to our house may be a 40-minute drive, but Lily *loves* her Chick-fil-A. So, when she's got a craving and we aren't leaving home, I'll bust out the food processor and the frying grease and make her happy. Now, I know this might not be the prettiest cooking process, but I'll be damned if these aren't some tasty nuggets. My secret is ginger ale for the batter, which makes 'em light and crispy, and that little bit of sugar and spice brings out all the other seasonings. We're always fighting over the last nugget.

❖ Gather Up

For the Chicken

2 boneless, skinless chicken breasts (1¼ to 1½ pounds total)

Garlic powder

Onion powder

Cayenne pepper

Sweet paprika

Fine sea salt and ground black pepper

For Frying

Vegetable oil

1 cup (120 grams to be exact) all-purpose flour

1½ cups (168 grams) cornstarch

Garlic powder

Onion powder

Cayenne pepper

Sweet paprika

Fine sea salt and ground black pepper

1 cup (248 grams) ginger ale

❖ Don't Forget

Your food processor

❖ Let's Make Some Nuggets

Go ahead and line your baking sheet with parchment paper.

Start with the chicken: Cut **2 boneless, skinless chicken breasts** into small chunks. Get out your food processor and add your chicken, then sprinkle in **a palmful each of garlic powder** and **onion powder,** plus **a couple pinches each of cayenne pepper, sweet paprika, fine sea salt,** and **black pepper.** Blend for about 1 minute, until it's pureed, smooth, and tacky.

Grab about 1 tablespoon full of chicken with your hands and form it into a nugget shape (so, basically, whatever shape you like). Put it on the baking sheet and keep going until you've shaped all the chicken, making sure none of them are touching on the baking sheet. You should get 32 or so. Place in the freezer for 30 minutes to set.

Time to get frying: Over medium, heat **3 inches of vegetable oil** in a large Dutch oven or heavy-bottomed pot until it reaches 350°F. (If you don't have a thermometer, a pinch of flour should sizzle immediately.) Put a wire rack on a baking sheet or put some paper towels on a plate.

Add **1 cup (120 grams to be exact) all-purpose flour** and **1 cup (112 grams) cornstarch** to a wide, shallow dish, then sprinkle in **a palmful each of garlic powder** and **onion powder,** plus **a couple pinches each of cayenne pepper, sweet paprika, fine sea salt,** and **black pepper** and mix well. Pour in **1 cup (248 grams) ginger ale** and stir until you get a smooth, thick batter. In a separate shallow dish, add the last ½ **cup (56 grams) cornstarch.**

Grab one nugget at a time and toss it in the cornstarch with your hands, then into the batter; let any excess batter drip off, and then put it immediately into the oil. Repeat this with a few more nuggets, making sure not to crowd the oil so it stays hot enough. Fry until they start floating and get golden brown, flipping once or twice—5 to 6 minutes total. Use a slotted spoon or spider strainer to move them over to the rack when you're done, and repeat with the rest of the nuggets. Sprinkle them with a little fine sea salt, if you like. Allow to cool for 5 to 10 minutes before eating the best nuggets of your life.

Luke the Duke's Corn Dogs

GETS YOU 10 CORN DOGS ❖ TAKES 1 HOUR

Yes, Luke is a dog, and no, these are not for dogs. They're named after our German shepherd Luke because anytime he sees a hot dog hitting fryer oil, he drools so much you'd think he was half Saint Bernard. Luke is the first pet I ever picked out for myself. He is my beloved, my pride and joy, and an accomplished counter surfer who has gotten ahold of more corn dogs than is good for him. As careful as I am when I'm frying these up, he somehow always manages to get his fill. This recipe uses up a whole package of hot dogs, which makes enough for the family, and if we happen to sacrifice one, well, no one is missing out.

❖ Gather Up

Vegetable oil, for frying

2 tablespoons salted butter, homemade if you want (see page 34)

1 cup (120 grams to be exact) all-purpose flour

½ cup (75 grams) yellow cornmeal

2 tablespoons sugar

2 teaspoons baking powder

Fine sea salt

All-purpose seasoning, like Everglades, or homemade if you want (see page 38)

Garlic powder

Onion powder

Dried mustard

⅔ cup (151 grams) whole milk

1 large egg

10 beef hot dogs (one 1-pound/497 gram package)

❖ Don't Forget

10 wooden skewers

❖ Let's Start Dippin' Some Dogs

Fill a large Dutch oven with **3 inches of vegetable oil.** Over medium, heat the oil to between 325° and 350°F. (If you don't have a thermometer, a drop of batter should start gently bubbling right away.) Put some paper towels on a plate.

In a small pot over low heat, or in a small bowl in the microwave, melt **2 tablespoons salted butter** and let it cool for a few minutes.

In a large bowl, stir together **1 cup (120 grams to be exact) all-purpose flour, ½ cup (75 grams) yellow cornmeal, 2 tablespoons sugar, 2 teaspoons baking powder, a couple pinches each of fine sea salt** and **all-purpose seasoning,** plus **a pinch each of garlic powder, onion powder,** and **dried mustard.** Now, pour in ⅔ **cup (151 grams) whole milk,** crack in **1 large egg,** and add the melted butter. Whisk until the batter is almost smooth. It should be nice and thick.

For easier dunking, you can pour the batter into a wide-mouth large mason jar so you can easily stick a hot dog into it, or just keep the batter in the bowl. Stick a wooden skewer into one end of each of the **10 beef hot dogs.** Dip each hot dog into the batter so it's coated with a nice thick layer, then place the corn dog in the oil and cook, turning every 30 seconds to prevent the batter from sliding off, until golden brown all over, 2 minutes or so total. Set it on the paper towel–lined plate. Repeat with the rest of the hot dogs, not frying more than a few at a time so the oil temperature doesn't drop and you get soggy corn dogs.

Let cool for a couple minutes, then dig in while you try to keep any four-legged family members away.

Rookie's Cookies

(Homemade Dog Treats)

GETS YOU 8 TREATS ❖ TAKES ABOUT 40 MINUTES, PLUS TIME TO COOL

When I met James, he had a dog named Rookie, an old German shepherd. We had her for the first three years we were together, and me and that dog bonded like crazy. Lily, too, since Rookie decided it was her bed that she was going to sleep in. When Rookie passed, it was devastating for all of us; we really could feel her absence. It was so hard on Lily, I realized I had got to get her another dog. I surprised the family with a new German shepherd puppy. When James saw her for the first time, sitting in the front seat of the car, he looked right at her and he said "Rookie," and her ears perked up and she started wagging her tail at him, and that was all she wrote. Rookie One and Rookie Two are part of the family, and there was no way I was going to cook all this delicious homemade food and not give some to my fur babies. This is the best recipe in this book that I've never actually eaten.

❖ *Gather Up*

- **4 bacon strips**
- **2 cups (240 grams to be exact) all-purpose flour**
- **1 cup (270 grams) creamy peanut butter**
- **1 cup (227 grams) chicken broth, homemade bone broth if you want (see page 54)**
- **1 large egg**

Note: *Store any extras in a bag in the freezer for up to 3 months.*

❖ *Let's Show Our Pups Some Love*

Cut **4 bacon strips** in half. Place the bacon in your 10-inch cast-iron skillet over medium heat. Let the strips fry, turning once, until crispy and browned; 1 to 2 minutes for each side once it's sizzling. Move the bacon to your cutting board, leaving the fat behind, and chop it into small pieces.

Meanwhile, in a large bowl, combine **2 cups (240 grams to be exact) all-purpose flour, 1 cup (270 grams) creamy peanut butter, 1 cup (227 grams) chicken broth,** and **1 large egg.** Mix well with a wooden spoon until thoroughly combined, then cover the bowl with beeswax wrap or a reusable bowl cover. Put in the fridge to chill for 30 minutes.

Preheat your oven to 350°F. Go ahead and line your baking sheet with parchment paper.

Once the dough has chilled, take it out of the fridge and turn it out onto your counter. Make sure you got your bacon bits, too.

You can either divide the dough into 8 equal pieces or work as you go and eyeball it (that's what I do). If you're doing it my way, grab a palm's worth of the dough, or grab one piece. Roll it around in your hand until you have a smooth ball, then flatten it out a bit between your hands. Make a little taco shell shape and add some of the bacon bits in the middle, then pinch the edges together so the bacon is sealed in the dough. Roll it back into a ball shape, then set that cookie on your baking sheet. Repeat with the rest of the dough and bacon bits. And make sure the treats aren't touching.

Bake until the dough is cooked through and the tops are light brown, 10 minutes or so. Move the cookies to a rack to cool to room temperature, then treat your doggo!

BREAKFAST

—◇—

The most important meal of the day,
because it's my favorite to cook.

Baked Cheesy Garlic Grits

FEEDS 6 TO 8 ❖ TAKES ABOUT 1 HOUR

I'm not gonna sugar-coat it (or put sugar in these), but cooking grits is *hard*. Making good grits is all in the technique so there aren't any lumps, and you're walking a fine line between watery and clumpy. It takes a lot of practice to perfect your skills, and in the meantime you have to scrub all those crusty pots! This is my answer for grit newbies. I'm not quite sure of the how or why, but something about starting them on the stove and finishing them in the oven will get them smooth and creamy every time. I made my grits this way when I was still learning, so we never went without them.

❖ Gather Up

- **4 cups chicken broth,** homemade bone broth if you want (see page 54)
- **8 tablespoons (1 stick) salted butter,** homemade if you want (see page 34), plus more for serving
- **Garlic salt**
- **Ground black pepper**
- **2 cups old-fashioned grits**
- **1 cup whole milk**
- **1 cup heavy whipping cream**
- **1 (5-ounce) package garlic and herb cheese** (Boursin or something like it)
- **½ cup (4 ounces) cream cheese**
- **2 to 4 cups shredded white Cheddar cheese (8 to 16 ounces),** up to you

❖ Let's Bake Some Grits

Preheat your oven to 350°F.

In a large pot over medium, combine **4 cups chicken broth, 8 tablespoons (1 stick) salted butter, a couple pinches of garlic salt,** and as much **ground black pepper** as you like. Bring it to a boil. Start stirring like crazy and slowly pour in **2 cups old-fashioned grits** and keep stirring until the lumps are gone (it's an arm workout). Bring the mixture back up to a boil, then reduce the heat to low and simmer, uncovered and stirring every so often, until the grits are starting to thicken, 10 minutes or so.

Take the pot off the heat and stir in **1 cup whole milk, 1 cup heavy whipping cream, 1 (5-ounce) package garlic and herb cheese,** and **½ cup (4 ounces) cream cheese,** and stir to combine and break up the cheese. Pour everything into an 8-inch square baking dish and spread it out nice and even. Cover the top with **2 cups shredded white Cheddar cheese,** then take a look at it and decide if you want more cheese on top. I do, so I add the other **2 cups shredded cheese.**

Bake until the grits are bubbling and both the grits and cheese are nice and lightly browned, 30 to 40 minutes. I like to serve it right out of the oven, with **a pat of cold butter** on each serving to help cool it down and make it even more tasty.

Sweet Meets Spicy
Supreme Omelet

FEEDS 1 OR 2 ❖ TAKES ABOUT 30 MINUTES

I knew me and James were meant for each other from the moment I laid eyes on him. But the *second* moment I knew that was when James was the first (and only) person in my life who was willing to try my eggs and grape jelly combo. He's so sweet and trusting and open-minded, though he did have to put some sriracha on his before it touched his lips. Everyone thinks it's freaky, but I swear, just try it once. This sweet and spicy sauce is like our private love language.

❖ Gather Up

- 4 ounces bulk breakfast sausage
- 4 bacon strips
- A couple handfuls of fresh spinach
- 4 large eggs
- ¼ cup whole milk
- All-purpose seasoning, like Everglades, or homemade if you want (see page 38)
- Fine sea salt and ground black pepper
- 2 tablespoons salted butter, homemade if you want (see page 34)
- ⅓ cup shredded cheese, any kind (1½ ounces or so)
- 2 tablespoons grape jelly
- 1 teaspoon sriracha

❖ Let's Crack Some Eggs

Heat your 10-inch cast-iron skillet over medium. Put some paper towels on a plate. When the pan is good and hot, add **4 ounces sausage.** Break up the sausage with your spoon into bite-size pieces and stir everything a few times. Fry until it's cooked all the way through and browned, 5 minutes or so. Move your sausage to a small bowl to cool and leave the grease in the pan, then pour it off. Put the pan back on medium and add **4 bacon strips.** Cook, flipping once or twice, until lightly browned, 5 to 7 minutes. Move the bacon to the paper towels to drain, and then chop it.

While the meats cook, chop up **a couple handfuls of fresh spinach** so you get ⅓ cup or so.

In a medium bowl, combine **4 large eggs, ¼ cup whole milk, a couple pinches of all-purpose seasoning,** and **a pinch each of fine sea salt** and **black pepper.** Whisk until the eggs are smooth.

Over medium, heat up your medium nonstick skillet (or cast-iron if it's really well seasoned) with **2 tablespoons salted butter.** When the butter is melted, pour in the egg mixture. Let it go without touching it until the bottom is set and cooked, 1 minute or so, then lift one side of the cooked eggs with your spatula and let the uncooked egg run underneath so it cooks too. Repeat this until the eggs are mostly all set, another minute or two. Sprinkle your bacon, sausage, and spinach on top of half of the eggs, then add ⅓ **cup shredded cheese.**

Fold the naked half of the eggs over to cover your filling. Cook for 2 minutes, then flip it and let it cook for another 2 minutes or so on the other side to melt the cheese. Slide it onto your plate.

In a small bowl, whisk up **2 tablespoons grape jelly** and **1 teaspoon sriracha** until smooth, then drizzle the spicy grape mixture over the omelet. Share if you dare, dig in, and let me know if you ended up wanting *more of* that grape goodness. I always do.

Hahira Breakfast Cups

GETS YOU 12 LITTLE CUPS ❖ TAKES 1 HOUR

I hope everyone reading treats this recipe with tender loving care. It's so dear to my heart because it's the first thing I ever cooked for James. I was living in Hahira, Georgia, when I met him, and by the time we got around to figuring out how we liked our eggs (you know what I mean), we knew we were in it for the long haul. He ate this breakfast like it was sent straight from heaven to his stomach. Now whenever I make it, we just get all googly-eyed while we eat and stare at each other.

There have been some changes over the years, so this recipe just keeps getting better, like our love. It used to be deep-fried, and now it's baked and, ahem, healthy. I like it with pico and cilantro, but James prefers it without. We love bacon and sausage, but you can go down to ½ pound each if you want to taste more egg than meat in your breakfast.

❖ Gather Up

Butter or bacon grease, for the pan

4 tablespoons (½ stick) **salted butter, homemade if you want (see page 34)**

1 **pound russet potatoes (2 or so big ones)**

½ **cup grated Parmesan cheese (2 ounces)**

Fine sea salt and ground black pepper

1 **pound bacon**

1 **(1-pound) roll of breakfast sausage**

6 **large eggs**

A handful of fresh parsley

❖ Let's Make My Favorite Breakfast

Preheat your oven to 400°F. Go ahead and grease a 12-cup muffin tin with **butter.**

In a small pot over low heat, or in a small bowl in the microwave, melt **4 tablespoons (½ stick) salted butter.**

Peel **1 pound russet potatoes.** You can either shred them babies with the largest holes on your box grater or in a food processor, or keep peeling the potatoes with your peeler to make long, thin strands. Gather them up into a clean cheesecloth or kitchen towel and, over the sink, twist both ends to squeeze all that extra water out. You may need to do this in 2 batches to get them as dry as possible. And you need to squeeze hard!

Add the potatoes to a medium bowl along with the melted butter and ¼ **cup grated Parmesan cheese,** then season with **a good pinch of fine sea salt** and as much **ground black pepper** as you like. Mix everything together. You can taste a bit to make sure the seasonings are good. Start packing those potatoes into the muffin cups tightly, dividing it evenly among all the cups and making sure to cover the bottoms and go up the sides.

Bake until the potatoes are tender and browned, 20 to 25 minutes. Then set those babies aside. Don't turn off that oven yet.

While the potatoes are cooking, chop **1 pound bacon.**

(recipe continues)

Heat a 12-inch cast-iron skillet over medium. When the pan is good and hot, add the bacon and **1 (1-pound) roll of sausage.** Break up the sausage with your spoon into bite-size pieces and stir everything a few times. Fry until everything is cooked through and nice and browned, 10 minutes or so. Put the bacon and sausage in a medium bowl and leave the grease in the pan.

Now, crack **6 large eggs** into the pan. Season them with a pinch each of sea salt and black pepper and fry them sunny side up, but don't cook them eggs all the way—just cook until the whites are set, a couple of minutes. Put the eggs in the bowl with the meat and stir to combine, breaking up the eggs with your spoon into bite-size pieces.

Now, top the potatoes with the egg, bacon, and sausage mixture, dividing it evenly. Sprinkle the last ¼ **cup grated Parmesan cheese** over it all.

Bake in the oven until the cheese is lightly browned on top and the smell is mouthwatering, 10 minutes or so. Let the breakfast cups cool in the pan for 5 minutes before you move them to a rack to cool for another 10 minutes.

Chop up **a handful of fresh parsley leaves** and sprinkle them all over your breakfast—you know why—and serve 'em up.

Sunrise Quiche

FEEDS 6 TO 8 ❖ TAKES 2 HOURS

One Christmas, my friend Preston brought over a breakfast quiche for us and ever since then we eat one on every holiday. But I'm gonna be me and even though this is a special-occasion treat, it still starts with me throwing whatever I have in the fridge into the mix—some shiitakes, a bell pepper, maybe a sweet potato, mozzarella, and maybe some Cheddar. Thankfully, it turns out great every time. Switch up the veggies with whatever you got, or don't—even if it's just egg, cheese, meat, and crust, that's still a damn special breakfast.

❖ *Gather Up*

For the Crust

- 2 cups (240 grams to be exact) all-purpose flour, plus more for rolling

- 1 teaspoon fine sea salt

- 8 tablespoons (1 stick/ 113 grams) cold salted butter, homemade if you want (page 34)

- ½ cup (114 grams) cold water

For the Filling

- ½ small Vidalia onion

- 5 garlic cloves

- 8 ounces fresh shiitake mushrooms

- 1 red bell pepper

- 1 medium sweet potato

- 5 bacon strips

- 1 (1-pound) roll of breakfast sausage

- 4 large eggs

- 1 cup whole milk

- Fine sea salt and ground black pepper

- 1 cup any shredded cheese (4 ounces)

- 2 tablespoons salted butter, for pan

❖ *Press Play on Some Aerosmith and Make This Nice, Sexy Quiche*

Preheat your oven to 400°F.

Start with the crust: In a large bowl, stir together **2 cups (240 grams to be exact) all-purpose flour** and **1 teaspoon fine sea salt.** Cube **8 tablespoons (1 stick/113 grams) cold salted butter** (make sure it's *cold*) and add them to the bowl. Use your hands to work the butter into the flour until the mixture resembles coarse crumbs. Add **½ cup (114 grams) cold water** and knead in the bowl just until everything comes together to form a firm, dry dough and there aren't any loose bits of flour left. If the dough is sticky, sprinkle on a little more flour, knead again, and repeat until it's not sticking at all. Cover the bowl and place the dough in the fridge to chill while you make the filling.

About that filling: Chop ½ **small Vidalia onion** and **5 garlic cloves** (and keep 'em separate). Now, cut the rest of your vegetables into small (about ½-inch) pieces: **8 ounces fresh shiitake mushrooms, 1 red bell pepper,** and **1 medium sweet potato.**

Heat your 12-inch cast-iron skillet over medium-high. While it heats, cut **5 bacon strips** into bite-size pieces. When the pan is hot, add the bacon and **1 (1-pound) roll of breakfast sausage.** Cook, breaking up the sausage with your spoon into bite-size pieces, until the meat is cooked through and nicely browned, 10 minutes or so. Add the garlic and cook, stirring regularly, until you can smell it, 1 minute more. Use a slotted spoon to take the meat out of the pan and set it aside in a bowl, but keep the grease in the pan.

Reduce the heat to medium and add all your chopped vegetables. Cook, stirring regularly, until the sweet potatoes are tender but not falling apart, 10 minutes or so. Move the vegetables to the bowl with the meat and stir them in.

In a medium bowl, whisk together **4 large eggs, 1 cup whole milk, a couple pinches of fine sea salt,** and **a pinch of black pepper** until completely smooth. Stir in **1 cup shredded cheese** and set aside.

(recipe continues)

Make and bake the quiche: Get the dough from the fridge and lightly flour your counter. Use your rolling pin to roll out the dough to make a 14-inch circle (the dough needs to be big enough to fill the bottom and go up the sides of your skillet). To keep it in a nice, even circular shape, turn your dough a quarter turn after every roll or two, and flour it lightly as needed to keep it from sticking—and most important, have fun with it!

Melt **2 tablespoons salted butter** in your 10-inch cast-iron skillet over medium heat, but don't burn the butter. Just make sure your butter is melted and the pan is warm. Tilt the pan to get the butter all over the bottom and up the sides. Carefully place the rolled-out dough in the pan and if there's any overhang on the sides, fold it under and in. Place the veggies and meats on top of the dough to fill the center of your pie. Pour the egg mixture into the dough and over all the ingredients. Give it a shake to make sure it's spread out.

Bake until the eggs are set and firm and the pie crust is golden brown, 30 to 35 minutes. Let cool on a rack for 15 to 20 minutes, but not any longer—you want it to be slightly warm. Slice it up and celebrate your special morning.

Recipe for Love

One of the comments I get most on my recipes isn't about my recipes at all. It's how much people love seeing me and James in love. And everyone wants to know the secret to our marriage.

Our secret is we're crazy.

We became that couple we used to make fun of, who were always finishing each other's sentences and just plain being gross. We miss each other after a couple minutes. We can never stay mad for very long, even when we were just *fuming*.

Sometimes you just get lucky and meet your person. A big part of our success is that we've been crazy about each other since the moment we first made eye contact. It's like our energies fell in love and then our bodies quickly followed. We have this magnetic attraction that makes all the frustration that comes with being in a relationship so much easier to handle. We keep things very spicy and sexy (wink), and that helps us get through the arguments and the disagreements and the exhaustion of parenting.

We're both hyper-independent. Even in our previous relationships, we could never give that up. We were going to do everything our way, on our own. But when we got together, part of just *knowing* it was right is that we were both finally ready to let that go. We became a team, and pretty soon we were doing everything together (probably too much). Part of that was learning to respect each other; that one was hard for me. We're both stubborn and hot-headed, and we'll both show our asses right away, and I've had to learn how to cool it. But we know each other so thoroughly, and care so deeply about the other's happiness, that we can always pull back and remember the big picture. One fight's not going to derail us . . . we're in this for the long haul.

And we've been keeping that energy up for nearly 6 years now by the time you're reading this. Day to day, we're always being each other's yes man. James wants a back rub: He's got it. I don't want to make dinner: James is on it. One of us is the lighter, the other is the flame, and that spark is always going to get lit. Sometimes it can take a lot of effort, but you just have to remind yourself that loving your person deeply means showing that love, day in and day out. Because it's all or nothing when you're married, and James and I are all in.

Breakfast Hash

Croissant Sandwiches

GETS YOU 2 SANDWICHES ❖ TAKES 1 HOUR

After I made my Flaky & Fluffy Croissants (page 219) for the first time and realized how easy it was, I was making them like a madwoman. We were eating croissants for breakfast, lunch, and dinner for weeks. It's unreal how many we ate, now that I think about it. Anyway, this was a recipe I came up with to use them when they were just a little past their prime. I've used one-, even two-day-old croissants and they were still fantastic after a quick bake.

These sandwiches have everything you want from a breakfast stuffed inside buttery pastries, but I have been known to add some grape jelly and sliced avocado to mine.

❖ *Gather Up*

1 **medium russet potato**

1 **small Vidalia onion**

Fine sea salt and ground black pepper

3 **large eggs**

2 **tablespoons all-purpose flour**

Vegetable oil, for frying

4 **bacon strips**

2 **breakfast sausage patties**

2 **croissants, homemade if you want (see page 219)**

Salted butter, homemade if you want (see page 34), room temperature

2 **slices pepper jack cheese**

❖ *You're Gonna Be Glad You Made Extra Croissants*

Preheat your oven to 350°F.

Peel **1 medium russet potato** and **1 small Vidalia onion.** Using the largest holes on your box grater, shred the potato. Gather it up into a clean cheesecloth or kitchen towel and, holding it over the sink, twist both ends to squeeze out all that excess water. You need to squeeze hard! Add the potato to a medium bowl, then repeat the grating and squeezing with the onion and add it to the bowl. Season with **a good pinch of fine sea salt** and as much **ground black pepper** as you like. Add **1 large egg** and **2 tablespoons all-purpose flour** and mix it up really good. Roll the mixture into 2 palm-size balls.

Over medium, heat up your 12-inch cast-iron skillet with **a thin layer of vegetable oil** covering the bottom. Put some paper towels on a plate. When the oil is good and hot, add your potato balls and gently flatten them with your spatula so they're ¼ inch thick or so. Fry your hash browns until they're golden brown, 5 minutes or so on each side, then move them over to the plate to drain. If they fall apart a little, that's just more crispy bits. Sprinkle them with salt while they're hot.

Now, fry **4 bacon strips** and **2 breakfast sausage patties** in the grease, flipping them once or twice, until they're crispy and golden, 5 minutes or so total. Move them over to the paper towels, too, but leave the grease in the pan. Finally, crack the last **2 large eggs** into the pan and fry until the whites are set and the yolks are however you like 'em (I like over easy), just a couple minutes.

While you're cooking the eggs, cut the croissants in half horizontally and spread each half with some **butter.** Put them cut side up on a baking sheet. Bake until they're soft and lightly golden, 5 minutes or so.

On the bottom half of each croissant, put a hash brown, then add 1 egg, half the bacon and sausage, and top each with **1 slice of the pepper jack cheese.** Stuff those babies full, close them up, and let's eat!

Chicken & Waffles

FEEDS 4 ❖ TAKES AT LEAST 2 HOURS

I wish I could show you the chaos in our house on mornings that I make chicken and waffles. I jump out of bed as soon as I have the thought because I know I have to get that chicken marinating immediately. By the time James wakes up a few hours later, I'm in the kitchen with flour in my hair and everywhere and one boob hanging out of my robe. If you can be a little more organized than me and plan ahead, you can get that chicken going in the evening and have yourself a pretty leisurely morning. Maybe you'll even have time to fry up a few slices of bacon to serve with it.

❖ *Gather Up*

For the Chicken

1 **cup buttermilk, homemade if you want (see page 34)**

All-purpose seasoning, like Everglades, or homemade if you want (see page 38)

Garlic salt, or garlic powder, if you like

Onion powder

Cayenne pepper

Fine sea salt and ground black pepper

2 **bone-in, skin-on chicken breasts (1½ to 2 pounds total)**

Vegetable oil, for frying

2 **cups all-purpose flour**

1 **tablespoon baking powder**

2 **large eggs**

❖ *Let's Get in the Kitchen and Get to It*

Start with the chicken: In a large bowl, add **1 cup buttermilk,** then sprinkle in **a palmful of all-purpose seasoning, a couple pinches each of garlic salt** and **onion powder, a pinch of cayenne pepper** (2, if you're feeling spicy), and as much **ground black pepper** as you like. Cut **2 bone-in, skin-on chicken breasts** in half through the bone, and add those pieces to the bowl. Cover the bowl, and refrigerate for at least 1 hour, or up to overnight.

Over medium, heat up your 10-inch cast-iron skillet with **1 inch of vegetable oil** until the oil is 350°F. (If you don't have a thermometer, a pinch of flour should sizzle right away.) Put a wire rack on a baking sheet or put some paper towels on a plate.

While the oil heats up, in a large bowl, mix **2 cups all-purpose flour, 1 tablespoon baking powder,** a couple pinches each of garlic salt and onion powder, a pinch or 2 of cayenne pepper, and as much ground black pepper as you like. In a separate shallow bowl, crack in **2 large eggs** and beat them until smooth.

Take your chicken from the marinade one piece at a time, let any extra drip off, and put in the dry coating. Then shake off any extra flour, put it in the egg to coat, let any extra egg drip off, and then put back in the dry coating one more time to get it good and covered.

Add the chicken to the hot oil and reduce the heat to medium-low. Cook, turning every so often with your tongs, until the chicken is golden brown and your thermometer reads 160°F on the inside (or cut one piece and make sure it's not pink by the bone), 10 to 15 minutes total. Use the tongs to move the chicken to the rack and sprinkle with as much **fine sea salt** as you like.

(recipe and ingredients continue)

For the Waffles

- 6 tablespoons (¾ stick/ 85 grams to be exact) salted butter, homemade if you want (see page 34)
- 2 cups (240 grams) all-purpose flour
- ⅓ cup (65 grams; don't pack it) brown sugar
- 1 tablespoon baking powder
- 1 teaspoon baking soda
- 1 teaspoon fine sea salt
- 2½ cups (568 grams) buttermilk, homemade if you want (see page 34)
- 2 large eggs

For Serving

- ⅓ cup maple syrup
- Ground cinnamon

While the chicken fries, start on your waffles: Heat your waffle iron however the instructions tell you to. Preheat the oven to 200°F or so to keep the waffles warm as you make them.

In a small pot over low heat or in the microwave, melt **6 tablespoons (¾ stick/85 grams to be exact) salted butter.**

In a large bowl, stir together **2 cups (240 grams) all-purpose flour, ⅓ cup (65 grams) brown sugar, 1 tablespoon baking powder, 1 teaspoon baking soda,** and **1 teaspoon fine sea salt.** Now, add ¼ cup (4 tablespoons/57 grams) of the melted salted butter (keep the other 2 tablespoons melted butter warm, for serving), then **2½ cups (568 grams) buttermilk** and **2 large eggs.** Stir just until it's all mixed but there's still some lumps. Cook in your waffle iron according to the instructions until golden brown, then move them to a plate in the oven to keep warm as you finish them one by one, until you've made 4 waffles.

Now, let's serve these: In a small bowl, mix together ⅓ **cup maple syrup,** the last 2 tablespoons melted butter, and **a pinch of ground cinnamon.** Mix well and taste to see if it needs more cinnamon. Put a waffle on each plate, top it with a piece of chicken, then drizzle the sauce all over. Now, ain't that one of the best bites of food you ever had?

Soufflé French Toast Casserole

FEEDS 6 ❖ TAKES AT LEAST 12 HOURS

Look at the name of this recipe, what do you think? Complicated? Impressive? Classy? Probably not "easy"—but that's why I make this! James loves French toast and I love James, so I'll make it when he requests it, but I'm not about to stand over the stove dippin' and flippin' individual slices. I'm going to throw everything together in one pan and bake it. Sometimes I'll dollop some softened cream cheese on the top before baking if I'm feeling extra decadent (he loves it when I do that). And don't you worry—if you just let it sit for a couple of hours in the morning instead of in the fridge overnight, it'll be just as good. The bread soaks up all that custard and puffs up real nice in the oven.

❖ *Gather Up*

- 8 tablespoons (1 stick/ 113 grams to be exact) salted butter, homemade if you want (see page 34), plus more for the pan

- 1 (12-ounce/340 gram) loaf French bread

- ¾ cup (170 grams) heavy whipping cream

- ¾ cup (170 grams) whole milk

- ½ cup (156 grams) maple syrup

- ¼ cup (50 grams; no need to pack it) brown sugar

- 6 large eggs

- Vanilla extract, homemade if you want (see page 33)

- Ground cinnamon

- Cayenne pepper

- Powdered sugar, for serving

- Fresh blueberries, for serving

❖ *Let's Get This Breakfast Going*

Go ahead and **butter** your 9 × 13-inch baking dish real good. Cut **1 (12-ounce/340 gram) loaf French bread** into 1-inch cubes. In a small pot over low heat, or in a small bowl in the microwave, melt **8 tablespoons (1 stick/113 grams to be exact) salted butter.**

In a large bowl, whisk together the melted butter with ¾ **cup (170 grams) heavy whipping cream,** ¾ **cup (170 grams) whole milk,** ½ **cup (156 grams) maple syrup,** ¼ **cup (50 grams) brown sugar, 6 large eggs, a splash of vanilla extract, a couple pinches of ground cinnamon,** and **a pinch of cayenne pepper** until smooth.

Spread the bread in your buttered dish in an even layer. Pour in the custard, and sprinkle the top with more cinnamon. Cover the dish and refrigerate overnight.

The next morning, preheat your oven to 350°F.

Uncover the baking dish and bake until the custard is set and the top is golden and crisp, 1 hour or so. Shower the top with **powdered sugar,** scatter over some **blueberries,** and slice it up. Don't you feel fancy now?

Mixed Berry Scones

GETS YOU 8 SCONES ❖ TAKES 1¼ HOURS

No one else is brave enough to say it: Scones and biscuits are the same thing! Sure, they may be different shapes, but they're flour, butter, and dairy baked to perfection. And okay, fine, I will admit that I do change my biscuit technique *a little bit* here, but it's just a few small things: shredded or cubed butter, cream or buttermilk, egg or no egg. So, if you reckon you're the type of person who wants a scone and tea in the morning versus a biscuit and coffee, well, I got some buttery and tender scones for you.

❖ *Gather Up*

- 8 tablespoons (1 stick/ 113 grams to be exact) cold salted butter, homemade if you want (see page 34)
- 2 cups (240 grams) all-purpose flour, plus more for dusting
- ½ cup (100 grams) granulated sugar, plus more for sprinkling
- 1 tablespoon baking powder
- 1 teaspoon fine sea salt
- 1 lemon
- 1½ cups (155 grams) mixed fresh or frozen berries
- ⅓ cup (114 grams) heavy whipping cream, plus 2 tablespoons for brushing
- 1 large egg
  Vanilla extract, homemade if you want (see page 33)
- 1 cup (113 grams) powdered sugar
- 3 or 4 tablespoons (78 grams) whole milk, as you need it

❖ *Your Breakfast Ain't Never Been This Fancy*

Make sure your **8 tablespoons (1 stick/113 grams to be exact) salted butter** is *cold* and use the biggest holes on a box grater to grate it into a medium bowl. Stick it back into the freezer for 10 minutes to chill again.

In a large bowl, whisk together **2 cups (240 grams) all-purpose flour, ½ cup (100 grams) granulated sugar, 1 tablespoon baking powder,** and **1 teaspoon fine sea salt.** Now, add the grated cold butter. Get in there with your hands and massage the butter into the flour until it looks like coarse crumbs. Grate the zest of **1 lemon** into the bowl. Add 1½ **cups (155 grams) mixed berries** to the flour and toss to coat them.

Pour ½ **cup (114 grams) heavy whipping cream,** the **1 large egg,** and **a splash of vanilla extract** into the bowl, and mix with a wooden spoon or your hands until a rough, shaggy dough forms—do not overmix; the less you work it, the lighter your scones will be.

Cover a plate with a square of parchment paper. Lightly flour your counter and turn out the dough onto it. Gently pat the dough into a disk about 2 finger-widths tall and 8 inches or so wide. Slice the dough into 8 wedges, then put the wedges on the plate. Freeze for 30 minutes to help make sure they're nice and flaky.

Meanwhile, preheat your oven to 400°F. Go ahead and line a baking sheet with parchment paper.

Put the scones on the baking sheet and brush with the other **2 tablespoons heavy whipping cream.** Add **a sprinkle of granulated sugar** to the top of each. Bake until the scones are golden brown and a toothpick poked into the middle of one comes out clean, 20 to 22 minutes. Move the scones to a wire rack to cool completely.

Meanwhile, in a small bowl, combine **1 cup (113 grams) powdered sugar, 3 tablespoons whole milk,** and another **splash of vanilla extract,** and whisk until the glaze is runny. If it's too thick, add a very small splash of milk and mix again; repeat until it's runny. Drizzle the cooled scones with the glaze and enjoy with one pinky up.

Hoe Cakes

with Cranberry Jam & Powdered Sugar

FEEDS 4 ❖ TAKES 30 MINUTES

If I could just eat a big ole breakfast every day and nothing else, I'd be happy as a clam. It's the meal I like to get most creative with. That's why people are always so impressed when I make hoe cakes for them. These cute pancakes are a real big thing down here, but no one ever wants to go through the effort of making them. For me, though, heating up just a bit of grease in the pan to get that perfect bite—crispy on the outside and doughy on the inside, with some real nice texture from the cornmeal—is the best part of my day. And I'm always trying to find a way to get my family to eat more cranberries, but you can also use another jam if it feels like too much work, too early for you.

❖ *Gather Up*

For the Cranberry Jam

2½ **cups fresh or frozen cranberries**

½ **cup granulated sugar**

Ground cinnamon

1 **lemon**

For the Hoe Cakes

1 **cup (150 grams to be exact) yellow cornmeal**

¾ **cup (170 grams) buttermilk, homemade if you want (see page 34)**

½ **cup (60 grams) self-rising flour (see my Note)**

1 **large egg**

2 **tablespoons granulated sugar**

Vegetable oil or bacon grease, or whatever you prefer, for frying

Powdered sugar, for dusting

❖ *Let's Fry Some Hoe Cakes*

First, we jam: In a small pot, combine **2½ cups cranberries** and ½ **cup granulated sugar,** and sprinkle in **a palmful of ground cinnamon.** Put the pot over medium-high and bring to a simmer, then cook, stirring regularly, until the cranberries have popped and the jam is thick and glossy, 10 minutes or so. Zest in **1 lemon** and stir. Taste and see if it needs more cinnamon. Set the jam aside to cool for now.

Now, get those cakes ready: In a medium bowl, combine **1 cup (150 grams to be exact) yellow cornmeal, ¾ cup (170 grams) buttermilk, ½ cup (60 grams) self-rising flour, 1 large egg,** and **2 tablespoons granulated sugar** and mix thoroughly.

Over medium, heat up your 10-inch cast-iron skillet with **enough vegetable oil to coat the bottom.** Put some paper towels on a plate.

When the oil is good and hot, drop heaping spoonfuls of the batter into the oil, making sure to give each one some personal space. Cook until they're browned on the bottom and you see some bubbles staying on the surface, 3 minutes or so per side. Move the finished hoe cakes to the paper towels and fry up the rest of the batter, adding more oil if you need to keep the bottom of the pan covered.

When you've cooked all the batter, plate your cakes, shower them with **powdered sugar,** and dollop some cranberry jam on top. Enjoy!

Note: If you don't have self-rising flour, use ½ cup (60 grams) all-purpose flour, ¾ teaspoon baking powder, and ⅛ teaspoon (or just a pinch) of fine sea salt.

Sour Cream Vanilla Coffee Cake

FEEDS 6 TO 8 ❖ TAKES 1¼ HOURS, PLUS TIME TO COOL

If you make only one recipe in this book, make this one. I love sweets, and cake is my favorite sweet, and this is my favorite cake. It tastes like heaven: the moistness of a Bundt cake mixed with a sweet crumb topping in every bite, plus a *ton* of cinnamon and sour cream for good measure. I picture the afterlife as me sitting in a rocking chair out on the porch, watching James and the kids play in the yard while I savor a slice of this cake.

❖ *Gather Up*

Butter, bacon grease, or your grease of choice, for the pan

For the Crumb Topping

12 tablespoons (1½ sticks) salted butter, homemade if you want (see page 34)

¾ cup (don't pack it) brown sugar

⅓ cup granulated sugar

Ground cinnamon

Fine sea salt

Cayenne pepper

2¼ cups all-purpose flour

For the Cake

1 cup (200 grams to be exact) granulated sugar

12 tablespoons (1½ sticks/ 170 grams) salted butter, room temperature

2 large eggs

½ teaspoon fine sea salt

1 cup (227 grams) sour cream

Vanilla extract, homemade if you want (see page 33)

❖ *Don't Start Brewing Your Coffee Just Yet (But Soon)*

Preheat your oven to 350°F. Go ahead and grease an 8-inch square cake pan with **butter** or whatever you like to use. Then, line it with parchment paper so that 2 inches of paper stick up and over two of the sides.

First, make the crumble: In a small pot over low heat, or in a small bowl in the microwave, melt **12 tablespoons (1½ sticks) salted butter.** In a medium bowl, mix together ¾ **cup brown sugar, ⅓ cup granulated sugar, a heaping palmful of ground cinnamon,** and **a couple pinches each of fine sea salt** and **cayenne pepper** (to bring out the cinnamon flavor). Stir in the melted butter. Taste it and see if it needs more salt or cinnamon. Using a fork, gently mix in **2¼ cups all-purpose flour** until large crumbles form—do not overmix or you won't have crumbs. Set them aside for now.

Now, make the cake: Grab your stand mixer (or a large bowl if you're using your handheld mixer), and put on the whisk attachment. In the bowl, combine **1 cup (200 grams to be exact) granulated sugar** and **12 tablespoons (1½ sticks/170 grams) softened salted butter.** Beat on medium-high speed until light and fluffy, 3 minutes or so. Add **2 large eggs** and ½ **teaspoon fine sea salt** and beat on medium-high speed until smooth and sugar begins to dissolve, 30 seconds or so. Now, beat in **1 cup (227 grams) sour cream** and **2 splashes of vanilla extract** until good and mixed, about a minute. Add **2 cups (240 grams) all-purpose flour, 1 tablespoon ground cinnamon, 1½ teaspoons baking powder,** and ¼ **teaspoon baking soda** and beat until just combined, 1 to 2 minutes.

Use a spatula to scrape half the batter into the prepared pan and spread it into an even layer. Evenly sprinkle half the crumb topping in large clumps over the batter, breaking up any really big crumbs if you need. Scrape out the rest of the batter over the crumb layer, then using your spatula, gently smooth it out. Sprinkle the remaining crumble over the batter. Use your spatula to gently press down the crumb topping into the batter so it stays put.

2 cups (240 grams)
 all-purpose flour

1 tablespoon ground
 cinnamon

1½ teaspoons baking powder

¼ teaspoon baking soda

For the Glaze (If You Like)

½ cup powdered sugar

2 tablespoons whole milk
 (or dark rum for adults)

❖ *Don't Forget*

Your stand mixer with
the whisk attachment,
or handheld mixer

Bake until a toothpick poked into the middle comes out clean, 1 hour or so. Let the cake cool in the pan on a wire rack for 30 to 45 minutes, just until warm.

While you wait, make the optional glaze: In a small bowl, combine **½ cup powdered sugar** and **2 tablespoons whole milk,** and whisk with a fork until smooth. Lift the cake out of the pan using the parchment overhang. Drizzle the glaze over the top, slice, and make sure you got some nice hot coffee. Any extra will keep covered in the fridge for a few days.

Cranberry-Orange Cinnamon Rolls

with Lemon Glaze

GETS YOU 12 ROLLS ❖ TAKES 5 HOURS

So much of my cooking is about satisfying my family's cravings, but these rolls are what I make when what I'm craving is to be alone. We have a rule in our house that when me or James is cooking, no one else (no kids, no spouse, though I do allow for pets) is allowed to come in the kitchen. That's how us parents get our me-time. I'm like an artist going into my studio, getting in the zone and losing track of the world. When I emerge hours later, my soul feels lighter, and my family's happy because they get to eat a whole pan of cinnamon rolls. You may have picked up on the fact that I love cranberries, and I will not apologize for getting you to eat them at every meal of the day. They're healthy, they're delicious, and they're my secret weapon in this recipe.

❖ *Gather Up*

For the Filling

1 orange

2 cups fresh or frozen cranberries (about 9 ounces)

¾ cup granulated sugar

3 tablespoons salted butter, homemade if you want (see page 34)

For the Dough

1 cup (227 grams to be exact) whole milk

1 (¼ ounce) packet instant or active dry yeast (2¼ teaspoons)

½ cup (100 grams) plus 1 tablespoon granulated sugar

2 large oranges

4 tablespoons (½ stick/ 57 grams) salted butter

4 cups (480 grams) all-purpose flour, plus more for rolling

❖ *You'll Want to Get Out of Bed for These*

Start with the filling: Zest **1 orange** so you have a heaping tablespoon or so of zest, then cut it in half and squeeze out 2 tablespoons juice. In a small pot, combine **2 cups cranberries, ¾ cup granulated sugar, 3 tablespoons salted butter,** the orange juice, and orange zest. Bring the mixture to a boil over medium-high, stirring every so often, then cook until it thickens and some of the cranberries have broken down, 10 to 15 minutes. Move the pan off the heat and set in the fridge to chill completely, which should take 4 hours or so.

Make the dough: In a small pot over low heat, or in a small bowl in the microwave, warm **1 cup (227 grams to be exact) whole milk** to a little warmer than body temperature (100° to 110°F). Pour the milk into a small bowl or a measuring cup and add **1 (¼ ounce) packet instant or active dry yeast (2¼ teaspoons)** and **1 tablespoon granulated sugar.** Set it aside to let the yeast do its thing (foam and froth) for 5 to 10 minutes. While you wait, zest **2 large oranges** so you have 2 tablespoons zest, and melt **4 tablespoons (½ stick/57 grams) salted butter** in a small pot over low heat or in a small bowl in the microwave.

Grab your stand mixer (or a large bowl if you're kneading by hand), and put on the dough hook. In the bowl, add **4 cups (480 grams) all-purpose flour,** the other **½ cup (100 grams) granulated sugar, 2 large eggs, 1 tablespoon vanilla extract (2 if you're sexy), 1 tablespoon ground cinnamon, 1 teaspoon fine sea salt,** the yeast mixture, the melted butter, and the orange zest. Mix on medium-high speed until it forms a smooth dough and starts to bang on the sides of the bowl, 10 minutes or so. Cover the bowl with a towel or bowl cover and let rest until doubled in size, which takes 1 hour or more in my kitchen.

2 large eggs

1 or 2 tablespoons vanilla extract, homemade if you want (see page 33), up to you

1 tablespoon ground cinnamon

1 teaspoon fine sea salt

Butter, bacon grease, or the fat of your choice, for the pan

For the Lemon Icing

4 tablespoons salted butter

1 lemon

1½ cups powdered sugar

❖ *Don't Forget*

Your stand mixer with the dough hook, or a large bowl

Grease your 12-inch cast-iron skillet with **butter** or the fat of your choice. Lightly flour your counter. Turn out the dough onto the counter and use a rolling pin to roll it out into a rectangle 12 inches by 16 inches or so. Be sure to flour the dough so it doesn't stick, and work from the center out to the edges to keep the shape even. Once it's rolled out, spread the cooled filling all over it generously, leaving a 1-inch border all around. Starting with the longer edge closest to you, gently and carefully roll it all the way up into a log, not pressing so hard the filling seeps out of the ends. Trim the ends so they're neat, then cut it into 1½-inch-thick rolls. You should get about 12 rolls.

Evenly space the rolls in the greased skillet, cover with a towel, and let them rise until they're puffy and touching, 30 minutes or so. Meanwhile, preheat your oven to 350°F.

Uncover the skillet and bake until the rolls are puffed up and lightly golden on top, 20 to 30 minutes. Let them sit in the pan for 10 minutes to cool a bit.

Now, let's make the icing: In a small pot over low heat or in a small bowl in the microwave, melt **4 tablespoons salted butter.** Zest **1 lemon** so you have 1 tablespoon or so, then cut it in half and squeeze the juice from half the lemon into a large bowl. Add the **1½ cups powdered sugar,** your melted butter, and the zest. Stir everything together until the icing is smooth.

After the rolls have cooled, ice them babies up and enjoy, my friend!

Apple Cinnamon Strudels

GETS YOU 8 PASTRIES ❖ TAKES ABOUT 6 HOURS

Warning: If you do not like being in the kitchen, do not make this recipe, because once you do, you're screwed. If you don't want to have to make breakfast pastries from scratch because your family now refuses to eat the store-bought ones after they've tasted yours, do not make this recipe. If you don't want to feel the intense sense of accomplishment that will make you shout "YEAH, I JUST MADE SOME FREAKIN' STRUDELS" while you flip ya hair and wait for the compliments to roll in, do not make this recipe.

❖ Gather Up

For the Dough

1½ cups (3 sticks/340 grams to be exact) cold salted butter, homemade if you want (see page 34)

1 cup (227 grams) whole milk, room temperature

4 tablespoons (50 grams) granulated sugar, plus more for sprinkling

1 (¼-ounce) packet instant or active dry yeast (2¼ teaspoons)

3½ cups (420 grams) all-purpose flour, plus more for rolling

1 teaspoon fine sea salt

1 large egg

For the Filling

2 tablespoons salted butter

2 medium apples

½ lemon

½ cup (no need to pack it) brown sugar

Vanilla extract, homemade if you want (see page 33)

Ground cinnamon

Ground nutmeg

1 teaspoon all-purpose flour

❖ Let's Get Rolling, and Let the Praise Roll In

Start with the dough: Make sure your **1½ cups (3 sticks/340 grams to be exact) salted butter** are *cold.* In your small pot over low heat, or in a small bowl in the microwave, warm **1 cup (227 grams) whole milk** and **½ cup (114 grams) water** to a little warmer than body temperature (100° to 110°F). Move the pan off the heat and add **1 tablespoon granulated sugar** and **1 (¼-ounce) packet instant or active dry yeast (2¼ teaspoons).** Stir to mix and set it aside to let the yeast do its thing (foam and froth) for 5 to 10 minutes.

In a large bowl, add **3½ cups (420 grams) all-purpose flour,** the last **3 tablespoons granulated sugar,** and **1 teaspoon fine sea salt,** and then pour in the yeast mixture. Mix everything together with your hands and then knead until a smooth dough forms, 5 to 7 minutes. Cover the bowl with a kitchen towel and set aside for a few minutes to hang out. In the meantime, we're about to have some fun.

Grab a foot or so of parchment paper. Unwrap your butter and place the sticks side by side on top of the parchment paper. Then grab another sheet of parchment paper (same length) and place on top of the butter. Get a wooden paddle or rolling pin or other hard object and start whacking that butter. You want to pound it until it's an evenly flattened block of butter that's 8 inches by 10 inches and ¼ inch thick or so. Once you've successfully let all your anger out onto those butter sticks, wrap them in the parchment and put the flattened butter and the bowl with the dough in the fridge for 1 hour to chill.

When the dough has chilled, grab the bowl and take off the towel. Lightly flour your counter and roll out the dough. It might be a little sticky, but that's what we want. Using a rolling pin, roll out the dough into a large rectangle that's 12 inches by 15 inches or so and ⅛ inch thick. Try to roll the dough out as much as possible without getting it so thin that it rips.

(recipe continues)

Next, grab your flattened butter block. Take off the parchment paper and place the butter in the center of the dough rectangle. Take one side of your dough and fold it onto the butter, so half of the butter's completely covered. Repeat with the other side, then stretch the dough to meet in the middle, press together, and fold over the shorter edges so you've still got a nice and even rectangle and the butter is completely enclosed. Roll out the dough again into a rectangle that's ½ inch thick and fold it over itself like you're folding a business letter. Wrap the dough in parchment paper and place it back in the fridge for 30 minutes.

Lightly flour your counter again. Unwrap the dough and roll it out to a ½ inch thick rectangle. Fold it again into thirds like a business letter and roll out again. Your dough should now look like a condensed, folded dough brick. Wrap it in the same parchment paper and put it back in the fridge to let the butter firm up again, 1 hour or so.

Now, you're going to roll the dough out one more time, but to a rectangle that's 15 by 22 inches or so and ¼ inch thick. Using a sharp knife, cut it into 8 rectangles, that are 7½ by 5½ inches or thereabouts.

Preheat your oven to 400°F. Go ahead and line a baking sheet with parchment paper.

Now, make your filling: In a small pot over low heat, or in a small bowl in the microwave, melt **2 tablespoons salted butter.**

Peel, core, and thinly slice **2 medium apples,** so you have 2 cups (any extra are snacks) and add them to a large bowl. Squeeze ½ **lemon** into the bowl just until you get 1 tablespoon juice. Add the melted butter, ½ **cup brown sugar, a small splash of vanilla extract,** and **a few pinches each of ground cinnamon** and **ground nutmeg,** and mix it all together. Taste it and see if it needs more of anything. Now, mix in **1 teaspoon all-purpose flour.**

Make and bake the strudels: Spoon ¼ cup of your filling on half of one piece of dough, leaving enough room to seal the strudel on one side. Fold the opposite short end over so now you have a littler square, and seal the 3 open sides with a fork. Repeat with all the dough pieces. Place each strudel on the baking sheet with 1 inch between them. Cut a couple of slits in the top of each to let the steam escape.

In a small bowl, whisk together **1 large egg** and **1 tablespoon water** until smooth. Brush the egg wash over the strudels, then sprinkle with granulated sugar.

Bake until golden brown and puffy, 15 to 20 minutes. Move the strudels to a wire rack to cool just until warm, then take a bite and let the praise begin. Any extras will keep in a container in the fridge for a few days.

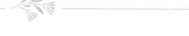

Whipped Chocolate Ganache Donuts

GETS YOU 6 DONUTS ❖ TAKES AT LEAST 14 HOURS

Oh my god, if I could make these donuts every week I would. But I don't because I can't stop myself from eating all of them. But even more than I love eating sweets, I love cooking breakfast. I am in my element in the kitchen in the morning: My hair is crazy, I'm not wearing makeup, I'm in my fabulous robe (and you know I'm not wearing anything underneath), and I feel like a true boss. If you haven't found your place in the kitchen yet, I highly recommend returning to this page, putting on your tunes, and start working some of this sweetened yeasty dough. You need to start the day before, so the donuts got time to rise and get nice and flavorful, but by the time you're eating a fresh-fried donut filled with an extra fluffy chocolate ganache, you'll feel like your best, most talented, hottest self.

❖ *Gather Up*

For the Donuts

- 4 tablespoons (½ stick/ 57 grams to be exact) salted butter, homemade if you want (see page 34)

- 3 large eggs

- ⅓ cup (76 grams) heavy whipping cream

- 1 tablespoon vanilla extract, homemade if you want (see page 33)

- 2½ cups (300 grams) all-purpose flour, plus more for rolling

- ¼ cup (50 grams) sugar

- 1 (¼-ounce) packet instant or active dry yeast (2¼ teaspoons; see my Note on page 215)

- 1 teaspoon fine sea salt

❖ *You're About to Fry Donuts, Friend!*

Start with the donut dough: In a small pot over low heat, or in a small bowl in the microwave, melt **4 tablespoons (½ stick/57 grams to be exact) salted butter.** Let it cool slightly.

Grab your stand mixer (or a large bowl if you're using a handheld mixer), and put on the whisk attachment. In the bowl, combine the melted butter, **3 large eggs,** ⅓ **cup (76 grams) heavy whipping cream,** and **1 tablespoon vanilla extract** (you can just eyeball a big splash of it). Mix on low speed until everything is nice and blended, 1 to 2 minutes, then add in **2½ cups (300 grams) all-purpose flour,** ¼ **cup (50 grams) sugar, 1 (¼-ounce) packet instant or active dry yeast (2¼ teaspoons),** and **1 teaspoon fine sea salt.**

Bump up the mixer speed to medium-high and mix until the dough comes together, 1 to 2 minutes more. Lightly flour your counter and turn out the dough. Knead it until it's a smooth ball that's not sticky at all, 5 minutes or so, sprinkling it with a little more flour only if you absolutely need to stop it sticking. Put the ball in a clean large bowl, cover with a bowl cover or towel, and refrigerate for at least 12 hours (you can go up to 24 hours).

Then make the ganache: Put ½ **cup bittersweet chocolate** into a medium heatproof bowl. In a small pot over medium heat, bring ½ **cup heavy whipping cream** and **2 tablespoons salted butter** to a simmer, stirring regularly. As soon as it's bubbling, pour the cream over the chocolate and let it sit, without messing with it, for 10 minutes. After you've been patient, stir everything together until it's smooth and creamy. Cover the bowl with a bowl cover and refrigerate until firm, 2 hours or so.

(recipe and ingredients continue)

For the Ganache

½ cup bittersweet chocolate
(you can buy disks
for baking or give a
bar a rough chop)

½ cup heavy whipping cream

2 tablespoons salted butter

Vegetable oil, for frying

Sugar

❖ *Don't Forget*

Your stand mixer with
the whisk attachment,
or handheld mixer

A 1-pint wide-mouth mason
jar, or a 3-inch round
biscuit or cookie cutter

A piping bag (or a big
zip top plastic bag)

When you're ready to fry, lightly flour your counter again. Gently turn out the dough onto it and use a rolling pin to roll it out until it's 2 finger-widths tall. Use your mason jar to cut as many donuts as you can, then re-roll the dough and repeat. You should get 6 total. Cover the dough with a towel and let it rise until very puffy and almost doubled in size, 1 hour or so.

Now we're frying: Fill your large Dutch oven with **2 to 3 inches of vegetable oil** over medium heat until the oil is 350° to 375°F (if you don't have a thermometer, a pinch of dough should start sizzling immediately). Put a wire rack on a baking sheet or put some paper towels on a plate.

When the oil is ready, reduce the heat to medium-low so the temperature stays steady, and add a few donuts to the oil—don't crowd the pan—and fry until they're nice and golden, 1 to 2 minutes per side. Use a spider strainer or tongs to move the finished donuts to the wire rack and repeat with the rest of the dough.

Cover a small plate with a thin layer of **sugar** and roll the donuts in the sugar to cover while they're still warm, then put them back on the rack to cool completely, 30 minutes or so. When they're cool, cut a little hole through the center of the top of the donut, just a little one to the middle so you can fill that baby with chocolate.

Fill the donuts: Get your stand mixer with the whisk attachment (or a large bowl and handheld mixer) back out, and add the ganache. Whip on medium speed until it's fluffy, 1 to 2 minutes. Scoop the ganache into a piping bag (or just a big zip top bag) and push all the ganache toward the tip. Twist the top to create some pressure, then cut off the bottom tip of the bag, a ½ inch or so.

Put the tip of the piping bag into the hole you cut in each donut and squeeze in the ganache until it comes out of the top and looks really pretty. Enjoy all your hard work right away!

SNACKS, APPS & SIDES

—— ◈ ——

The bites may be small,
but the flavors are *big*.

Aunt Teisha's Cowboy Caviar

FEEDS A CROWD (GETS YOU 8 CUPS) ❖ TAKES 45 MINUTES

My Mama, Leisha, and my Aunt Teisha are twins. At every single family gathering, whether it's Christmas, Thanksgiving, or a kid's birthday party, Teisha is bringing her cowboy caviar—and tequila. Those evenings go something like this: Mama, Teisha, and their two sisters set themselves down to drink tequila and get to chatting. Then when they're good and ready, they head into the kitchen to prepare the meal. Only after I was old enough to join them in the drinking did they invite me in for the second part of their ritual. That first get-together is one of my fondest memories. They were in the kitchen dancing and singing and *cackling;* they were having such a good time, and that's when I knew I was going to love cooking. This is my ode to Teisha, one of the family members I can lean on the most. She's finding out her signature dip of seasoned-up beans, avocado, and all sorts of goodness scooped up with chips is in this book, the same way you are.

❖ *Gather Up*

1 cup frozen sweet corn

1 (15-ounce) can black beans

1 (15-ounce) can black-eyed peas

3 plum tomatoes

1 jalapeño pepper

¼ small red onion

1 yellow bell pepper

A handful of fresh cilantro

⅓ cup olive oil

1 lemon or lime

Sugar

Garlic salt

Onion powder

All-purpose seasoning, like Everglades, or homemade if you want (see page 38)

Cayenne pepper

2 ripe avocados

Fine sea salt and ground black pepper

Tortilla chips, for serving

❖ *Let's Get in the Kitchen*

First, thaw **1 cup frozen sweet corn.** Drain and rinse **1 (15-ounce) can black beans** and **1 (15-ounce) can black-eyed peas.** Set them all aside to drain while you chop all your vegetables. Get out your knife and toss what you chop into a large bowl as you go: Scoop out the seeds and dice (meaning make those pieces nice and even and small) **3 plum tomatoes** and **1 jalapeño pepper** (leave the seeds in if you can handle the heat!). Dice ¼ **small red onion** and **1 yellow bell pepper.** Chop **a handful of fresh cilantro** so you get about ¼ cup, and leave a few sprigs for garnish later. Phew, that was a lot of chopping! Add your corn and beans to the bowl now, too.

In a small bowl, combine ⅓ **cup olive oil,** the juice of ½ **lemon, a couple pinches each of sugar, garlic salt, onion powder,** and **all-purpose seasoning,** then add **a pinch cayenne pepper** (2, if you're feeling spicy) and whisk together. Taste it and add the juice from the other lemon half if you think it needs it, or any other seasonings, until you're happy.

Pour the dressing into the large bowl and stir to coat everything. Dice **2 ripe avocados** and gently stir them in. Taste and season with **fine sea salt** and **ground black pepper.** Garnish with some of that cilantro you set aside to make it fancy. Enjoy with plenty of **tortilla chips** (and tequila).

Smoked Salmon Dip

FEEDS 4 HUNGRY PEOPLE ❖ TAKES AT LEAST 10 MINUTES (IDEALLY 1 DAY)

My friend Luke's dad is famous for his fish dip. Everyone brings him their fish, he smokes it and makes this dip with it, and no one can ever stop talking about it. I finally had to try this dip for myself, and you know how I am—I thought, "*Well, hell, I could make this.*" Plus I didn't have a choice since Luke's dad told me he was taking that recipe to the grave. Here's my version, with some Hannah touches (dill) that make it a little different but just as tasty. I hope that someday everyone starts coming to my house to hang out with me and eat my dip, if I can ever stop James from eating all of it first.

❖ Gather Up

A handful of fresh dill

A handful of fresh chives

1 **(8-ounce) package cream cheese, room temperature**

¼ **cup sour cream**

¼ **cup mayonnaise, homemade if you want (see page 42)**

Tabasco

Garlic salt

Ground black pepper

½ **lemon**

Liquid smoke, if you like

8 **ounces hot-smoked salmon (or another smoked fish, like trout, if you want)**

Ritz crackers or potato chips, for serving

❖ Don't Forget

Your food processor, or a medium bowl

❖ Let's Make Some Dip

Chop **1 handful of fresh dill** and **a handful of fresh chives.** Measure out a heaping spoonful of each and put them in your food processor (or a medium bowl). Save the rest of the chopped dill and chives for garnish. To the food processor, add **1 (8-ounce) package softened cream cheese, ¼ cup sour cream, ¼ cup mayo, a couple shakes of Tabasco,** and **a pinch each of garlic salt** and **black pepper.** Squeeze in the juice from ½ **lemon** and if you like an intense smoky taste, add **a small splash of liquid smoke.** Mix until smooth and combined. Scrape into a medium bowl.

Chop **8 ounces hot-smoked salmon** into bite-size pieces and stir into your cream cheese base. Taste it and add more of any of the seasonings until you're happy.

This dip is best if it's made the night before and served cold, so if you got the time, cover the bowl and refrigerate it for up to 24 hours.

When you're ready to dig in, spread the dip in your best serving dish and top it with the dill and chives you set aside ('cause we fancy). Serve cold with **crackers or potato chips** for dipping. I don't know if this dip keeps because we never have leftovers.

Mama's Classic Fried Deviled Eggs

GETS YOU 12 ❖ TAKES 1 HOUR

I dressed up my Mama's fried deviled eggs with herbs and a touch of sweetness from some honey, and use panko bread crumbs instead of regular because they fry up so nicely. Now, I can't usually be bothered with a piping bag, but if you want to get decorative with your deviled eggs, by all means, be my guest.

❖ *Gather Up*

Ice water

Distilled white vinegar

8 large eggs

Vegetable oil, for frying

¼ cup mayonnaise, homemade if you want (see page 42)

1 teaspoon mustard, homemade if you want (see page 45) or Dijon

1 teaspoon honey

Hot sauce (I like Tabasco)

Fine sea salt and ground black pepper

A handful of fresh dill

1 cup panko bread crumbs

Cayenne pepper

Sweet paprika

❖ *Let's Devil Some Eggs*

Add about 4 cups of water to a medium pot so your eggs will be covered. Fill a medium bowl with **ice water.** Bring the water in the pot to a boil over medium-high and add **a splash of distilled white vinegar.** Add **6 large eggs** and boil for 5 minutes, then move the pot off the heat and let the eggs sit in the hot water for 5 more minutes. Move the eggs to the ice water for 10 minutes. Drain and peel the eggs, and pat them real dry so the breading sticks.

Heat **2 inches of vegetable oil** in a large heavy-bottomed pot to between 350°F and 360°F. (If you don't have a thermometer, a pinch of panko should sizzle right away.) Put some paper towels on a plate.

Halve the cooked eggs lengthwise, then separate the egg whites from the yolks, placing the yolks in a small bowl. To the egg yolks add **¼ cup mayonnaise, 1 teaspoon mustard, 1 teaspoon honey, a couple shakes of hot sauce, a pinch of fine sea salt,** and **a big pinch of black pepper.** Chop **a handful of fresh dill** to get 3 tablespoons or so, and add most of it to the bowl (save the rest for later). Use a fork to mix the ingredients until they're smooth and creamy. Taste and add more of any of the seasonings until you're happy. Cover the bowl.

In a small shallow bowl, beat together the last **2 large eggs** until smooth. In another small shallow bowl, mix together **1 cup panko bread crumbs, a couple pinches of fine sea salt,** and **a pinch of ground black pepper,** and then add **a small sprinkle of cayenne pepper.** Take each egg white half and coat all over in the bread crumb mixture, then dip in the beaten egg, let the excess drip off, then place it back in the panko mixture to coat it one more time.

Use a slotted spoon or spider strainer to carefully lower the breaded egg whites into the hot oil, without adding too many at once to drop the temperature, and fry until golden brown, 2 minutes or so per side. Using your slotted spoon, put them on the paper towels. Sprinkle with fine sea salt and repeat with the other eggs. Let the eggs cool until warm.

Add a heaping spoonful of the egg yolk mixture to each egg white, making sure to use up all the filling. Garnish with the dill you set aside and **a sprinkling of sweet paprika.** Snap a picture, they look so good.

Fry Me a River, Corny Fritters!

FEEDS 4 TO 6 ❖ TAKES 1 HOUR

When I figured out how to make my own corn fritters at home, well, that was a life milestone, up there with becoming a mother and meeting James. As a kid, if there were corn fritters on a menu, you better believe I was ordering them. They were, and continue to be, my favorite food (or one of them, anyway). This recipe is perfection. They're sweet, creamy, spicy, and crunchy—everything I want from a fritter. I had to mess around with the ingredients quite a bit to get everything perfect, so I suggest you try it once as is, before you get to experimenting yourself.

❖ Gather Up

- 4 ears of fresh sweet corn, or 3 cups frozen sweet corn (no need to thaw it)
- ½ small Vidalia onion
- 2 garlic cloves
- 1 cup shredded sharp white Cheddar cheese (4 ounces)
- ½ cup heavy whipping cream
- ½ cup all-purpose flour
- 2 large eggs
- 1 tablespoon sugar
- 1 teaspoon baking powder
- All-purpose seasoning, like Everglades, or homemade if you want (see page 38)
- Onion powder
- Garlic powder
- Cayenne pepper
- Vegetable oil, for frying
- Fine sea salt and ground black pepper
- A couple fresh chives

❖ Let's Fry Some Fritters

Slice the kernels off **4 ears of sweet corn,** or use the **3 cups frozen sweet corn.** Chop up ½ **small Vidalia onion** nice and small so you get ¼ cup or so, and chop **2 garlic cloves.**

Add the corn, onion, and garlic to a large bowl, then add **1 cup shredded sharp white Cheddar cheese,** ½ **cup heavy whipping cream,** ½ **cup all-purpose flour, 2 large eggs, 1 tablespoon sugar, 1 teaspoon baking powder, a couple pinches each of all-purpose seasoning, onion powder,** and **garlic powder,** and **a pinch of cayenne pepper.** Mix together until you get a batter that's a little thicker than pancake batter.

Pour enough **vegetable oil** into your 12-inch cast-iron skillet to cover the bottom by ½ inch. Heat the oil over medium until it reaches 300° to 350°F. (If you don't have a thermometer, a drop of batter should start sizzling immediately. While you're at it, eat your test fritter and make sure you're happy with the seasoning.) Put some paper towels on a plate.

When the oil is ready, add heaping tablespoons of the batter to the pan, making sure not to crowd the fritters; I can usually get 8 to 10 in the pan at a time. Fry the fritters, not messing with them except to flip them once so they get good and crisp, until golden brown and cooked through, 3 to 4 minutes on each side. You'll know it's time to flip them when the tops start to bubble and the bottoms release easily from the pan. Using tongs or a slotted spoon, move the finished fritters to the paper towels. Repeat with the rest of the batter.

Sprinkle the hot fritters with **fine sea salt** and **black pepper.** Chop **a couple fresh chives** up nice and small and shower them on top. Aren't they just perfect?

Loaded-Up Potato Skins

Me and James are absolute freaks for potatoes, and when one of us gets the itch, you better believe I'm making loaded potato skins. With all due respect for any other way to cook potatoes, these have captured our hearts and stomachs. They're crispy on the outside, soft and fluffy on the inside, covered in melted cheese—and the best part is, the kids don't want anything to do with them, so we don't have to share.

❖ Gather Up

- **6 medium baking potatoes (like russets)**
- **Olive oil**
- **Fine sea salt and ground black pepper**
- **6 bacon strips**
- **1 cup shredded Cheddar cheese (4 ounces)**
- **½ cup shredded Colby jack cheese (2 ounces)**
- **A couple fresh chives**
- **Salted butter, homemade if you want (see page 34), for serving**
- **Sour cream, for serving**

❖ Let's Load Up Some Potato Skins

Preheat your oven to 400°F. Go ahead and line your baking sheet with foil.

Scrub and clean **6 medium baking potatoes,** then dry them off real good; any water left will keep them from getting crispy. Place the potatoes on the baking sheet and drizzle with enough **olive oil** to coat. Then sprinkle all over with **fine sea salt.** Bake until the skins are dark and crispy, and the potatoes are soft all the way through, 1 hour or so. Let cool out of the oven for 10 minutes before you mess with them. Switch the oven to broil.

While they're baking, heat your 10-inch cast-iron skillet over medium. Put some paper towels on a plate. When the pan is hot, add **6 bacon strips** and cook, flipping a few times, until they're cooked and crisp, 5 to 7 minutes total. Put the bacon on the paper towels and let drain for a couple minutes. Chop the bacon into small pieces.

Once the potatoes are cool enough to touch, cut them in half longways. Use a spoon to scoop out the middle of each potato to make room for the filling; leave ½ inch or more of potato next to the skin. (Save the potato scraps for your littles.) Put the potatoes back on the baking sheet, scooped sides up. Sprinkle them with salt and **ground black pepper.**

Sprinkle the potatoes evenly with **1 cup shredded Cheddar cheese** and **½ cup shredded Colby jack cheese.** Broil until the cheese is good and melted, 3 minutes or so, but keep an eye on it because every broiler has a mind of its own.

Chop **a couple fresh chives** nice and small and add your toppings! Top each potato skin with **a pat of salted butter** to start to cool things down, then **a dollop of sour cream,** then sprinkle with the chopped bacon and chives. Enjoy, my friend.

Hot, Sweet & Sexy Wings

FEEDS 4 ❖ TAKES JUST OVER 1 HOUR

James is a wing man. And the best kind of wingman, may I add. He took us girls out to the bar one night, and it ended very well for everyone involved (you already know who I went home with). My wingman likes his sweet and spicy, but not *too* spicy. They're on the sweeter side, just like him.

❖ *Gather Up*

- 3 **pounds whole chicken wings**
- **Onion powder**
- **Sweet paprika**
- **Garlic salt**
- **Garlic powder**
- **Ground black pepper**
- **Cayenne pepper**
- 1 **tablespoon baking powder**
- 4 **tablespoons (½ stick) salted butter, homemade if you want (see page 34)**
- ½ **cup (no need to pack it) brown sugar**
- ⅓ **cup Tabasco**

❖ *Let's Get Sweet and Spicy*

Preheat your oven to 425°F. Go ahead and line your rimmed baking sheet with foil and put a wire rack inside. Wash and dry **3 pounds chicken wings.** (I wash my chicken! You can skip it if you want.)

In a large bowl, sprinkle in **a palmful each of onion powder** and **sweet paprika,** and then **a couple pinches each of garlic salt, garlic powder,** and **black pepper,** and **a pinch of cayenne pepper,** then whisk until thoroughly combined. That's your dry rub. Taste a little bit and add more of any of the seasonings until you're happy. Now, stir in **1 tablespoon baking powder.** Add the chicken wings and get in there to make sure they're all good and covered with the seasoning.

Spread out the chicken wings on the rack without touching one another. Bake, turning the wings every 20 minutes, until they're lightly browned, 1 hour or so. Take them out of the oven and let cool on the rack for 5 to 10 minutes.

While the wings bake, in a small pot over medium, melt **4 tablespoons (½ stick) salted butter.** Add **½ cup brown sugar** and **⅓ cup Tabasco.** Cook, stirring every so often, until the sugar is completely dissolved, 3 to 4 minutes. Move the pan off the heat and let the sauce cool a bit so it's just warm, 5 to 10 minutes.

Once everything is good and cool, put the wings in a clean large bowl, pour the sauce over, and toss them up. You're about to get real messy, in a good way.

Spring Creek Boat Rolls

GETS YOU ABOUT 12 ROLLS ❖ TAKES ABOUT 2 HOURS

Most of the water in our part of Georgia is dark and dirty, and there's no way in hell I'm going swimming in it. James is a dedicated boat captain, and so from the beginning he was insisting I get out and enjoy the water with him. Well, Spring Creek is the only place by us with crystal-clear water (there's still gators, though), so that's where we always end up in the summer. We go with a big group of friends in their boats, and everyone brings something to share for lunch. These little bites of flaky pie crust stuffed with my favorite sandwich fillings are always my contribution. I like Black Forest ham and turkey, Gouda cheese, and sometimes mozzarella, but you can get totally creative with the fillings. Go with the flow, as they say.

❖ *Gather Up*

For the Dough

2 cups (240 grams to be exact) all-purpose flour, plus more for rolling

1 or 2 tablespoons sugar, up to you

1 teaspoon fine sea salt

8 tablespoons (1 stick/ 113 grams) cold salted butter, homemade if you want (see page 34)

½ cup (114 grams) ice cold water

For the Filling

A couple big handfuls of fresh baby spinach

1 (8-ounce) package cream cheese, room temperature

¼ cup mustard, homemade if you want (see page 45) or Dijon

1 cup any shredded cheese (4 ounces)

¼ to ½ pound thinly sliced deli meat, up to you

❖ *Plan Something Fun So You Got a Reason to Make These*

First, let's make the dough: In a large bowl, whisk together **2 cups (240 grams to be exact) all-purpose flour, 1 tablespoon sugar (2, if you're sexy),** and **1 teaspoon fine sea salt.** Cube **8 tablespoons (1 stick/113 grams) salted butter** (make sure it's *cold*), then add the butter cubes to the bowl. Use your fingers to mix the butter into the flour until it resembles coarse crumbs. Add **½ cup (114 grams) ice cold water** and knead in the bowl just until everything comes together to form a firm, dry dough and there aren't any loose bits of flour. If the dough is sticky, sprinkle on a little more flour, knead again, and repeat until it's not sticking at all.

Pat the dough into any size square, then fold the square in half and pat it down in half again to create some layers. Cover tightly with beeswax wrap or parchment paper. Let it chill in the fridge until all the other ingredients are ready.

Meanwhile, work on that filling: Take **a couple big handfuls of fresh baby spinach** and chop it so you have 1 cup or so. In a medium bowl, combine **1 (8-ounce) package room-temperature cream cheese** and the chopped spinach and mix well.

Now, layer and fill the dough: Go ahead and line a baking sheet with parchment paper. Lightly flour your counter and unwrap the dough. Use your rolling pin to roll the dough into a 12-inch-ish square about ¼-inch thick. Keep flouring the dough and turning it as needed to keep the shape even, the sides mostly straight, and stop it from sticking.

Smear the dough with ¼ **cup mustard.** Add the cream cheese mixture in an even layer, keeping a ½-inch border around the edges, then cover the cream cheese with **1 cup shredded cheese.** Now, on top of the cheese arrange ¼ **to ½ pound thinly sliced deli meat**—how much you like is up to you—making sure you keep that border all the way around.

For Baking and Serving

1 large egg

¼ cup mayonnaise, homemade if you want (see page 42)

Dill pickles, plus 2 tablespoons pickle brine

Fine sea salt and ground black pepper

A handful of fresh parsley

Once the dough is covered with your toppings, start at any end and tightly roll it up all the way into a log. Trim ½ inch or so off each end, move the log to the baking sheet, cover with beeswax wrap, and let rest in the fridge for 30 minutes.

Meanwhile, preheat your oven to 425°F.

Bake the rolls: Unwrap your log and cut it into 1-inch-thick or so slices; you should get about 12 slices. In a small bowl, whisk together **1 large egg** and **1 tablespoon water** until completely smooth. Arrange the slices evenly on your baking sheet, then brush the tops with the egg wash. Bake until the dough is cooked through and the tops and bottoms are browned, 20 to 25 minutes.

Meanwhile, in a medium bowl, mix ¼ **cup mayonnaise** and **2 tablespoons dill pickle brine.** Season with **a pinch each of fine sea salt** and **black pepper** and mix. Add more seasonings until you're happy.

When the rolls are done, arrange them on a platter and garnish with the mayo. Chop up enough **dill pickles** nice and small to get 1 cup or so. And then chop up **a handful of fresh parsley.** Shower the rolls with the pickles and parsley, and dig in!

Mini Pizza Pies

GETS YOU 6 MINI PIZZAS ❖ TAKES 2 HOURS

When we're not picking up a pie to go, I'll make my pizza-loving babies these little pizzas. In terms of size, they're halfway between a Hot Pocket and a pizzeria calzone, and way tastier than either. (I said it.) Fill them with whatever you and your family like, or the vegetables or meat you have around. The ham and pepperoni are what we go for, but you know some pineapple would be good in there, too, or sausage, or extra cheese. You won't use all the sauce in the filling and that's on purpose: Dip these pies in that sauce as you enjoy.

❖ *Gather Up*

❖ *Let's Throw Some Pizza Pies*

For the Dough (see my Note)

- 1 cup (227 grams to be exact) warm water
- 1 tablespoon sugar
- 1 (¼-ounce) packet instant or active dry yeast (2¼ teaspoons)
- 2½ cups (300 grams) all-purpose flour, plus more for rolling
- 1 teaspoon fine sea salt

For the Filling

- 1 small Vidalia onion
- 2 plum tomatoes
- 1 boneless ham steak or a few pieces of thick-sliced ham
- ½ cup pepperoni slices
- Olive oil
- ¼ cup tomato paste
- Dried basil
- Garlic salt
- Onion powder
- Dried oregano
- Dried rosemary
- Dried parsley

Start with your dough: Grab your stand mixer (or a large bowl if you're kneading by hand), and put on the dough hook. In the bowl, combine **1 cup (227 grams to be exact) warm water** (a little warmer than body temperature, 100° to 110°F), **1 tablespoon sugar,** and **1 (¼-ounce) packet of instant or active dry yeast (2¼ teaspoons).** Stir with a fork and set it aside to let the yeast do its thing (foam and froth) for 5 to 10 minutes.

Add **2½ cups (300 grams) all-purpose flour** and **1 teaspoon fine sea salt.** Mix on medium speed or knead by hand until the dough comes together and stops sticking to the sides of the bowl, 5 minutes or so. The dough will be very sticky at first, but trust that it will eventually become smooth and less sticky as you work it. Place the dough in a clean large bowl. Cover and let sit in a warm place to puff up a little and just slightly rise, 30 minutes or so.

Meanwhile, get your filling going: Chop up **1 small Vidalia onion** nice and small to get 1 cup. Roughly chop **2 plum tomatoes.** Chop **1 ham steak or thick-sliced ham** until you have ½ cup of that, and you can either leave them whole or chop the ½ **cup pepperoni slices.**

Add **a splash of olive oil** to your 10-inch cast-iron skillet and heat over medium. When the oil is good and hot, add the onion. Cook, stirring every so often, until the onion is soft, 5 minutes or so. Add ¼ **cup tomato paste** and cook, stirring without stopping now, until the paste is brick red, 2 to 3 minutes. Add the plum tomatoes, ¼ **cup water,** and **a couple pinches each of dried basil, garlic salt, onion powder, dried oregano, dried rosemary,** and **dried parsley.** Stir together, reduce the heat to medium-low so the sauce simmers, and cook, stirring every so often, until the tomatoes are broken down, 10 minutes or so. Taste it and add any more of the seasonings until you're happy.

(recipe and ingredients continue)

2 cups shredded mozzarella cheese (8 ounces)

1 large egg

❖ *Don't Forget*

Your stand mixer with the dough hook, or a large bowl

Preheat your oven to 375°F. Go ahead and line a baking sheet with parchment paper.

Divide the dough into 6 equal pieces. Lightly flour your counter. Working with one dough ball at a time, and using your fingers or a rolling pin, press the dough out from the center until you have a 6-inch circle. Repeat until you have 6 dough circles.

Lift one circle onto the baking sheet and spread a heaping spoonful of the sauce on the dough, leaving a ½-inch border all around. In the middle of the sauce, add a couple slices of pepperoni and a heaping spoonful of ham, and top with some of the **2 cups shredded mozzarella cheese** (you want about ⅓ cup on each). Fold the dough circle in half and crimp the edge closed with a fork so you got a half-moon shape.

Repeat with the other dough circles, sauce, and the rest of the pepperoni, ham, and mozzarella, forming the pizzas on the baking sheet, until you've filled the sheet up (you can use 2 baking sheets, or you can bake in batches, if you need to). Keep the sauce you got left warm.

In a small bowl, use a fork to whisk **1 large egg** until smooth. Brush the tops of the pizza pies with the egg wash.

Bake until the crust is golden brown, 25 to 30 minutes. Move the pizza to a wire rack to cool (and bake the next batch, if you need). Either way, give them 5 to 10 minutes to cool so no one burns their mouths! Make sure you got the leftover sauce on the side for dipping.

Note: *If you want to skip making your own dough, you can use 1 pound (454 grams) of store-bought dough and make your pizzas a little smaller, or hit up your local pizza place—they'll sell you some!*

Bebop's
Sweet Bacon Collard Greens

FEEDS 4 TO 6 ❖ TAKES 2 HOURS

This recipe is from my Aunt Bebop, my Mama's sister. And just like Aunt Teisha was known for her Cowboy Caviar (page 114), Bebop brings these greens to every gathering. These sweet, salty, smoky greens are the only way anyone in my family eats collards now, and I have a feeling they're going to convert you, too.

❖ Gather Up

3 pounds collard greens

3 tablespoons distilled white vinegar

5 or 6 bacon strips

¼ cup sugar

All-purpose seasoning, like Everglades, or homemade if you want (see page 38)

❖ Let's Stew Some Greens

You want to start by washing your greens real well. I personally like using my sink (make sure it's clean and there are no dishes in there!) so there's enough room to wash the greens. First, pull out the center veins from **3 pounds collard greens**—you want the leaves, not the veins. Rip the leaves a little to help them cook down—not too small, like lasagna noodle size.

Put the stopper in the sink and fill it up with water. (If you don't want to use your sink or can't, you can use the largest tub or bowl you got.) Add **1 tablespoon distilled white vinegar** to the water and the greens, and swish around with your hands, almost like they're in your laundry washer. Drain and repeat two more times, using up the other **2 tablespoons distilled white vinegar.**

Once the greens are thoroughly washed, grab **5 or 6 bacon strips.** You want to cut them into tiny chunks, like bacon bits. Put them in your large pot and put the pot over medium. Let the bacon fry, stirring regularly, until they turn golden brown, 5 to 7 minutes. Add **¼ cup sugar** and stir. Reduce the heat to low and let it sizzle for about a minute, without stirring, to cook the sugar a bit.

Now, add in one handful of your collard greens. You want to slowly add the entire bushel over time, not all at once. Stir the greens into the bacon and sugar, and let them start to wilt. Once your first handful of greens has wilted, add another handful. Repeat, adding a little at a time, until all your greens are in the pot and wilted.

Sprinkle in **a palmful of all-purpose seasoning,** then pour in at least 6 cups water. Make sure there's enough water to cover the greens; add more if you need to. Raise the heat to medium-high and bring to a boil, then reduce the heat to low and simmer, uncovered and stirring maybe just once or twice, until the greens are so silky and tender you could eat the whole pot, and the liquid is mostly gone, 1 hour. Pour into a bowl for serving and eat up!

Smokin' Honey Bacon Green Beans

FEEDS 4 ❖ TAKES 30 MINUTES

I hated green beans growing up, and the only way my Mama could get me to eat them was if they were cooked with bacon. When I got older and started cooking for myself, I said "Screw this, I'm adding honey, too" because everything is better with honey. Now, my kids love their sweet, salty, and smoky green beans way more than I did when I was growing up. In the summer when the beans are coming in, and around the winter holidays, you can find me cooking up these beans in no time, and them disappearing just as fast.

❖ *Gather Up*

1 **pound fresh green beans**

2 **garlic cloves**

2 **tablespoons salted butter, homemade if you want (see page 34)**

5 **bacon strips**

Fine sea salt and ground black pepper

1 **tablespoon honey**

❖ *Let's Cook These Green Beans*

Cut the stem ends off **1 pound fresh green beans.** Chop **2 garlic cloves.** Set them aside for now.

In your 10-inch cast-iron skillet, melt **2 tablespoons salted butter** over medium. Put some paper towels on a plate. When the butter is melted, add **5 bacon strips** and cook, flipping a few times, until browned and crisp, 5 to 7 minutes total. Move the bacon to the plate, leaving the grease in the pan. When the bacon is cool, crumble it up.

Add the green beans, garlic, and **a pinch of fine sea salt** to the pan. Cook, stirring to coat the green beans in all those flavorings, then leave them alone until they're starting to brown in spots, 5 minutes or so. Add **2 tablespoons water** and **1 tablespoon honey** and stir to mix everything. Cover the pan with a lid and steam the green beans until they're bright green, 2 minutes or so.

Take the pan off the heat, sprinkle with **ground black pepper,** then taste a green bean and add more salt if you think it needs it before you add the bacon. Sprinkle with the bacon and eat hot!

The Absolute Best Sweet Potatoes

FEEDS 4 ❖ TAKES 1 HOUR

You know how every recipe tells you to poke holes in your sweet potatoes before you put them in the oven? You know me; once I was in a rush or not paying attention or just plain forgot. Well, damned if those weren't the best sweet potatoes I've ever eaten—and I've been crazy for them since I was a kid. Something happens when you let them steam and cook in their own juices. The flavor is more concentrated, the sugars get caramelized, and all that sweet potato-y goodness doesn't get diluted. The skins will puff up, and some of them might pop in places, and that's what you want. I haven't had one explode on me (yet), but if it does, it won't go nowhere but the oven. After you try one of these, the toasted pecans and honey butter is really just gilding the lily.

❖ *Gather Up*

½ **cup pecans**

4 **large sweet potatoes (6 to 8 ounces each)**

Olive oil

Fine sea salt

6 **tablespoons (¾ stick) salted butter, homemade if you want (see page 34), room temperature**

¼ **cup honey**

Ground cinnamon

❖ *Don't Forget*

Your stand mixer with the whisk attachment, or handheld mixer

❖ *Let's Roast Some Sweet Potatoes*

Preheat your oven to 450°F. Roughly chop ½ **cup pecans** while you wait.

Scrub and clean **4 large sweet potatoes,** then dry them off. Put them on a baking sheet and drizzle with enough **olive oil** to coat them nicely. Sprinkle the outsides all over with **fine sea salt.** Bake until charred on the outside and tender all the way through, 45 minutes or so.

While the potatoes are in the oven, melt **2 tablespoons softened salted butter** in a small skillet over medium. Add the chopped pecans and toast them, stirring regularly to make sure they're coated in butter, until they're golden and smell amazing, 2 to 3 minutes. Set them aside to cool.

Grab your stand mixer (or a medium bowl if you're using a hand mixer), and put on the whisk attachment. In the bowl, combine the last **4 tablespoons softened salted butter,** ¼ **cup honey,** and **a pinch of ground cinnamon.** Whip on medium speed until light and fluffy, 2 to 3 minutes. Taste and see if it needs more cinnamon.

Once the potatoes are done, split them open longways. Sprinkle the insides with salt, then spread with your honey butter, top with the pecans, and enjoy your new favorite sweet potato.

Ultimate Mashed Potatoes

Put these under, over, or in between pretty much every dish in the Mains chapter (pages 139–201). There's no meal some potatoes with garlic and herbs can't improve.

❖ *Gather Up*

4 **pounds medium Yukon Gold potatoes**

4 **cups chicken broth,** homemade bone broth if you want (see page 54)

A handful of fresh parsley leaves

1 **fresh rosemary sprig**

2 **fresh sage leaves**

2 **garlic cloves**

6 **tablespoons (¾ stick) salted butter,** homemade if you want (see page 34)

½ **cup heavy whipping cream**

½ **cup whole milk**

½ **cup sour cream**

2 **tablespoons ranch seasoning**

Fine sea salt and ground black pepper

❖ *Let's Mash Some Potatoes*

Peel **4 pounds medium Yukon Gold potatoes** and cut them into quarters. Put the potatoes and **4 cups chicken broth** in a large pot and set it over medium. Cook the potatoes until they're fork-tender, 25 to 30 minutes. Scoop out ½ cup or so of the broth to save, then drain the potatoes and return them to the pot.

While you're waiting on the potatoes, chop **a handful of fresh parsley leaves,** the leaves from **1 fresh rosemary sprig,** and **2 fresh sage leaves.** Chop up **2 garlic cloves** nice and small.

Over medium, heat up your 10-inch cast-iron skillet with **2 tablespoons salted butter.** When the butter is melted, add your garlic and cook, stirring regularly, until it smells amazing, 2 to 3 minutes. Add the garlic butter to your potato pot.

Smash and mix your potatoes with a masher until there aren't any big chunks, then add the other **4 tablespoons salted butter,** plus ½ **cup heavy whipping cream,** ½ **cup whole milk,** ½ **cup sour cream, 2 tablespoons ranch seasoning,** and all your chopped herbs. Keep mixing until you get the consistency of mashed potatoes you like. Sometimes I like mine chunky and sometimes I like mine smooth—see what you're feeling tonight! You can add the chicken broth you saved if you like your mashed potatoes a little less thick—completely up to you. Taste a bite and season with **fine sea salt** and **black pepper** until you're happy. Serve warm and enjoy all that garlicky goodness.

MAINS

———◆———

You're going to be eatin'
good every night now.

Mama's Chicken Pot Pie

FEEDS 4 TO 6 ❖ TAKES ABOUT 2 HOURS

My pot pie isn't your everyday version; it's a special-request chicken pot pie. It's for when you want to show someone you love them (and, yes, showing love for yourself counts!) by spending a good couple of hours in the kitchen boiling the chicken, rolling out the dough, assembling the filling, and bringing it all together. I make everything I can from scratch, and that's how I've put my own special spin on my Mama's recipe. Growing up, whenever me and my brother asked for it, she'd grant our wish and make it. She used canned soup and canned dough, and so it all happened much faster, but I love the extra steps. Plus, it's so good you don't need to serve it with anything else on the side. Just a slice of this is all I need for dinner.

❖ *Gather Up*

For the Crust

- 2 cups (240 grams to be exact) all-purpose flour, plus more for rolling
- 1 or 2 tablespoons sugar, up to you
- 1 teaspoon fine sea salt
- 8 tablespoons (1 stick/ 113 grams) cold salted butter, homemade if you want (see page 34)
- ½ cup (114 grams) ice cold water

For the Filling

- ½ small Vidalia onion
- 1 medium head of broccoli
- 1 pound boneless, skinless chicken breasts (about 2 medium)

❖ *It's Always a Special Occasion When You're Eating Pot Pie*

Preheat the oven to 350°F. Put a 10-inch cast-iron skillet in the oven while it preheats.

Start with the crust: In a large bowl, whisk together **2 cups (240 grams to be exact) all-purpose flour, 1 tablespoon sugar (2, if you're sexy),** and **1 teaspoon fine sea salt.** Cube **8 tablespoons (1 stick/113 grams) salted butter** (make sure it's *cold*), then add the butter cubes to the bowl. Use your fingers to mix the butter into the flour until it resembles coarse crumbs. Add ½ **cup (114 grams) ice cold water** and knead in the bowl just until everything comes together to form a firm, dry dough and there aren't any loose bits of flour. If the dough sticks to your hands a bit, sprinkle on a little more flour, knead again, and repeat until it's not sticking at all.

Cut the dough into 2 equal pieces and shape them into rounds. Cover tightly with beeswax wrap or parchment paper. Let chill in the fridge until all the other ingredients are ready.

Start on the filling: Roughly chop ½ **small Vidalia onion** and cut **1 head of broccoli** into bite-size pieces. Wash and dry **1 pound boneless, skinless chicken breasts.** (I wash my chicken! You can skip it if you want.) You can also trim any excess fat, if desired.

(recipe and ingredients continue)

Fine sea salt and
ground black pepper

2 tablespoons salted butter

2 cups frozen mixed
vegetables

1 (8-ounce) package cream
cheese, room temperature

½ to 1 cup chicken broth,
homemade bone broth if
you want (see page 54),
as you need it

Garlic powder

Onion powder

For Baking and Finishing

3 tablespoons salted butter

In a medium pot, add enough water so that the chicken will be covered, and keep adding **pinches of fine sea salt** until it's salty like broth. Add the chicken. Bring the water to a boil over high heat. Once the water is boiling, cover the pot with a lid and immediately take it off the heat. Allow the chicken to sit until it reaches 160°F in the center, 5 to 10 minutes. (If you don't have a thermometer, cut one open to make sure there's no pink inside.) Once the chicken is cooked, use tongs to get it from the pot and onto on a cutting board or plate. Let it rest for 5 minutes before shredding the meat with 2 forks.

In a medium skillet over medium-high, melt **2 tablespoons salted butter.** Add the onion and cook, stirring regularly, until softened, 5 minutes or so. Add the broccoli and **2 cups frozen mixed vegetables** and cook, stirring, until the vegetables are tender and slightly browned, 8 to 10 minutes.

Move the pan off the heat, add **1 (8-ounce) package room-temperature cream cheese** and ½ **cup chicken broth.** Stir together until good and mixed, and the cream cheese has melted. Season with **a couple pinches each of garlic powder, onion powder, and fine sea salt,** and **a pinch of black pepper** and mix them in. Fold in the shredded chicken. If the filling is really thick, add the last ½ **cup chicken broth.** Taste it and make sure you're happy with the seasoning.

Make and bake the pie: Get just one of the dough pieces from the fridge and lightly flour your counter. Use your rolling pin to roll out the dough to make a ½-inch-thick disk. Fold it over itself two or three times. Use your rolling pin to roll out the dough to make a 14-inch circle. To keep it in a nice, even circular shape, turn your dough a quarter turn after every roll or two, and flour it lightly as needed to keep it from sticking—and most important, have fun with it! Repeat with the other dough piece to make another 14-inch circle.

Carefully take the skillet out of the oven and add **2 tablespoons salted butter** so it melts, but don't burn the butter. Spread the butter all over the bottom and up the sides of the skillet. Carefully place one rolled-out dough in the skillet so it sits flat on the bottom and goes up and over the sides.

Fill the dough with the chicken mixture, then drape the other piece of dough over the top. Press the edges together with your fingers to seal the dough, or crimp them with a fork (sometimes I do, sometimes I don't). Cut a slit in the top to let steam escape, if you want. However you make it, it'll be tasty!

Bake until the crust is golden brown and crisp, around 50 minutes. Grab the last **1 tablespoon salted butter** and wipe it over the crust while it's still hot. Let the pie cool for 10 minutes before you cut it up and serve. I just know you're going to love it!

Butter-Roasted Chicken

FEEDS 4 ❖ TAKES 2 HOURS

We eat a lot of chicken in this family, maybe too much. And as much as we love chicken and dumplings (James) and fried chicken (me), sometimes I do want to shake things up a bit. So, every now and then I'll roast us a chicken in a big pot in the oven with lots of flavorful goodies in there with it. I love an herb butter on anything and everything. One summer I was out sunning, and I even thought about lathering myself up with some! A better use of a garlicky, herby butter, though, is this chicken. Rosemary is my favorite herb, but change it up with whatever herbs you got—they're all good here.

❖ Gather Up

- 1 medium Vidalia onion
- 8 garlic cloves
- 3 fresh rosemary sprigs
- 1 small bunch of fresh thyme
- 1 lemon
-   Olive oil
- 1 cup chicken broth, homemade bone broth if you want (see page 54)
-   Chicken bouillon base
-   All-purpose seasoning, like Everglades, or homemade if you want (see page 38)
-   Garlic salt
-   Onion powder
-   Dried oregano
- 8 tablespoons (1 stick) salted butter, homemade if you want (see page 34), room temperature
-   Fine sea salt
- 1 (3-pound) whole chicken

❖ Let's Roast the Best Chicken You've Had

Preheat your oven to 425°F.

Roughly chop **1 medium Vidalia onion** and **4 garlic cloves,** and throw them into a large Dutch oven. Take **3 fresh rosemary sprigs** and **1 small bunch of fresh thyme** and chop enough leaves nice and small to get about 1 tablespoon of each, then put the chopped herbs in a medium bowl. Now, roughly chop whatever's left of the herbs and throw them into the Dutch oven.

Zest half of **1 lemon** into the bowl with the herbs, then halve the lemon and toss the lemon halves into the pot. Drizzle everything in the pot with **a couple glugs of olive oil,** enough to coat it all, and mix.

In a small bowl or measuring cup, combine **1 cup chicken broth** and **1 spoonful of chicken bouillon base,** then sprinkle in **a palmful each of all-purpose seasoning, garlic salt,** and **onion powder** and **a couple pinches of dried oregano.** Stir until the bouillon is good and blended. Taste it and make sure you're happy with the seasoning. Pour that into the Dutch oven.

Chop up the other **4 garlic cloves** nice and small and add them to your medium bowl with the herbs and lemon zest. Now, add **8 tablespoons (1 stick) softened salted butter** and **a couple pinches of fine sea salt.** Mix with a fork until it's all nice and blended. Taste it and see if it needs more of anything. Rub the garlic-herb butter all over and inside **1 (3-pound) whole chicken.** Tuck the wing tips under.

Place the chicken, breast side up, on the vegetables in the Dutch oven and cover. Roast for 45 minutes, then uncover and continuing roasting until the chicken is nice and browned on top and cooked through (either it's 165°F in the thickest part of the thigh or you cut it and if there's no pink inside, it's good), 15 to 30 minutes or so more. Set the Dutch oven on the counter and let the chicken rest in the pot for 15 minutes before carving it and shredding the meat. Serve it with the buttery, herby, oniony, garlicky sauce drizzled over.

Good Ole Fish Tacos

FEEDS 4 TO 6 ❖ TAKES 1 HOUR

This is hands-down our favorite way to make fish. We're usually frying up bass from our pond, but you can use whatever white fish you can find, like halibut, tilapia, or cod. The secret ingredient is my homemade mustard that helps the breading stick. Now it's not so much of a secret, I guess.

❖ Gather Up

1 green or red cabbage, or one of each (or a 14-ounce bag coleslaw mix)

1 large or 4 small ripe tomatoes

1 medium cucumber

Pickled jalapeño slices

½ cup mayonnaise, homemade if you want (see page 42)

6 tablespoons mustard, homemade if you want (see page 45) or Dijon

All-purpose seasoning, like Everglades, or homemade if you want (see page 38)

Fine sea salt and ground black pepper

½ cup yellow cornmeal

½ cup all-purpose flour

1 pound boneless, skinless firm white fish fillets

Vegetable oil, for frying

12 tortillas

1 cup shredded pepper jack cheese (4 ounces)

❖ Let's Fry Up Some Fish Tacos

Start with the slaw: Shred **1 green or red cabbage** until you have 8 cups. Chop up **1 large ripe tomato** and **1 medium cucumber** nice and small. Chop up **a few pickled jalapeño slices**—enough to equal a heaping spoonful.

In a large bowl, stir together **½ cup mayonnaise, 2 tablespoons mustard,** and the pickled jalapeños until combined. Add the cabbage, tomato, and cucumber and toss to coat. Sprinkle in **a palmful of all-purpose seasoning,** then add a little more for good measure, plus **a couple pinches each of fine sea salt** and **black pepper.** Mix well and taste it; make sure you're happy with the seasoning. Store the slaw in the fridge until you're ready to eat.

Now, get to this fish for the tacos: In a shallow dish, stir together **½ cup yellow cornmeal, ½ cup all-purpose flour, a couple pinches of all-purpose seasoning,** and **a pinch each of fine sea salt** and **black pepper** until evenly combined. Rub **1 pound boneless, skinless firm white fish fillets** all over with the last **4 tablespoons mustard.** Coat the fillets all over with the cornmeal mixture, pressing to help it stick, shake off any excess, and put them on a plate.

Fill your 12-inch cast-iron skillet with ½ **inch of vegetable oil** and heat over medium-high. Put some paper towels on a plate. Once the oil is hot—throw a pinch of the flour mixture in and if it sizzles immediately, but not crazy, it's ready—then reduce the heat to medium. Add the fillets, working 2 at a time if you need to keep the pan from getting crowded, and fry until lightly golden brown, crispy, and cooked through, 2 to 5 minutes per side, depending on the thickness of the fish. Move the fish to the paper towels and sprinkle with fine sea salt. Break or cut the fish into bite-size pieces.

Warm **12 tortillas** until they're soft and browned in spots. If you have a gas stove, you can do this right on the burner for a few seconds on each side. You can also heat them in a dry cast-iron skillet over medium, 1 minute or so.

Divide the coleslaw among the tortillas, then the fish pieces, sprinkle them all with the **1 cup shredded pepper jack cheese,** and dive in!

Jazzy Jambalaya

FEEDS 4 TO 6 ❖ TAKES ABOUT 1 HOUR

I lived in Louisiana for a year, and a real honest-to-God native Louisianan taught me how to make jambalaya and gumbo (see page 197). It's been so long I can't remember what they taught me that makes this *authentic,* except that you have to season the hell out of it. It may seem like a lot of ingredients, but this is truly one of the original one-pot meals. Once you're done chopping up some vegetables, you're halfway to dinner and the sink's still clear.

❖ *Gather Up*

- 1 (1-pound) package of your favorite smoked sausage (I use Conecuh hickory smoked)
- 2 boneless, skinless chicken breasts (1 to 1½ pounds total)
- 1 medium Vidalia onion
- 1 pint cherry tomatoes
- 2 garlic cloves
- 1 green bell pepper
- 4 green onions (scallions)
- 6 tablespoons (¾ stick) salted butter, homemade if you want (see page 34)
- Garlic salt
- Ground black pepper
- 2 tablespoons all-purpose flour
- Cajun seasoning (I use Slap Ya Mama)
- Onion powder
- Cayenne pepper
- 2 cups chicken broth, homemade bone broth if you want (see page 54)
- 1 cup white or yellow rice

❖ *Let's Head on Down to the Bayou*

First, you're gonna need to chop: Slice **1 (1-pound) package of smoked sausage** into ¼-inch-thick slices. Cut **2 boneless, skinless chicken breasts** into 1-inch pieces. Chop **1 medium Vidalia onion, 1 pint cherry tomatoes,** and **2 garlic cloves.** Chop up **1 green bell pepper** nice and small. Slice up **2 green onions.**

Over medium-high, heat up your 12-inch cast-iron skillet with **2 tablespoons salted butter.** When the butter is melted, add your chopped chicken and season with **a couple pinches each of garlic salt** and **black pepper.** Brown the chicken on all sides, flipping the pieces as they finish, but don't worry about cooking the chicken through yet. This will take 3 to 4 minutes per side. Put the chicken in a medium bowl.

Add another **2 tablespoons salted butter** to the skillet plus the sausage and cook, stirring every so often, until browned all over, 5 minutes or so total. Add that to the bowl with the chicken.

Add the last **2 tablespoons salted butter** to the skillet, then add **2 tablespoons all-purpose flour** and cook, stirring without stopping now, until the flour is lightly browned, 1 to 2 minutes. Then add in your onion, cherry tomatoes, green pepper, garlic, and the chopped green onions. Sprinkle in **2 palmfuls of Cajun seasoning, a palmful of onion powder, a couple pinches of cayenne pepper,** and **a pinch of black pepper.** Stir everything together, then reduce the heat to medium. Cook, stirring every so often, until the tomatoes release their juices, 10 minutes or so. Taste and see if it needs some more seasonings (I always think it does).

Add **2 cups chicken broth** and **1 cup white or yellow rice** and bring to a boil, scraping the bottom of the skillet with your spoon to get all the browned bits off. Now, add back in the chicken and sausage, stir it, and reduce the heat to low. Cover the skillet and cook until the rice is nice and tender and all the liquid is gone, 20 minutes or so. Take the skillet off the heat and let it rest for 5 to 10 minutes, then fluff it with a fork. Slice up the last **2 green onions** and sprinkle them all over ('cause we fancy) before serving.

Sloppy James

Cheese on a Sloppy Joe may be controversial, but this is a Sloppy James and the cheese is a *requirement.* James loves to cook just as much as I do. But while I love a big ole project during the day that takes hours and gets me into my zone, James is the master of quick-and-easy dinners. And these couldn't be quicker, or easier. In fact, if it's James's night to cook, he's probably making these.

❖ Gather Up

1 small Vidalia onion

1 small green bell pepper

2 garlic cloves

1 jalapeño pepper

1 (15-ounce) can tomato sauce

Brown sugar

Worcestershire sauce

Mustard, homemade if you want (see page 45), yellow mustard, or Dijon if you're feeling frisky

Tomato paste

Olive oil

Onion powder

Garlic salt

Ground black pepper

1 pound ground beef (I like 80/20)

4 hamburger buns

Salted butter, homemade if you want (see page 34), for the buns, room temperature

4 slices Cheddar cheese (I like medium, but you do you)

❖ Let's Get Sloppy

Start by chopping up nice and small **1 small Vidalia onion, 1 small green bell pepper,** and **2 garlic cloves.** Take out the seeds from **1 jalapeño pepper,** then chop that up real small, too.

In a medium bowl, combine **1 (15-ounce) can tomato sauce, 2 spoonfuls of brown sugar, about 1 tablespoon each of Worcestershire sauce, mustard, tomato paste,** and **olive oil,** then sprinkle in **a palmful of onion powder** and **a couple pinches each of garlic salt** and **ground black pepper** until smooth. Taste and make sure you're happy with the seasoning. Set that aside for now.

Set your 12-inch cast-iron skillet over medium, and add a splash of olive oil. When the oil is good and hot, add all the chopped vegetables. Cook them, stirring every so often, until they're lightly browned and tender, 4 to 5 minutes. Add **1 pound ground beef** and start breaking it up with your spoon. Keep cooking, stirring and breaking up the meat, until the meat is cooked through and browned, 3 to 5 minutes more.

Pour the seasoning mixture over the meat and bring to a boil, then reduce the heat to low so the sauce simmers. Cook uncovered, stirring every so often, until nice and thick and the flavors have come together, 15 to 20 minutes. Taste it and see if it needs more of anything your heart tells you.

Meanwhile, toast **4 hamburger buns,** baby! We like to **butter** ours before toasting them, but that's up to you. When the meat mixture is ready, top each bottom bun with a big spoonful, then add the **4 slices Cheddar cheese,** 1 slice on top of each sandwich so they start to melt a bit. Close 'em up, and enjoy the mess!

Finger Lickin' Fried Chicken

FEEDS 4 TO 6 ❖ TAKES AT LEAST 4 HOURS

I would fry every single chicken that comes through this house, if it were up to me. I use my Mama's Mama's recipe, who left the seasoning pretty plain so her family could flavor their pieces as they please. My Mama added a little bit more spice to hers, and then I took the cap off and dumped a whole jar into my recipe. There really isn't a trick to fried chicken except this: Do not be serving raw chicken. While you're learning, cut at least one piece open and check to make sure there's no pink anywhere on the meat. I speak from experience, as I have served some raw chicken in my day, but I've learned (and James is still alive). Leave the chicken in the grease longer than you think and pull it when it's dark brown—just before it goes too far—and finish it in the oven, if you got extra-large chicken pieces.

❖ *Gather Up*

1 whole (2- to 3-pound) chicken (or 2 breasts, 2 thighs, 2 drumsticks, and 2 wings; see my Note)

2 cups buttermilk, homemade if you want (see page 34)

Tabasco

Garlic salt

Onion powder

Sweet paprika

All-purpose seasoning, like Everglades, or homemade if you want (see page 38)

Fine sea salt and ground black pepper

Cayenne pepper

2 large eggs

Vegetable oil, for frying

2 cups all-purpose flour

⅓ cup cornstarch

2 tablespoons baking powder

Flaky sea salt, if you want

❖ *Let's Fry Some Chicken*

If you're starting with **1 whole chicken,** cut it up into 2 breasts, 2 thighs, 2 drumsticks, and 2 wings. If you're starting with parts, you're ready to brine!

To a large bowl, add **2 cups buttermilk,** then shake in a **good amount of Tabasco** (about 2 tablespoons) and sprinkle in **a palmful each of garlic salt, onion powder, sweet paprika, all-purpose seasoning,** and **black pepper,** and **a couple pinches of cayenne pepper** and mix it up. Taste it and make sure you're happy with your seasonings. Add **2 large eggs** and whisk until smooth. Add your chicken to the bowl, cover, and refrigerate for at least 2 hours, or up to 24 hours.

Over medium-high, heat up your 12-inch cast-iron skillet with **1 inch of vegetable oil,** until the oil is 350°F. (If you don't have a thermometer, a pinch of flour should sizzle immediately.) Put a wire rack on a baking sheet. Preheat your oven to 350°F, too.

To a wide, shallow bowl, add **2 cups all-purpose flour, ⅓ cup cornstarch,** and **2 tablespoons baking powder,** and then sprinkle in **a palmful each of garlic salt, onion powder, sweet paprika, all-purpose seasoning,** and **black pepper,** and **a couple pinches of cayenne pepper** and mix well.

When the oil is ready, get your chicken from the fridge. Starting with the biggest pieces, one by one, lift them out of the bowl and let the extra buttermilk drip off first, then coat the pieces in the flour completely. Now, dip them back into the buttermilk, and back again into the flour, making sure each piece is completely coated. Place the chicken pieces in the pan with the oil but don't crowd them; add in batches. Adjust the stove to keep the oil at 300°F while you're frying, so our chicken can cook nice and even.

(recipe continues)

Note: *Our chickens are 2 to 3 pounds, but I know they can be a lot bigger from the store. If you got a big ole 4-pound chicken, you may need to finish the pieces in the oven. Check the biggest pieces with a thermometer or by cutting close to the bone, and making sure there's no pink.*

Cook until each side of each piece is deeply golden brown, 10 to 15 minutes total, then move it to the rack. If your chicken isn't cooked through (meaning either it's 165°F or you cut it and if there's no pink inside, it's good), put the baking sheet in the oven and bake until the chicken is done. Meanwhile, continue to fry up the rest of that chicken and finish any pieces in the oven if you need to.

Let the chicken cool for 5 to 10 minutes (we don't want any burned mouths), then sprinkle with some **fine** or **flaky sea salt** and enjoy.

Note: Here in Georgia we got cube steaks at every store. They might be called minute steaks by you, or you might not have them. That's okay—you can make your own! They're cut from top or bottom round, so get you four 4-ounce steaks, then pound the living hell out of them until they're ¼ inch thick or so. If you have a meat tenderizer with the spikes, you'll get that classic "cube" look.

Chicken Fried Steak

with Gravy

FEEDS 4 ❖ TAKES 45 MINUTES

Next time you're looking to have a real celebratory meal, you're going to want to fry up some steak. James says you better make the gravy with it—don't half-ass it now, since you got the juice right there in your pan! This is an old family recipe we don't make as much as we used to (maybe for obvious reasons), but when that steak does hit the grease, we know we're in for something good. Despite seeming complicated, it comes together pretty fast, and you're eating in under an hour.

❖ *Gather Up*

For the Steaks

Vegetable oil, for frying

1½ cups all-purpose flour

1 teaspoon baking powder

Garlic salt

Garlic powder

Onion powder

All-purpose seasoning, like Everglades, or homemade if you want (see page 38)

Fine sea salt and ground black pepper

Cayenne pepper

1 cup buttermilk, homemade if you want (see page 34)

2 large eggs

Tabasco

4 cube steaks (about 1 pound total; see my Note)

For the Gravy

2 tablespoons all-purpose flour

1 cup whole milk, plus more if you need it

½ cup heavy whipping cream

Fine sea salt and ground black pepper

❖ *Chicken-Fried is the Best Kind of Fried*

First, the steaks: Over medium-high, heat up your 12-inch cast-iron skillet with **1 inch of vegetable oil.** Put some paper towels on a plate.

In a wide, shallow dish, mix together **1½ cups all-purpose flour** and **1 teaspoon baking powder,** then sprinkle in **a palmful each of garlic salt, garlic powder, onion powder,** and **all-purpose seasoning,** plus **a couple pinches of black pepper** and **a pinch of cayenne pepper** (2, if you're feeling spicy). In another shallow dish, whisk together **1 cup buttermilk, 2 large eggs,** and **a couple good shakes of Tabasco** until smooth.

One at a time, dip **4 cube steaks** into the buttermilk mixture. Let any extra drip off, then put it into the flour mixture and make sure it's coated all over, then move it to a plate.

Once your oil is heated and shimmering (it should be 300°F if you got a thermometer. If not, a steak should sizzle immediately), add the steaks without crowding the pan, cooking them two at a time if you need. Fry until beautifully golden brown, 2 to 3 minutes on each side. Move them over to the paper towels and sprinkle with **fine sea salt.** Let them rest for a few minutes.

Now, make your gravy: Drain off all but 2 tablespoons or so of the grease from the pan. Add **2 tablespoons all-purpose flour** and cook, stirring without stopping, until the flour starts clumping, 1 minute or so. Slowly pour in **1 cup whole milk** and ½ **cup heavy whipping cream,** and keep whisking until all the clumps are gone—just a minute or so. Add **a pinch each of fine sea salt** and **black pepper.** Taste and see if it needs more of either. Bring it to a simmer, whisking all the while, and cook until it's nice and thick, 3 to 5 minutes. You want to be able to pour your gravy; add a splash or two more milk if your gravy is too thick.

Move the steaks to a serving plate and drizzle over the gravy to your heart's desire. Serve it up hot.

Mary's Meatloaf

FEEDS 4 TO 6 ❖ TAKES 2 HOURS

My Granny Mary loved to cook, and she put her whole heart into it. The thing she loved to make most of all was meatloaf. She loved it so much she'd make two loaves at a time, every week, for weeks, and weeks . . . and weeks on end. She loved meatloaf a little too much. But now that I'm thinking about her recipe chock full of herbs, my mouth is watering a little bit. The best part was the leftovers; we'd heat up a slice and sandwich it in a biscuit, then drizzle it with some honey. Damn, it's good.

❖ *Gather Up*

1 **small Vidalia onion**

1 **small red bell pepper**

1 **jalapeño pepper**

  A handful of fresh parsley

  A couple fresh sage leaves

3 **garlic cloves**

  Butter, for the pan

2 **large eggs**

1½ **cups fresh bread crumbs**

1 **pound ground beef** (I like 80/20)

1 **pound ground pork**

¼ **cup tomato sauce**

2 **tablespoons honey**

2 **tablespoons tomato paste**

  All-purpose seasoning, like Everglades, or homemade if you want (see page 38)

  Cayenne pepper

  Fine sea salt and ground black pepper

½ **lemon**

½ **cup heavy whipping cream**

1 **teaspoon all-purpose flour**

  A couple fresh thyme sprigs

❖ *Don't Forget*

  Your thermometer

❖ *Let's Make Some Meatloaf*

Preheat your oven to 375°F. Line 9 × 13-inch baking dish with parchment or aluminum foil.

Chop **1 small Vidalia onion, 1 small red bell pepper,** and **1 jalapeño pepper** (take the seeds out, if you want) nice and small. Chop **a handful of fresh parsley** so you get 2 tablespoons, and **a couple fresh sage leaves** to get 1 tablespoon. Chop **3 garlic cloves,** too.

Over medium, heat up your 10-inch cast-iron skillet with enough butter to coat the bottom. When the butter is melted, add the onion, bell pepper, jalapeño, and garlic. Cook, stirring regularly, until they just start to soften, 3 to 5 minutes. We still want some texture.

In a large bowl, whisk **2 large eggs** until smooth, then stir in **1½ cups fresh bread crumbs** until they're all mixed in with the egg. Add the cooked vegetables, parsley, and sage, then stir in the **1 pound ground beef, 1 pound ground pork,** ¼ **cup tomato sauce, 2 tablespoons honey,** and **2 tablespoons tomato paste.** Sprinkle in **a palmful of all-purpose seasoning, a couple pinches of cayenne pepper,** and a **pinch of black pepper.** Grate the **zest of** ½ **lemon** into the bowl. Use your hands to mix everything until just evenly combined.

Form the mixture into a loaf around 9 inches by 5 inches and 2 inches thick (you don't have to be too exact, but that's what you're aiming for). Place it in the lined baking dish and into the oven it goes. Bake until a thermometer stuck right into the middle reads 160°F, which should take 1 hour or so. Let it rest for 15 minutes.

Pour any juices from the baking dish into a small skillet and stir in ½ **cup heavy whipping cream** and **1 teaspoon all-purpose flour.** Strip the leaves from **a couple fresh thyme sprigs** and chop enough to get 1 teaspoon or so, then add that to the skillet. Put the skillet over medium heat and cook, stirring every so often, until slightly thickened, around 5 minutes. Season with **fine sea salt** and ground black pepper until you're happy. Slice the meatloaf. I know it looks almost too good to eat—but go on and dig in with the gravy on the side.

Slow Cooker BBQ Ribs

FEEDS 4 ❖ TAKES 6 TO 8 HOURS

If you do not have a slow cooker, this recipe is my argument that you need one. Do you see how short the instructions are? And do you *see* how fall-apart tender that meat is in the picture over there? I got the idea from my Aunt Teisha to make ribs in my slow cooker, but these seasonings are all mine. When James and I first got together, we were constantly going over to his mom Diane's house because she loved it when James cooked his ribs for her. Y'all the first time I tasted James's ribs I was horrified—they were dry and chewy, and nothing like mine. So next time we went over to Diane's we had a cook-off, and I'm happy to say this is the recipe she's using to this day. James says, "no comment."

❖ *Gather Up*

1 medium Vidalia onion

2 garlic cloves

1 rack of baby back ribs
 (2 pounds or so)

1 (16-ounce) bottle of your
 favorite barbecue sauce,
 plus plenty more for dipping

1 cup beef broth, homemade
 bone broth if you want
 (see page 53)

Brown sugar

Garlic salt

Cayenne pepper

Ground black pepper

❖ *Don't Forget*

Your slow cooker (hard
 to forget for this one!)

❖ *Stock Up on Napkins and Let's Make Some Ribs*

Thinly slice **1 medium Vidalia onion.** Slice **2 garlic cloves.** Cut **1 rack of baby back ribs** to fit into the cooker.

Pour **1 (16-ounce) bottle of barbecue sauce** and **1 cup beef broth** into your slow cooker, then sprinkle in **2 spoonfuls of brown sugar, a palmful of garlic salt,** and **a couple pinches each of cayenne pepper** and **black pepper.** Add your onion, garlic cloves, and then the ribs. Toss and stir everything so the ribs are coated in the sauce.

Cover the slow cooker and cook on low for 6 to 8 hours, until the ribs are falling-off-the-bone tender. This one's for everyone who loves a whole lot of sauce in their meal: Serve with more barbecue sauce for dipping!

My Go-To Pot Roast

FEEDS 4 TO 6 ❖ TAKES 4 TO 5 HOURS

Several generations of busy moms before me in my family have relied on pot roast. I grew up in a blue-collar family, and my mom worked, so she had to get creative with the slow cooker meals. This pot roast was in constant rotation when I was growing up. Now that I'm grown with kids of my own, when I know I'm going to be busy all day I'll throw all those same ingredients into the oven and walk away. If you want to use the slow cooker, this is great after 6 to 8 hours on low. Either way, it's so tender you could cut it with a spoon. Serve with Ultimate Mashed Potatoes (page 136) and boom! You got a classy family dinner. Eat it plain, and you still have a complete dinner.

❖ *Gather Up*

1 medium Vidalia onion

4 garlic cloves

1 boneless beef chuck roast (3 pounds or so)

Fine sea salt and ground black pepper

4 tablespoons (½ stick) salted butter, homemade if you want (see page 34)

1 cup beef broth, homemade bone broth if you want (see page 53)

1 bunch of fresh rosemary

1 bunch of fresh thyme

1 sprig of fresh sage

2 bay leaves

Garlic salt

Onion powder

All-purpose seasoning, like Everglades, or homemade if you want (see page 38)

Cayenne pepper

4 medium carrots

2 celery stalks

1½ pounds little red potatoes

❖ *Let's Pot Up This Roast*

Preheat your oven to 300°F.

Chop up **1 medium Vidalia onion** and **4 garlic cloves.** Season your **boneless beef chuck roast** generously with **fine sea salt** and **ground black pepper**—make sure it's seasoned all over!

Over medium, heat up your large Dutch oven with **4 tablespoons (½ stick) salted butter.** When the butter is melted, add your roast and sear it on both sides, 7 to 10 minutes total. When that's done, add your onion and garlic, **1 cup beef broth, 1 bunch of fresh rosemary, 1 bunch of fresh thyme, 1 sprig of fresh sage,** and **2 bay leaves,** then sprinkle in **a palmful each of garlic salt, onion powder,** and **all-purpose seasoning,** plus **a couple pinches each of cayenne pepper** and **black pepper.**

Bring everything to a simmer, cover the pot, and put it in the oven. Bake for 2 hours. Right before the time is up, chop **4 medium carrots** and **2 celery stalks.** Cut 1½ **pounds little red potatoes** in half.

After 2 hours, add your carrots, celery, and little red potatoes. Bake for 1½ to 2 more hours, until the vegetables are tender and the meat is practically falling apart. Check the seasoning to make sure you're happy with it, toss those bay leaves, then serve it up!

James's Smash Burgers

FEEDS 4 ❖ TAKES 20 MINUTES

I hadn't thought to ask James about his famous burgers until I decided to put them in this book. He makes them all the time, and I just get to sit back and enjoy. It never occurred to me how he learned to make such a damn good burger, how he gets those edges so perfectly charred they're crispy and crunchy, how he gets the seasoning into each bite, or how he learned to handle his meat so well (you know what I mean!!). So, now I'm finding out the same way you are that his very first job when he was 15 was at a restaurant, shaping burgers! His boss Tim taught him to cook with love, and most important, to smash the burger *before* you put it on the griddle.

❖ *Gather Up*

For the Sauce

½ cup mayonnaise, homemade if you want (see page 42)

¼ cup ketchup

2 tablespoons mustard, homemade if you want (see page 45), yellow mustard, or Dijon if you're feeling frisky

For the Burgers

2 pounds ground beef (I like 80/20)

Dale's Seasoning (see my Note)

A.1. Sauce

Worcestershire sauce

All-purpose seasoning, like Everglades, or homemade if you want (see page 38)

Ground black pepper

Salted butter, homemade if you want (see page 34)

4 hamburger buns

8 slices sharp Cheddar cheese

Any of your favorite hamburger toppings

❖ *Let's Smash Some Burgers*

Make your sauce: In a small bowl, mix **½ cup mayonnaise, ¼ cup ketchup,** and **2 tablespoons mustard** until well combined. We call this sauce our "mixed up stuff." Refrigerate it until you're ready to eat.

Move on to the burgers: In a large bowl, combine **2 pounds ground beef** with **2 glugs each of Dale's Seasoning, A.1. Sauce,** and **Worcestershire sauce** (we're aiming for 2 tablespoons each here). Mix just until combined and no more. Divide the mix into 8 equal-size balls, then patty them out by putting them one at a time between 2 pieces of parchment paper and smashing with a cast-iron skillet until they're less than ½ inch thick—get them as thin and round as possible. Once you've smashed them all, take off the parchment and sprinkle the patties all over with **a couple pinches each of all-purpose seasoning** and **black pepper.**

Heat a big ole griddle if you got one, or your 12-inch cast-iron skillet over high. **Butter** the insides of **4 hamburger buns.** When the griddle or skillet is hot, toast the buns until golden brown, 1 to 2 minutes. Move them to a plate.

Add the burgers to the griddle, working in batches if you need to. Sear, pressing down with a spatula to help create those crispy edges, until they're real browned and crusty, 2 minutes or so on each side. When you flip them the first time, add the **8 slices of sharp Cheddar cheese,** 1 slice on each burger, so the cheese is melted by the time the bottom is crisped.

Put 2 burgers each on the toasted buns, and serve with the mixed up stuff and any other toppings you like. Now, ain't that a perfect burger?

Note: *James seasons his meat with both Dale's Seasoning (his secret ingredient; grab it if you see it at the store) and A.1., but you can just double up on one or the other if that's all you got.*

You Butter Believe

Butternut Squash Casserole

FEEDS 4 TO 6 ❖ TAKES ABOUT 90 MINUTES

We choose the vegetables we eat by going by what's in season. I think you might be able to get a butternut squash in a grocery store year-round now, but I only want to eat it when I'm feeling cozy. I grew up eating butternut squash and didn't think much of it. It wasn't until I was making my own baby food for the kiddos that I discovered I had a real taste for it. Of course, this ain't no baby food—it's adult food. It's got enough garlic and garlic salt, and a healthy amount of cheese, to make me think twice about kissing James goodnight. Well, that's a lie . . . you butter believe he always gets a kiss and then some.

❖ Gather Up

1 **large butternut squash (2 pounds or so)**

2 **garlic cloves**

2 **cups heavy whipping cream**

2 **tablespoons salted butter, homemade if you want (see page 34)**

Onion powder

Garlic salt

Ground black pepper

1½ **cups shredded white Cheddar cheese (6 ounces)**

❖ If It's Sweater Weather, I'm Making This Casserole

Preheat your oven to 350°F.

Trim the ends off **1 large butternut squash** and, using a peeler or a sharp knife, peel off all the skin. Cut the squash in half longways, then use a spoon to scoop out the seeds. Now, use your sharpest knife to cut the squash as thin as you can manage into crosswise slices (like potato chips) so they're about ⅛ inch thick. (If you have a mandoline, that will work perfectly.) Roughly chop **2 garlic cloves.**

In a medium pot, combine the garlic, **2 cups heavy whipping cream, and 2 tablespoons salted butter,** then sprinkle in **a palmful each of onion powder** and **garlic salt,** and **a couple pinches of black pepper.** Bring it to a simmer over medium-high, stirring every so often, for 5 minutes or so, then take it off the heat right away. Taste and make sure you're happy with the seasoning.

Make the squash slices look pretty in a 9 × 13-inch baking dish by putting them in rows and overlapping them slightly. Pour the hot cream mixture over the squash, then sprinkle with 1½ **cups shredded white Cheddar cheese.** Cover the pan with foil.

Bake until the squash is tender, 40 minutes or so. Take off the foil and raise the oven to 425°F and cook until the casserole is bubbling away and the cheese is melted and browned, 25 minutes or so more. Let it cool for 5 minutes before you dig in and get *extra* cozy.

BBQ Pineapple Chicken Bake

FEEDS 4 ❖ TAKES 1 HOUR

My "screw around and find out" or "throw whatever I got in a pan" meals are always my best. I'm telling you, this is the real joy of being in the kitchen: listening to your intuition, treating the kitchen like a playground, and then getting to see your family's faces when they taste your creation. I dreamed up this chicken right here when I had a craving for something sweet and savory for dinner. I happened to have some pineapple, plus I always have an unbelievable amount of chicken, and this is what I came up with. It hits all my cravings: sweet, spicy, bacon, and seasoned to the hilt. It's great over white rice or my Ultimate Mashed Potatoes on page 136.

❖ *Gather Up*

1 **(20-ounce) can diced pineapple (or use 2 cups fresh)**

6 **bacon strips**

4 **boneless, skinless chicken breasts (about 2 pounds total)**

Fine sea salt and ground black pepper

1 **cup of your favorite barbecue sauce (I like Sweet Baby Ray's)**

Brown sugar

Tabasco

Garlic salt

Onion powder

❖ *Let's Bake Up This Chicken*

Preheat your oven to 350°F.

Drain **1 (20-ounce) can diced pineapple,** or dice (meaning make sure the pieces are nice and even) enough fresh pineapple so you get 2 cups total. Roughly chop **6 bacon strips.**

Put the bacon in your 12-inch cast-iron skillet and put that over medium-high. Cook the bacon, stirring regularly, until it's well browned, 5 to 7 minutes. Use a slotted spoon to move the bacon to a medium bowl, leaving the grease in the pan.

Season **4 boneless, skinless chicken breasts** all over with **a big pinch each of fine sea salt** and **black pepper.** Put the chicken in the skillet, still over medium-high, then add in your diced pineapple and leave the chicken to cook until everything is nice and browned on the bottom, 1 to 2 minutes, then flip and repeat, another 1 to 2 minutes. The chicken won't be fully cooked yet but that's okay. Move the chicken and the pineapple to the bowl with the bacon.

Make sure your skillet is off the burner, then add **1 cup barbecue sauce, 2 spoonfuls of brown sugar, a couple dashes of Tabasco, a palmful of garlic salt,** and **a couple pinches each of onion powder** and black pepper. Add ¼ **cup water** and stir it real well. Taste it and see if it needs any more seasonings.

Put the chicken, pineapple, and bacon back into the skillet and spoon the sauce over the chicken to cover it. Bake in the skillet, uncovered, until the chicken is cooked through (either it's 165°F or you cut it and if there's no pink inside, it's good), 25 to 30 minutes. Dish it up! And you only gotta wash one pan!

Chicken & Rice Casserole

FEEDS 4 TO 6 ❖ TAKES ABOUT 1 HOUR

I started making this casserole at a pretty young age, when my parents were working late and I was in charge of dinner for my brother and me. It's my Mama's recipe that she'd make all the time, then she taught me how to make it, and now my kids love it, too. I included some measurements here, but it really couldn't be simpler: You cook up some yellow rice however the box tells you, shred some leftover chicken, and chop enough broccoli to get your fiber in for the evening. Just use however much your heart tells you of each; it's always gonna be good.

❖ *Gather Up*

2 cups boxed yellow rice (or 4 cups cooked)

Cooked chicken (12 ounces should get you 2 cups shredded; boiled, pan-seared, or rotisserie—I've tried them all and they are all good)

1 head of broccoli

2 cups chicken broth, homemade bone broth if you want (see page 54)

2 cups shredded Cheddar cheese (8 ounces)

½ cup (4 ounces) cream cheese, room temperature

Onion powder

All-purpose seasoning, like Everglades, or homemade if you want (see page 38)

Garlic salt

Ground black pepper

Cayenne pepper

❖ *I Have Never Been So Excited for a Casserole*

Preheat your oven to 350°F.

While that's happening, cook the **2 cups yellow rice** according to the directions on the package. Shred **12 ounces cooked chicken** so you get 2 cups. Chop up **1 head of broccoli** into real small pieces (you should have 2 cups or so).

In a large bowl, combine the cooked rice, chicken, broccoli, **2 cups chicken broth, 1 cup shredded Cheddar cheese,** ½ **cup (4 ounces) softened cream cheese, a couple pinches each of onion powder** and **all-purpose seasoning,** and **a pinch each of garlic salt, black pepper,** and **cayenne pepper.** Mix it all together and make sure you're happy with the seasoning.

Put your mixture into a 9 × 13-inch baking dish, then sprinkle the other **1 cup shredded Cheddar cheese** on top. Cover the baking dish with foil.

Bake for 20 minutes, then take off the foil and continue baking until the broccoli is tender, the liquid is gone, and the cheese is browned, another 20 minutes or so. Let it rest for 5 minutes before you dish it up. Is that not the best damn casserole you've ever had?

Crispy Creamy Mac 'n' Cheese

FEEDS 4 TO 6 ❖ TAKES 45 MINUTES

I know I say you should always do you, go with your gut, and measure with your heart, but this recipe is all about the cheese, so don't you dare think about skimping on it. The more cheese, the better—consider this your permission to pile it on. And then pile on some more. You *want* to reach for the Lactaid pills when you eat it.

When I realized the kids were eating way too much boxed mac and cheese, I dug up my distant relative Hazel's recipe (to be completely honest with you, I'm not even sure how we're related) and have been using it ever since. So, now we all eat mac and cheese, but a lot less often and it's so much better than that bright orange nonsense.

❖ *Gather Up*

Fine sea salt

1 pound cellentani or cavatappi pasta or your favorite fancy pasta shape

1 (8-ounce) block Cheddar cheese, plus more if you want

1 (8-ounce) block Gouda cheese, plus more if you want

1 (4-ounce) block Colby jack cheese

1 (2-ounce) block Parmesan cheese

2 cups heavy whipping cream

1 (8-ounce) package cream cheese

8 tablespoons (1 stick) salted butter, homemade if you want (see page 34), plus more for the pan

Onion powder

Garlic salt

Garlic powder

❖ *Let's See Just How Much Cheese We Can Fit into This Dish*

Fill a large pot with water and bring to a boil over medium-high. **Generously salt** it—don't be shy now—to season your pasta. Stir in **1 pound cellentani or cavatappi pasta.** Cook according to the package directions for al dente, or add another minute if you like your pasta softer. Drain your pasta and set it aside for now.

Grate your cheese now; **8 ounces sharp Cheddar cheese** and **8 ounces Gouda cheese** should get you 2 cups of each, **4 ounces Colby jack cheese** will get you 1 cup, and **2 ounces Parmesan cheese** will get you ½ cup. Set aside 1 cup each of the Cheddar and Gouda for the topping—or shred even more for the topping, the more cheese the better here.

Preheat your broiler on low, if that's an option; if not, keep the rack in the middle of the oven.

While your pasta cooks, grab your second large pot and add **2 cups heavy whipping cream, 1 (8-ounce) package cream cheese, 8 tablespoons (1 stick) salted butter,** and **a pinch each of onion powder, garlic salt,** and **garlic powder.** Set over medium-low and cook, stirring regularly, until everything is melted and you get a homogenous creamy blend.

Move the pot off the stove and place it on a heat-safe surface. Add in all the Colby jack, all the Parmesan, 1 cup of the Cheddar, and 1 cup of the Gouda. Mix together until the cheeses are melted into a smooth sauce. If your sauce is really thick, stir in up to ½ **cup water.** Taste and make sure you're happy with the seasonings.

Next, add your cooked pasta to the cheesy sauce. Mix well and fold the sauce and pasta into one another so the pasta is entirely covered in cheesy goodness.

Butter your 12-inch cast-iron skillet. Spread your mac and cheese in the pan in an even layer with your spoon. Then sprinkle the Cheddar and Gouda cheese you set aside on top.

Broil the mac 'n' cheese until the topping is golden brown, which usually takes 3 to 5 minutes in my oven, but keep an eye on it, as every broiler has a mind of its own. Let sit for 10 minutes before enjoying all this cheesy goodness!

Sauced Up Shrimp Linguine

FEEDS 4 ❖ TAKES 30 MINUTES

After I made that lasagna on page 178, I had to try my hand at more Italian cooking. James has Italian roots (his mom's dad is from Italy), but I didn't grow up eating much—or really any—Italian food. Turns out, it usually checks all the boxes we need for a family dinner: carbs and protein (I guess that actually ain't that many boxes). This is one of the few recipes where I want you to grate your own Parmesan—Parmigiano-Reggiano, if you will—since we're honoring the Italian side of the family.

❖ Gather Up

- 1 medium Vidalia onion
- 2 garlic cloves
- A hunk of Parmesan cheese, about 1 ounce (or ¼ cup grated)
- Fine sea salt and ground black pepper
- 1 pound linguine
- 4 tablespoons (½ stick) salted butter, homemade if you want (see page 34)
- 1 pound cherry tomatoes
- ½ cup heavy whipping cream
- Garlic salt
- Onion powder
- Dried rosemary
- Dried oregano
- Dried basil
- 1 pound peeled and deveined medium shrimp
- A handful of fresh parsley

❖ Let's Get Extra Saucy

Bring a large pot of water to a boil over high heat. While you're waiting, chop **1 medium Vidalia onion** and **2 garlic cloves.** Grate the **hunk of Parmesan cheese** until you have ¼ cup (or just use pre-grated).

When the water comes to a boil, add **a couple big pinches of fine sea salt**—don't be shy now—to season the pasta water. Add **1 pound linguine** and cook according to the directions on the package for al dente. Scoop out and save about ½ cup of the pasta water, then drain the pasta.

Meanwhile, over medium-high, heat up your 12-inch cast-iron skillet with **4 tablespoons (½ stick) salted butter.** When the butter is melted, add your onion, season with fine sea salt and **ground black pepper,** and cook, stirring regularly, until the onion is soft, 5 minutes or so. Add the garlic and **1 pound cherry tomatoes** and cook, stirring every so often, until the tomatoes split and release their juices, 5 to 7 minutes. Add ½ **cup heavy whipping cream,** then sprinkle in **a palmful each of garlic salt, onion powder, dried rosemary, dried oregano,** and **dried basil** and another pinch each of salt and pepper. Bring the mixture to a simmer, stirring regularly, then reduce the heat to medium-low. Cook, stirring every so often, until the sauce is thickened and the tomatoes are very soft, another 5 to 7 minutes.

Add **1 pound peeled and deveined medium shrimp** and cook, stirring every so often, until the shrimp are just barely pink and cooked through, 3 minutes or so. Now, add your cooked pasta, a splash of the pasta water, and half your grated Parmesan cheese. Get in there and toss it. The more you can toss and mix that pasta and sauce together, the better the sauce will coat the pasta. You're looking for a glossy sauce that covers the pasta evenly. If it's too thick, add another splash of pasta water. If it's too runny, keep cooking and tossing until it's not. Taste and check the seasoning one last time.

Serve it right away with the rest of the grated Parmesan to sprinkle over. Chop **a handful of fresh parsley** and sprinkle it over, too ('cause we *fantasiosi*—that's Italian for fancy).

Scalloped Potatoes & Ham Casserole

FEEDS 8 ❖ TAKES 2 HOURS

We had a bumper crop of potatoes from our garden one season, and we were getting pretty sick of them. I love potatoes, but you can only eat so many, you know? We gathered up a whole load of them to give to our neighbors, and do you know what they had waiting to give to us? THEIR OWN POTATOES. So, we smiled real big and thanked them and ended up with just as many potatoes at home as we started the day with. I had to get real creative during our Potato Era, so I turned scalloped potatoes into a one-dish meal by adding some ham.

❖ Gather Up

- 4 **bacon strips**
- 12 ounces cooked ham (a boneless ham steak or real thick-sliced ham)
- 1 small Vidalia onion
- 2 garlic cloves
- 3 pounds Yukon Gold potatoes
- 4 tablespoons (½ stick) salted butter, homemade if you want (see page 34)
- ¼ cup all-purpose flour
- 1 cup chicken broth, homemade bone broth if you want (see page 54)
- 1½ cups heavy whipping cream
- 1 cup whole milk
- Garlic salt
- Onion powder
- Fine sea salt and ground black pepper
- 1 cup shredded sharp Cheddar cheese (4 ounces)
- 1 cup shredded white Cheddar cheese (4 ounces)

❖ Let's Scallop Some Potatoes

Preheat your oven to 350°F.

Heat up your 10-inch cast-iron skillet over medium. Put some paper towels on a plate. Add **4 bacon strips** to the pan and cook, flipping once or twice, until crisp and golden, 5 to 7 minutes total. Move them over to the paper towel, then chop up the bacon.

Dice (meaning your pieces are nice and even) **12 ounces of cooked ham,** so you have 2 cups or so. Chop **1 small Vidalia onion** and **2 garlic cloves.** Peel (or not!) **3 pounds Yukon Gold potatoes.** Slice the potatoes as thin as you can manage.

Over medium, melt **4 tablespoons (½ stick) salted butter** in your medium pot. Cook the onion and garlic, stirring regularly, until they're soft, 5 to 7 minutes. Add ¼ cup **all-purpose flour** and stir until it stops smelling like raw flour, 1 minute or so.

Reduce the heat to low and gradually add **1 cup chicken broth** while stirring. Pour in **1½ cups heavy whipping cream** and **1 cup whole milk,** then sprinkle in **a palmful each of garlic salt** and **onion powder,** and add **a pinch of black pepper,** then stir well. Raise the heat to medium-high and let the sauce just barely come to a simmer, then take the pan off the heat. Check the seasoning.

Spoon a little sauce onto the bottom of a 9 × 13-inch baking dish. Spread one-third of the potatoes in an even layer and season them **a pinch of fine sea salt** and a pinch of black pepper. Now, sprinkle over one-third of the cooked bacon and one-third of the diced ham. Spread one-third of the sauce over everything, and sprinkle with one-third of the **1 cup shredded sharp Cheddar cheese** and one-third of the **1 cup shredded white Cheddar cheese.** Now, do this twice more so you use up everything. Cover the dish with foil.

Bake for 30 minutes. Take off the foil and bake until the potatoes are tender, the sauce is bubbling, and the cheese is browned, another 40 minutes or so. Let it rest for 15 minutes before slicing and enjoying.

Lover's Lasagna

FEEDS 8 TO 10 ❖ TAKES 3 TO 4 HOURS

Making lasagna is a labor of love. One Valentine's Day, I thought I'd really lean into that and put my whole heart into making something for my people. The pasta is homemade, the sauce is homemade, even the cheese is homemade! I know it seems like a lot, but what you want to do is read everything through once, maybe twice for good measure, then just kind of get it all going at the same time. I'll start the sauce, then while I'm waiting for it to simmer, I'll make the pasta dough; and while the dough is chilling, I'll make the cheese. If you're organized, make the dough and cheese first. And if you don't want to make pasta or cheese, I got you covered, too. There's options for buying them, because even if you make lasagna from store-bought ingredients, you're still showing you care.

❖ Gather Up

For the Sauce

- 1 large Vidalia onion
- 4 or 5 garlic cloves
- Olive oil
- 1 pound ground beef (I like 80/20)
- Fine sea salt and ground black pepper
- 1 (28-ounce) can tomato puree
- 1 (14-ounce) can diced tomatoes
- Garlic salt
- Garlic powder
- Onion powder
- Dried parsley
- Dried oregano
- Dried basil
- Dried rosemary

❖ Clear Your Afternoon: We're Makin' Lasagna

Start with your sauce: Chop **1 large Vidalia onion** and **4 or 5 garlic cloves.** In your 10-inch cast-iron skillet over medium, heat **a splash of olive oil.** When the oil is good and hot, add **1 pound ground beef** and season with **a pinch each of fine sea salt** and **black pepper.** Start stirring, breaking up the beef into small pieces, and cook until the meat is cooked through and you don't see any pink, 5 minutes or so. Add your chopped onion and garlic and cook, stirring every so often, until the onion and garlic are softened and start to brown, another 5 minutes or so.

Pour in **1 (28-ounce) can tomato puree** and **1 (14-ounce) can diced tomatoes,** juices and all. Stir and let sit for a minute until it starts bubbling again, then sprinkle in **a palmful of garlic salt** and **a couple pinches each of garlic powder, onion powder, dried parsley, dried oregano, dried basil,** and **dried rosemary.** Stir again and scrape up the browned bits from the bottom, then reduce the heat to low so your sauce simmers, uncovered and stirring every so often, while you get your other ingredients.

Now, for putting it all together: If you're using my **Pasta Dough,** boil the noodles according to the directions on page 52. If you're not making your own noodles, boil 1 (1-pound) box lasagna noodles according to the package directions, and I suggest adding **a glug of olive oil** to the cooking water to prevent sticking.

For the cheese layer, you'll need **1 batch of Homemade Fresh Cheese,** which is 3 balls. If you don't want to make your own cheese, in a large bowl combine 1 pound of ricotta cheese and an 8-ounce package softened cream cheese, and mix until smooth.

For Putting It All Together

1 batch Pasta Dough (page 50) or 1 pound store-bought lasagna noodles (not no-boil or oven-ready)

Olive oil

1 batch Homemade Fresh Cheese (page 49) or use 1 pound ricotta and 1 (8-ounce) package room-temperature cream cheese

1 (1-pound) package shredded mozzarella cheese

1 cup grated Parmesan cheese (4 ounces)

Preheat your oven to 350°F. Grease a 9 × 13-inch baking dish with olive oil.

Let's assemble this baby: Have your noodles, meat sauce, soft cheese mixture, **1 (1-pound) bag of shredded mozzarella cheese,** and **1 cup grated Parmesan cheese** within reach. Line the bottom of your greased baking dish with one layer of lasagna noodles, so they completely cover the bottom without overlapping. If you have to rip or cut a few noodles to fit, that's fine. Spread 2 cups of the meat sauce evenly over the noodles, edge to edge. Then, crumble 1 ball of fresh cheese evenly over the top (or dollop one-third of the ricotta mixture), and sprinkle with 1 heaping cup mozzarella and ⅓ cup Parmesan. Repeat this twice more, for a total of 3 layers that end with the Parmesan cheese. If you have any extra mozzarella, sprinkle that on top. Cover the dish tightly with aluminum foil.

Bake for 30 minutes, then take off the foil and bake until the top is golden brown and the sauce is nice and bubbly, another 30 minutes or so. Let it cool in the dish for 10 to 15 minutes before slicing and showing all your loved ones how much you care.

Knock-Out

Ham Hock Lima Bean Soup

FEEDS 4 ❖ TAKES 12 TO 14 HOURS

This soup right here will send you straight to the couch. This is not a soup you can do anything after eating. Once I made it for lunch and took James a bowl, and he looked at me and said "I'm not eating this." I asked him why not and he said "'Cause I got work to do this afternoon!" Well, he ended up eating the soup, and it wasn't 10 minutes before he was lying on the couch. I say this all with love, because I have nothing but fond memories from getting knocked out by it. The first time I make it every year is after Thanksgiving, when I need to use up the ham bone from our feast. Any time you have a leftover holiday ham all through the winter, head straight for this page, but make sure you got everything crossed off your chore list first.

❖ *Gather Up*

1 **(1-pound) bag dried lima beans**

1 **medium Vidalia onion**

2 **garlic cloves**

4 **cups chicken broth, homemade bone broth if you want (see page 54)**

1 **pound ham hocks (probably 2, smoked or not, up to you) or a ham bone**

All-purpose seasoning, like Everglades, or homemade if you want (see page 38)

Fine sea salt and ground black pepper

❖ *Don't Forget*

Your slow cooker (I've made this on the stove, but it takes *forever*)

❖ *The Couch Will Be Calling Your Name Soon*

Rinse **1 (1-pound) bag dried lima beans** and put them in a medium bowl with enough water to cover by a couple inches. Let them soak for 8 hours or you can leave them overnight, then drain.

Chop **1 medium Vidalia onion** and **2 garlic cloves.** Throw them into your slow cooker, then add the drained beans, **4 cups chicken broth,** and **1 pound ham hocks or your ham bone,** then sprinkle in **a palmful of all-purpose seasoning.** Add **a big pinch each of fine sea salt** and **black pepper.**

Cover the cooker and cook on high for 4 hours. After 4 hours, check and see if the beans are tender. If they are, you're good to go. If not, turn the cooker to low and cook for another 2 hours. By the time the beans are ready, the ham should be falling off the bone.

Taste and make sure there's enough seasoning in there for you, then serve it up, picking out any bone if you happen to scoop one up, and ideally in close proximity to the couch.

Nice & Creamy Crab Bisque

FEEDS 4 ❖ TAKES 1 HOUR

Me and James were out to eat in Savannah, or somewhere close by, and I ordered crab bisque for the first time in my life. I knew I had to make it as soon as we got home. I just follow my taste buds when I'm trying to recreate a dish. I start with what I know is in there (in this case, crab and cream), add a little bit of seasoning, a little bit of onion and garlic, taste it, and if I say "Well, that ain't it," I remember what I did and do something else next time. Once I get the seasoning down, I keep listening to my heart and make it just how I want. Use whatever crabmeat you can find: canned, from crab legs you cooked yourself, plain ole lump crabmeat, I've used it all, and it's all good.

❖ Gather Up

1 small Vidalia onion

2 garlic cloves

1 pound crabmeat, any kind

4 tablespoons (½ stick) salted butter, homemade if you want (see page 34)

¼ cup all-purpose flour

¼ cup tomato paste

Seafood seasoning (I use Chef Paul Prudhomme's Blackened Redfish Magic)

Garlic salt

Onion powder

Fine sea salt and ground black pepper

2 to 4 cups seafood or vegetable stock (you could even use clam juice), up to you

1 cup heavy whipping cream

1 lemon

¼ cup grated Parmesan cheese (1 ounce)

A handful of fresh parsley

❖ Don't Forget

Your handheld blender or regular blender

❖ Let's Whip Up Some Bisque

Chop up **1 small Vidalia onion** and chop up **2 garlic cloves** nice and small. Drain **1 pound crabmeat** if you need to, then pick through it to make sure there's no stray shell bits.

Over medium, heat up your large Dutch oven or pot with **4 tablespoons (½ stick) salted butter.** When the butter is melted, add the onion and cook, stirring regularly, until it's softened but not at all browned, 5 minutes or so. Add your garlic and cook, stirring all the while, until you can smell it; 1 minute is all it should take. Add ¼ **cup all-purpose flour** and ¼ **cup tomato paste,** and stir to coat the onion, then sprinkle in **a palmful each of seafood seasoning, garlic salt,** and **onion powder,** and add **a pinch of black pepper.** Stir constantly for 2 minutes, to cook the flour and tomato paste.

Pour in **2 cups seafood stock** and raise the heat to medium-high to bring it to a simmer. Then reduce the heat to low and cook, stirring regularly, until the soup has thickened and the flavors have all come together, 20 to 30 minutes. Take the pot off the heat. You can blend it right in the pot with a handheld blender. (Or, if you don't have one, move it over to a regular blender. But be careful! Let the soup cool more, fill the blender only halfway, and make sure the blender lid is cracked open away from you to let the steam escape.) Blend until smooth.

Pour the soup back into the pot if you need and add the crabmeat (save a little for the top) and **1 cup heavy whipping cream.** Zest **1 lemon** into the pot, then cut the lemon in half and squeeze just a bit of juice in there as well (call it 1 tablespoon). Put the pot back over low heat and bring to just barely a simmer. If you like your soup thinner, add up to another **2 cups seafood stock.** Taste and make sure you're happy with the seasoning and add some **fine sea salt** if it needs it.

Scoop the soup into bowls and sprinkle with ¼ **cup grated Parmesan cheese** and the crab you saved. Chop **a handful of fresh parsley** and sprinkle that over, too, before serving. Now, don't that taste good?

Won't Make You Cry

Onion Soup

FEEDS 4 TO 6 ❖ TAKES 2 HOURS

I could eat an onion like an apple—just take a big ole bite out of one side. That's how much I love them. And when I learned there was a whole soup made with just onions . . . well, you know I had to try making it. It's one of my favorite winter dishes to cook, a little bit of France-meets-Georgia, by way of Italy (I love my Parmesan cheese). Don't forget to grab you a piece of garlic toast before you dig in, my friend.

❖ *Gather Up*

4 large Vidalia onions

2 garlic cloves

4 tablespoons (½ stick) salted butter, homemade if you want (see page 34)

Brown sugar

4 cups chicken broth, homemade bone broth if you want (see page 54)

Garlic salt

Onion powder

All-purpose seasoning, like Everglades, or homemade if you want (see page 38)

Fine sea salt and ground black pepper

1 cup heavy whipping cream

1 cup grated Parmesan cheese (4 ounces), plus more for serving

A handful of fresh parsley

❖ *Let's Get Some Tunes Going and Get Chopping*

Start by cutting **4 large Vidalia onions** in half longways, peeling them, and then thinly slicing them longways. Chop **2 garlic cloves.**

Over medium, heat up your large pot or Dutch oven with **4 tablespoons (½ stick) salted butter.** When the butter is melted, add the onions and cook, stirring every so often, until they are tender, 10 to 15 minutes. Sprinkle over **a spoonful of brown sugar** and keep cooking for 15 to 20 minutes more, until the onions are dark brown and caramelized. Add the garlic and cook until you can smell it, 1 minute or so.

Raise the heat to medium-high and start adding **4 cups chicken broth,** 1 cup at a time, while stirring without stopping. Once you've added all the broth, sprinkle in **a palmful each of garlic salt, onion powder,** and **all-purpose seasoning,** and add **a couple pinches of black pepper.** Bring it back to a boil. Reduce the heat to low so it simmers and cook, uncovered and stirring every so often, for 30 minutes so the flavors can combine.

Stir in **1 cup heavy whipping cream** and **1 cup grated Parmesan cheese.** Raise the heat to medium and cook for another 15 minutes, stirring every so often, until it reduces and gets a beautiful caramel color. Taste it and make sure you're happy with the seasonings, adding some **fine sea salt** if it needs it.

Ladle the soup into bowls and **sprinkle with more Parmesan cheese.** Chop **a handful of fresh parsley** and sprinkle that on, too. I know I said this soup won't make you cry, but that first bite makes me shed a tear of joy!

Cream of Mushroom Soup

FEEDS 4 ❖ TAKES 1 HOUR

I have tried many types of mushrooms in this soup and all of them are wonderful, so I say get the ones you enjoy the most. My favorites are shiitakes and lion's mane. Lion's mane aren't that easy to find at a store, but they're one of the few mushrooms we feel confident foraging (once we got a lion's mane that was the size of James's head!). It's real humid and damp here, and the mushrooms go crazy, but we're never going to pick them unless we are absolutely certain we know what we're getting. Anyway—I'm off on a tangent—whether you use foraged mushrooms or white button mushrooms from the store, this soup will warm you right up.

❖ *Gather Up*

8 ounces fresh mushrooms

1 medium Vidalia onion

2 garlic cloves

4 tablespoons (½ stick) salted butter, homemade if you want (see page 34)

2 tablespoons all-purpose flour

2 to 3 cups chicken broth, homemade bone broth if you want (see page 54), up to you

1 cup heavy whipping cream

Garlic salt

Onion powder

All-purpose seasoning, like Everglades, or homemade if you want (see page 38)

❖ *Don't Forget*

Your handheld blender, or regular blender

❖ *Let's Make Some Magical Mushroom Soup*

Clean and roughly chop **8 ounces fresh mushrooms.** Chop **1 medium Vidalia onion** and **2 garlic cloves.**

Over medium, heat up your large Dutch oven with **4 tablespoons (½ stick) salted butter.** When the butter is melted, add your onion and cook, stirring regularly, until the onion is softened but not at all browned, 5 minutes or so. Add all the mushrooms and cook, stirring regularly, until they've released their liquid, it's cooked off, and then they've had a chance to brown in the butter, 12 to 15 minutes total. (You can pick out a few pretty mushrooms now and save them for garnish if you want to get fancy.) Add the garlic and **2 tablespoons all-purpose flour** and stir without stopping until the flour no longer smells raw, 2 minutes or so.

Keep stirring while you pour in **2 cups chicken broth,** then add **1 cup heavy whipping cream,** and sprinkle in **a palmful each of garlic salt, onion powder,** and **all-purpose seasoning.** Raise the heat to medium-high to bring the soup to a simmer, then cook, stirring regularly, until it thickens, 5 minutes or so.

Take the pot off the heat. You can blend it right in the pot with a handheld blender. (Or, if you don't have one, move it over to a regular blender. But be careful! Let the soup cool off more, fill the blender only halfway, and make sure the blender lid is cracked open facing away from you to let the steam escape.) Blend until smooth. I like my soup thick, but if you want yours thinner, add up to another **1 cup chicken broth.** Taste the soup to make sure you're happy with the seasoning, then serve it up!

Chicken & Dumplings

for My Dumplin'

Have I mentioned that we have around 70 chickens on our property at any given moment? One summer, we wanted to process and stock our freezer with some quality, home-grown chickens. So after we did that, I decided to surprise James for the first time with his favorite meal: chicken and dumplings. We both grew up eating it, made from cream of mushroom soup and frozen dumplings, and it was hearty, but if you've ever had those frozen dumplings, you know sometimes the texture can be, well, slimy. These dumplings, though, are made from scratch and are creamy and melt-in-your mouth tender. This is James's favorite recipe in the whole book. He's looking over my shoulder right now, reminding me I don't make it nearly enough for him.

❖ *Gather Up*

For the Stew

½ **small Vidalia onion**

4 **garlic cloves**

1 **rotisserie chicken (about 3 pounds)**

2 **tablespoons salted butter, homemade if you want (see page 34)**

2 **cups heavy whipping cream**

2 **cups chicken broth, homemade bone broth if you want (see page 54), plus more if you like**

Garlic powder

All-purpose seasoning, like Everglades, or homemade if you want (see page 38)

Fine sea salt and ground black pepper

❖ *Let's Show Your Dumplin' You Care*

First, do some chopping for the stew: Chop ½ **small Vidalia onion** and **4 garlic cloves.** Pick off all the meat from **1 rotisserie chicken** and shred it (save the bones for your next batch of bone broth if you like; see page 54). That should get you 3 to 4 cups of chicken.

Start the stew: In a large Dutch oven or pot over medium, melt **2 tablespoons salted butter.** When the butter is melted, add the chopped onion and garlic, and cook, stirring regularly, until soft but not at all browned, about 5 minutes. Pour in **2 cups heavy whipping cream** and **2 cups chicken broth** and stir. Add the shredded chicken, then sprinkle in **a palmful of garlic powder, a couple pinches of all-purpose seasoning,** and **a pinch each of fine sea salt** and **black pepper.** Raise the heat to medium-high and bring to a boil.

While the chicken comes to a boil, make your dumpling dough: In a large bowl, combine **2 cups (240 grams to be exact) all-purpose flour, 4 tablespoons (½ stick/57 grams) softened salted butter,** and **1 tablespoon baking powder.** Sprinkle in **a palmful each of garlic powder** and **onion powder.** Massage the butter into the dry ingredients until the mixture looks like coarse crumbs. Pour in **1 cup (227 grams) whole milk** and mix and fold it in with your hands— don't be afraid to get dirty now—until a soft, dry dough forms. If your dough is at all tacky (meaning it sticks to your hand a little), sprinkle it with a little more flour and knead it in until it's dry.

(recipe and ingredients continue)

For the Dumplings

2 cups (240 grams to be exact) all-purpose flour, plus more for rolling

4 tablespoons (½ stick/ 57 grams) salted butter, room temperature

1 tablespoon baking powder

Garlic powder

Onion powder

1 cup (227 grams) whole milk

A handful of fresh parsley, for serving

Lightly flour your counter and turn out the dumpling dough. Use a rolling pin to roll it out to about, oh, let's say ¼ inch thick—you know I always eyeball it. Cut the dough into bite-size pieces. You can make them whatever shape you want, just make sure they're about the size of a quarter so they can fit on your spoon.

Put it all together: When the broth is at a boil on the stove, add in all the dumpling pieces. Reduce the heat to medium and make sure to stir often until the dumplings are done so they cook evenly and don't stick together. Usually that takes anywhere from 8 to 10 minutes; you know they're done when they're light and fluffy all the way to the middle.

If the broth is too thick for your liking, add more chicken broth to thin it out. These are *your* chicken and dumplings, make them how you like! Taste and make sure you're happy with the seasoning. Chop **a handful of fresh parsley** and sprinkle it all over ('cause we fancy).

First Night Chili

FEEDS 4 TO 6 ❖ TAKES 2 HOURS

James's and my first date was supposed to be dinner out at a restaurant, but I was running late from something (who even knows what) and he had already waited 45 minutes, so I called him up and said "Do you want to just come over and eat chili and watch a movie?" I didn't even make the chili fresh—it was leftovers! (But we all know chili is better on the second day anyway.) I know it was this chili that locked James in, in all its boozy glory. Adding half a can of beer in the last few minutes of cooking is my special trick. I don't drink too often, but sometimes I still have a taste for alcohol, and this is a way to scratch that itch. I heated us up two bowls, put *Star Wars* on the TV, and we both started the next phase of our lives right then.

❖ *Gather Up*

½ **small Vidalia onion**

1 **small jalapeño pepper (only if you like heat)**

3 **garlic cloves**

1 **(14-ounce) can sweet corn**

Vegetable oil or bacon grease, for the pan

1 **pound ground beef (I like 80/20)**

1 **(15-ounce) can chili beans**

1 **(15-ounce) can kidney beans**

1 **(15-ounce) can black beans**

1 **(14-ounce) can diced tomatoes**

1 **(14-ounce) can tomato sauce**

Chili powder

Garlic salt

Garlic powder

Onion powder

Ground cumin

Cayenne pepper

❖ *This Chili Is So Special, Y'all*

First, chop ½ **small Vidalia onion** (chop the other half for topping your chili, if you're into that) and **1 small jalapeño pepper** (you can skip this), then thinly slice **3 garlic cloves.** Drain **1 (14-ounce) can of sweet corn.** Set that aside for now.

Over medium, heat up your large Dutch oven with **a splash of vegetable oil** to coat the bottom. When the oil is good and hot, add in **1 pound ground beef** and let it start browning without messing with it. After it gets nice and browned on the bottom, 5 minutes or so, start stirring and breaking it up into small pieces with your spoon. When the meat is almost cooked through and browned, another 5 minutes, add your onion, jalapeño if using, and garlic and keep cooking until the meat is completely cooked and the vegetables are soft, 5 minutes or so more.

Add the drained corn to the meat, then add to the pot, liquid and all, **1 (15-ounce) can chili beans, 1 (15-ounce) can kidney beans, 1 (15-ounce) can black beans, 1 (14-ounce) can diced tomatoes, and 1 (14-ounce) can tomato sauce.** Sprinkle in **a palmful of chili powder, a couple pinches each of garlic salt, garlic powder, onion powder, ground cumin,** and **cayenne pepper.** Mix it all together.

Pour in **half of the 25-ounce Busch Beer tall boy.** I like a real strong alcohol taste in my chili, so I save the other half to pour in at the end. If that doesn't sound appealing to you, go ahead and add the whole thing now. Reduce the heat to low so the chili simmers. Cover the pot and cook, stirring every so often, until thickened, about 1 hour. Taste and make sure you're happy with the seasoning.

(recipe and ingredients continue)

1 (25-ounce) Busch Beer tall boy (or the beer of your choosing)

A handful of fresh cilantro, or however much you like

Shredded cheese, for serving, if you want

Sour cream, for serving, if you want

When the chili is nice and thick, pour in what's left of your **Busch Beer tall boy.** Chop up **a handful of fresh cilantro** (or however much you like) and add that, too. Stir and let simmer for another 15 minutes just to let the flavors mingle.

Scoop the chili into bowls; you can add **shredded cheese** and **sour cream,** if that's how you like your chili. However you eat it, it's gonna be a special night. Any extra will keep beautifully in the fridge for a few days.

Damn Good Chicken Gumbo

FEEDS 4 TO 6 ❖ TAKES ABOUT 1 HOUR

When I moved to Louisiana, I didn't know anything about their cooking, but thanks to all the gravy I'd made, I already knew how to make a roux. You can jump right in the kitchen and make this, too! Just keep stirring and don't stop until it's milk chocolate colored. Your roux is going to turn out just fine, and if you do happen to burn it, start over. Life's too short to cry over burnt flour.

❖ Gather Up

- 1 (1-pound) package of your favorite smoked sausage (I used Conecuh hickory smoked)
- 1 medium Vidalia onion
- 1 green bell pepper
- 2 large celery stalks
- 3 garlic cloves
- 1 jalapeño pepper
- 1 bunch of fresh parsley
- 6 tablespoons (¾ stick) salted butter, homemade if you want (see page 34)
- 2 tablespoons vegetable oil
- 2 pounds boneless, skinless chicken (any cut)
- Fine sea salt and ground black pepper
- ¾ cup all-purpose flour
- 6 to 8 cups chicken broth, homemade bone broth if you want (see page 54), as you need it
- 2 cups shelled and deveined medium shrimp (1 pound or so)
- Cajun seasoning (I use Slap Ya Mama)
- Cooked white rice, for serving

❖ Let Me Show You All My Gumbo Secrets

Slice **1 (1-pound) package smoked sausage.** Dice up (meaning make sure your cuts are nice and even and small) **1 medium Vidalia onion, 1 green bell pepper, 2 large celery stalks,** and **3 garlic cloves.** Take the seeds out of **1 jalapeño pepper** and chop that up real small, too. Chop up the leaves from **1 bunch of fresh parsley** nice and small. That was a lot of chopping; get some water!

Over medium, heat up your large Dutch oven with **2 tablespoons salted butter** and **2 tablespoons vegetable oil.** Season **2 pounds boneless, skinless chicken** all over with **a couple pinches each of fine sea salt** and **black pepper.** When the fat is hot, sear the chicken until it's cooked through, 4 to 5 minutes per side. Remove the chicken and leave the fat in the pan. Let the chicken cool for 10 minutes, then shred it with 2 forks.

While the chicken cools, add another **2 tablespoons salted butter** to the pot and put in your sliced sausage, diced onion, green pepper, celery, and jalapeño. Cook, stirring every so often until the vegetables are tender, 7 to 10 minutes. Add the garlic and cook, stirring regularly, until you can smell it, 1 minute or so. Season with fine sea salt and black pepper. Use a slotted spoon to move everything to a large bowl, leaving the fat in the pan.

To the same pot, add the last **2 tablespoons salted butter** and **¾ cup all-purpose flour.** Cook and stir without stopping until the flour is a milk chocolate color, up to 5 minutes. Start adding **6 cups chicken broth,** 1 cup at a time and stirring regularly after each. Raise the heat to high and bring to a simmer. Add the sausage and vegetables back in, plus the shredded chicken and **2 cups shelled and deveined medium shrimp.** Sprinkle in **a palmful of Cajun seasoning.** Simmer until the shrimp is cooked through and looks pink, 5 to 7 minutes more, then take the pot off the heat.

If the gumbo is too thick for you, stir in up to another **2 cups chicken broth,** a splash at a time, until it's just how you like it. Stir in your chopped parsley, then taste it and make sure you're happy with the seasoning. Serve it up piping hot, over **white rice.**

Slow Cooker Brunswick Stew

FEEDS 4 TO 6 ❖ TAKES 8 HOURS

This is the easiest recipe in the cookbook, I swear. Sear some meat, season it up, and walk away for eight hours. It's one of my Mama's best, but I got a little tired of it always being beef when she made it. So I added some chicken to a batch and never looked back. Cooking really can be that simple sometimes—and nothing feels better than experimenting and finding out your idea is even *more* delicious. I'll serve it over rice, or maybe even mashed potatoes if I feel like putting some more effort into dinner that night. If not, it's still good with bread. If you can remember to cook it ahead, the next day it will be even tastier, and you'll have to do zero work.

❖ Gather Up

- 2 tablespoons salted butter, homemade if you want (see page 34)
- Vegetable oil
- 1 whole boneless beef chuck roast (2 pounds or so)
- 6 boneless, skinless chicken thighs (2½ pounds or so total)
- Fine sea salt and ground black pepper
- 2 cups chicken broth, homemade bone broth if you want (see page 54)
- 1 medium Vidalia onion
- 2 garlic cloves
- ¼ cup (no need to pack it) brown sugar
- 2 tablespoons tomato paste
- Worcestershire sauce
- A.1. sauce
- Tabasco sauce
- Onion powder
- Garlic salt
- All-purpose seasoning, like Everglades, homemade if you want (see page 38)
- Cayenne pepper
- 1 pound baby red potatoes
- 1 pint cherry tomatoes
- 1½ cups frozen lima beans
- 1 cup frozen sweet corn

❖ Don't Forget

Your slow cooker

Over medium, heat up your 12-inch cast-iron skillet with **2 tablespoons salted butter** and **a splash of vegetable oil.** While it heats, season **1 whole beef chuck roast** and **6 boneless, skinless chicken thighs** nice and thoroughly with a **couple pinches each of fine sea salt** and **black pepper.** When the oil is good and hot, add the meat (sear the chicken separately, if you need to, so nothing's crowded) and sear on both sides until golden brown, 5 to 7 minutes total. Put the roast and the chicken into your slow cooker. Pour **2 cups chicken broth** into the skillet and scrape up all the browned bits from the bottom. Pour all that into the cooker.

Chop up **1 medium Vidalia onion** and **2 garlic cloves** and put those into the cooker. Now, add ¼ **cup brown sugar, 2 tablespoons tomato paste, a good dozen shakes of Worcestershire sauce** (call it 2 tablespoons), **a glug of A.1. Sauce** (about 1 tablespoon), and **a couple shakes of Tabasco sauce,** then sprinkle in **a palmful each of onion powder, garlic salt,** and **all-purpose seasoning,** plus **a couple pinches each of cayenne pepper** and black pepper. Stir it all together.

Cover and set your cooker to high, and cook for 6 hours. Right before the 6 hours are up, halve **1 pound baby red potatoes** and chop **1 pint cherry tomatoes.** Add the potatoes, tomatoes, **1½ cups frozen lima beans,** and **1 cup frozen sweet corn,** then stir, cover, and continue cooking for another 2 hours on low, until the potatoes are tender and the meat is falling apart. Taste it and make sure you're happy with the seasoning, adding some fine sea salt if you think it needs it. Shred the beef and chicken with 2 forks and thank your slow cooker for all it does for you.

BISCUITS, BREADS & ROLLS

———◇———

Classic Southern carbs and
everything else that makes life
so damn delicious.

Classic Biscuits & Milk Sausage Gravy

FEEDS 6 ❖ TAKES 1 HOUR

For generations in my family—me, my Mama, my grandmother—whenever we're cooking a big breakfast, these biscuits have always been on the menu. They're a staple and we probably eat them once a week still. And just like my Mama and grandmother, I'd been making the gravy with Jimmy Dean sausage all my life. Recently, though, I've been getting my meat from a local farm that does all grass-fed beef and pork; and let me tell you, this sausage made me forget about Jimmy Dean (which is saying something). Use the best sausage you can find, and if that happens to be Jimmy Dean, you'll be eating well. When you make these biscuits, make sure your butter and buttermilk are *cold* so the biscuits will rise tall and flake up in the oven.

❖ *Gather Up*

Butter, bacon grease, or the fat of your choice, for the pans

For Your Biscuits

4 tablespoons (½ stick/ 57 grams to be exact) cold salted butter, homemade if you want (see page 34)

2 cups (240 grams) all-purpose flour, plus more if you need it

1 tablespoon baking powder

1 to 2 teaspoons sugar, up to you

1 teaspoon fine sea salt

¾ cup (170 grams) cold buttermilk, homemade if you want (see page 34)

❖ *Ooooh Get Ready to Taste the Love in Every Bite*

Preheat your oven to 425°F. **Butter** a 10-inch cast-iron skillet (or you can line a baking sheet with parchment paper).

Start with your biscuit dough: Cube up **4 tablespoons (½ stick/ 57 grams to be exact) salted butter** and make sure it's *cold.* Stick it back in the fridge or freezer if you need to.

In a large bowl, whisk together **2 cups (240 grams) all-purpose flour, 1 tablespoon baking powder, 1 teaspoon sugar (2, if you're sexy),** and **1 teaspoon fine sea salt.** Add your cold cubed butter and using your hands, work the butter into the flour mixture. Gently press the butter into the dry ingredients and keep working it together until it looks like coarse crumbs; you want the butter to be as evenly spread out as best you can. Pour in ¾ **cup (170 grams) cold buttermilk** and knead all the ingredients in the bowl until the dough comes together and there isn't any more loose flour. If it feels sticky to you, just add in a spoonful of flour at a time and mix until the dough feels tacky (it shouldn't stick to your hands). Just feel it out, you'll get it!

Lightly flour your counter and turn out the dough. With your hands, gently pat down the dough and flatten it until it's about 3 finger-widths thick (the shape doesn't matter). Fold it in half, and pat it back down to 3 finger-widths thick. Do this two more times to make your biscuits flaky. After your last fold, you want your piece of dough to be 1 finger-width thick, or a little thicker. Use your mason jar to cut out as many biscuits as you can. Place the biscuits in your buttered cast-iron pan. Reroll the dough scraps and repeat to get 6 biscuits total.

Bake the biscuits until golden brown on top, 10 to 12 minutes. Move the biscuits over to a wire rack and allow them to cool until just warm.

1 **pound ground sausage**

4 **tablespoons (½ stick) salted butter**

½ **cup all-purpose flour**

3 **to 4 cups whole milk, as you need it**

Fine sea salt and ground black pepper

❖ *Don't Forget*

A 1-pint regular mason jar for cutting biscuits, or a 3-inch cookie or biscuit cutter

Meanwhile, make your gravy: Add a good amount of grease to another 10- or 12-inch cast-iron skillet so it's nice and coated, and heat it over medium. When the grease is melted and hot, add **1 pound ground sausage.** Cook, breaking it up into small pieces, until it's completely cooked through, 5 to 7 minutes. Move the meat to a plate or bowl, leaving the fat in the pan.

Put the skillet over medium-low and add in your **4 tablespoons (½ stick) salted butter.** Once the butter is completely melted, add ½ **cup all-purpose flour** and whisk together. It should start to form a clump and look doughy, but keep stirring until it lightens in color and starts bubbling a bit, 1 to 2 minutes.

Slowly whisk in **3 to 4 cups whole milk** (depending on how thick you like your gravy), adding a splash at a time and stirring all the while. You want to get a nice creamy and thick consistency, almost like an Alfredo sauce. Until you get there, keeping adding the milk slowly, gently stirring everything. Ultimately, it's up to you; I like mine thick so I don't add the full 4 cups.

When you're happy with your consistency, add your sausage meat back in and mix together. Taste it and add **pinches of fine sea salt** and **ground black pepper** until you're happy.

Put the warm biscuits on your plates, slowly drizzle the gravy all over, and pat yourself on the back!

Cinnamon Raisin Biscuits

GETS YOU 8 BISCUITS ❖ TAKE 45 MINUTES, PLUS TIME TO COOL

I worked at Hardee's for exactly one day. They just threw me on the register with no training and no supervision, and I was so mad about it I just started giving away free food. I can't forget how poorly they treated me, but I also can't forget their cinnamon raisin biscuits. I couldn't stop craving those biscuits even if I never stepped foot in a Hardee's again. So, I tried to recall the taste from memory and I swear to god, when I took my first bite—you know that moment in *Ratatouille* when the critic takes a bite of food and he couldn't help himself and started crying? That's what this biscuit is for me.

❖ Gather Up

Butter, bacon grease, or the fat of your choice, for the pan, if you like

For Your Biscuits

4 tablespoons (½ stick/ 57 grams to be exact) cold salted butter, homemade if you want (see page 34)

2 cups (240 grams) all-purpose flour, plus more for rolling

1 tablespoon granulated sugar, plus more for sprinkling

1½ teaspoons cream of tartar

1½ teaspoons baking powder

1 teaspoon fine sea salt

1 teaspoon ground cinnamon, plus more for sprinkling

¾ cup (170 grams) cold whole milk

Vanilla extract, homemade if you want (see page 33)

Distilled white vinegar (or use apple cider vinegar, homemade if you want; see page 41)

½ cup (75 grams) raisins

❖ *If These Don't Butter Your Biscuit, I Don't Know What Will*

Preheat your oven to 425°F. Go ahead and line a baking sheet with parchment paper or lightly **butter** your 10-inch cast-iron skillet.

Make the biscuit dough: Cube **4 tablespoons (½ stick/57 grams) salted butter** and make sure it's *cold.* Stick it in the fridge or freezer if you need to.

Into a large bowl, sift together **2 cups (240 grams) all-purpose flour, 1 tablespoon granulated sugar, 1½ teaspoons cream of tartar, 1½ teaspoons baking powder, 1 teaspoon fine sea salt, and 1 teaspoon ground cinnamon.** Whisk until all the dry ingredients are good and mixed.

Add your cubed butter to the dry ingredients and using your hands, work the butter into the dry mixture until it resembles coarse crumbs. You want the butter to be as evenly spread out as best you can throughout the flour mixture. Pour in ¾ **cup (170 grams) cold whole milk, a small splash of vanilla extract** (2 if you're sexy), and **a few drops of distilled white vinegar.** Stir, with a spatula or wooden spoon, until everything comes together and the dough is soft and beautiful and easy to work with. Then add ½ **cup (75 grams) raisins** and mix until they're evenly distributed.

Lightly flour your counter, turn out the dough, and gently knead it a few times so there's no stray bits of flour. Use a rolling pin to roll out the dough to 1 finger-width thickness; the shape doesn't matter, just the thickness. Use your mason jar to cut out biscuits from the dough, dipping the rim in flour to prevent sticking. Place the biscuits on the baking sheet or in the skillet, leaving a little space between them. Reroll the scraps and repeat the rolling and cutting one more time; you should get 8 biscuits. If you like, sprinkle a pinch of cinnamon and a pinch of granulated sugar on top of each biscuit for extra flavor.

For Your Vanilla Drizzle

2 tablespoons salted butter

½ cup powdered sugar

Vanilla extract

Fine sea salt

❖ *Don't Forget*

A 1-pint regular mason jar, or a 3-inch cookie or biscuit cutter

Bake until the biscuits are golden brown on top and cooked through, 12 minutes or so. Move them to a wire rack to cool completely.

Meanwhile, make the drizzle: In a small pot over low heat, or in a small bowl in the microwave, melt **2 tablespoons salted butter.**

Grab a small bowl and add the melted butter, ½ **cup powdered sugar, 1 tablespoon water, a small splash of vanilla extract,** and **a pinch of fine sea salt.** Whisk together with a fork until it gets smooth and creamy.

Drizzle over the cooled biscuits and maybe you'll have your *Ratatouille* moment, too!

Southern Sweet Cornbread

with Honey Butter

FEEDS 6 TO 8 ❖ TAKES 45 MINUTES

My Mama was big into cooking anything easy and filling she could rely on her trusty Crock-Pot to make while she was at work. Whatever she was slow-cooking up that night (Brunswick Stew, on page 198, was a favorite), she always made a batch of cornbread to go with it. You know how some families have bread or rolls with their meals? For us, it was cornbread and biscuits. My Mama's cornbread already had some sugar in it because we like a sweet cornbread in this family, but for me it needs honey, too. Hell, everything needs honey. I especially like to serve this with My Go-To Pot Roast (page 162) or Jazzy Jambalaya (page 149).

❖ Gather Up

- **1 cup (120 grams to be exact) all-purpose flour**
- **1 cup (150 grams) yellow cornmeal**
- **⅓ cup (67 grams) sugar**
- **1 tablespoon baking powder**
- **1 teaspoon fine sea salt**
- **Cayenne pepper**
- **1 cup (227 grams) heavy whipping cream**
- **⅓ cup (66 grams) vegetable oil, plus more for the pan**
- **2 large eggs**
- **⅓ cup honey**
- **2 tablespoons salted butter, homemade if you want (see page 34), room temperature**

❖ Don't Forget

- **Your 9-inch cast iron skillet (this is the only thing I use it for!)**

❖ *Just Wait 'Til You Try This Cornbread*

Preheat your oven to 400°F. Place your 9-inch cast-iron skillet in the oven to get good and hot, too.

In a medium bowl, combine **1 cup (120 grams to be exact) all-purpose flour, 1 cup (150 grams) yellow cornmeal, ⅓ cup (67 grams) sugar, 1 tablespoon baking powder, 1 teaspoon fine sea salt,** and **a pinch of cayenne pepper** (2, if you're feeling spicy). Whisk all the dry ingredients together. Add **1 cup (227 grams) heavy whipping cream** and ⅓ **cup (66 grams) vegetable oil,** then crack **2 large eggs** right in there—no need to beat them. Stir everything together until just barely combined; be relaxed about it, you want some lumps.

Carefully put the hot skillet on the stovetop. Add a **good glug of vegetable oil** and swirl it around to coat all the sides. Scrape in all the batter and use your spoon to spread it out nice and even.

Bake until the cornbread is golden brown and a toothpick poked into the middle comes out clean, 20 to 25 minutes.

While the cornbread bakes, in a small bowl, mix ⅓ **cup honey** (or use less if you don't want so much honey!) and **2 tablespoons softened salted butter** until smooth.

When the cornbread is out of the oven, spread the top with the honey butter, and make sure you eat the cornbread while it's nice and hot.

Butter My Rolls

GETS YOU 12 ROLLS ❖ TAKES 3 HOURS

I'm gonna let you in on some very important information: These rolls are my secret weapon. When I want to impress our guests, I make them. When I want to flex on someone and show them just how good I am in the kitchen, I make them. When I'm feeling real competitive, I make them. My family now asks me *not* to bring these to get-togethers because they know I'd be showing off. So, next time you find yourself invited over to the house of someone you got a thing for, or for whatever reason are going to the same barbecue as your ex, or a potluck with that one neighbor you can't stand, make these. These are your mic-drop rolls.

❖ *Gather Up*

For the Rolls

- 4 tablespoons (½ stick/ 57 grams to be exact) cold salted butter, homemade if you want (see page 34)
- 2½ cups (300 grams) all-purpose flour, plus more if you need it
- ¾ cup (170 grams) warm water
- ¼ cup (84 grams) honey
- 1 tablespoon fine sea salt
- 1 (¼-ounce) packet instant or active dry yeast (2¼ teaspoons; see my Note)
- Vegetable oil, for greasing
- 1 large egg

For the Topping

- 2 tablespoons salted butter
- 1 tablespoon honey
- Ground cinnamon
- Flaky sea salt

❖ *Don't Forget*

Your stand mixer with the dough hook, or a large bowl

❖ *You're Gonna Want to Dog-Ear This Page*

Start with the rolls: Cut **4 tablespoons (½ stick/57 grams to be exact) salted butter** into cubes and make sure it's *cold.*

Grab your stand mixer (or a large bowl if you're kneading by hand), and put on the dough hook. In the bowl, combine **2½ cups (300 grams) all-purpose flour, ¾ cup (170 grams) warm (a little warmer than body temperature, 100° to 110°F) water, ¼ cup (84 grams) honey, 1 tablespoon fine sea salt,** and **1 (¼-ounce) packet instant or active dry yeast (2¼ teaspoons),** then add the cold butter. Mix together on low speed to work the butter into the flour so it's evenly distributed and the mixture looks crumbly, 1 to 2 minutes.

Continue to knead the dough on low speed until it comes together into a smooth dough that bounces back when poked with your finger, 5 minutes or so. The dough shouldn't be sticky at all; if it is, sprinkle on a little more flour and mix until it's not. (If you're mixing by hand, knead in the bowl first to bring it together, then lightly flour your counter, turn out the dough, and knead until it's smooth and bounces back when poked, 10 minutes or so.)

Grease a large bowl generously with **vegetable oil,** add the dough, and toss to coat, then cover with a kitchen towel or a bowl cover and let proof until it's doubled in size, about 1 hour here in Georgia (it may be longer if it's colder where you are).

Scoop the dough out of the bowl, and punch it down to deflate it a bit. Cut the dough into 12 equal pieces and roll them into smooth balls between your hands. Grease a baking sheet with more vegetable oil, then line it with parchment paper and space out the rolls 1 inch apart (or you can grease your 10-inch cast iron skillet and use that instead). Grab a kitchen towel, and loosely cover the dough. Let the rolls proof again until they're almost doubled in size, 45 minutes or so.

Preheat your oven to 400°F.

Note: If you want to be sure your yeast is good to go, or you're using active dry yeast, mix the water and yeast first, plus a bit of the sugar or honey in your recipe so it's got something to feed on, then let sit for 5 to 10 minutes until it becomes frothy. This means that the yeast is active and ready to use. If it doesn't froth, your yeast is too old to work.

Crack **1 large egg** into a small bowl and whisk with **1 teaspoon water** until smooth. Brush the egg wash over the tops of the rolls. Bake the rolls until they're nice and golden brown, 12 to 14 minutes.

While they're baking, make the topping: In a small pot over low heat, or in a small bowl in the microwave, melt **2 tablespoons salted butter.** If you need to, pour it into a small bowl, then mix in **1 tablespoon honey** and **a pinch of ground cinnamon,** stirring until smooth. Taste it and see if it needs more cinnamon.

Once the rolls come out of the oven, lightly brush the honey butter on top. Sprinkle the hot rolls with a little **flaky sea salt** and prepare yourself for the best rolls you ever had.

Cheddar Jalapeño Bagels

Holy hell, these are good. When I got into making our own bagels, I tried all sorts of different flavor combinations, but none were as good as this one. Since it's just me and James that eat them, I can get a little creative—and hot ('cause you know we like it spicy). If you're not into it, though, you can get in there and mess around; maybe do a cinnamon raisin bagel, or load it up with sesame seeds, or do Cheddar and garlic—whatever your heart and your stomach desire. We think they taste like a bakery bagel, but if you're sensitive to salt, you can bump it down a bit. Don't let anything stop you from getting into the kitchen and making your bagels, which couldn't be easier or more delicious.

❖ *Gather Up*

1 cup (227 grams to be exact) warm water

1 (¼-ounce) packet instant or active dry yeast (2¼ teaspoons)

1 tablespoon sugar

2 jalapeño peppers

2½ cups (300 grams) all-purpose flour, plus more for rolling

1 tablespoon fine sea salt, plus more for sprinkling

1 cup (4 ounces/113 grams) shredded Cheddar cheese, plus more for sprinkling

1 large egg

Cream cheese, for serving

❖ *Don't Forget*

Your stand mixer with the dough hook or a large bowl

❖ *Let's Spice Up Your Breakfast*

In a small bowl, combine **1 cup (227 grams to be exact) warm water** (a little warmer than body temperature, 100° to 110°F), **1 (¼-ounce) packet instant or active dry yeast (2¼ teaspoons),** and **1 tablespoon sugar.** Stir really good and set aside to let your yeast wake up and bubble, 5 to 10 minutes.

While you're waiting, take the seeds out of **2 jalapeño peppers,** then chop the peppers up real small. If you like, you can leave some slices to decorate the top.

Grab your stand mixer (or a large bowl, if you're kneading by hand), and put on the dough hook. To the bowl, add **2½ cups (300 grams) all-purpose flour, 1 tablespoon fine sea salt,** and the yeast mixture. Mix on medium speed until the dough is no longer sticky, 5 minutes or so. (If you don't have a mixer, you can mix everything by hand and knead. It will take longer than the mixer, but keep on working the dough until all the ingredients are all good and mixed and you have a consistent dough; your arms will get a nice workout.)

Sprinkle **1 cup (4 ounces/113 grams) shredded Cheddar cheese** and the chopped jalapeño over the top of the dough and then knead the dough on low speed until it's evenly mixed, just a minute or so. Lightly flour your counter and turn out the dough. Cover the dough with a kitchen towel and let it rise at room temperature until it's doubled in size, about 1 hour here in Georgia (it may be longer if it's colder where you are).

Cut the dough into 6 equal pieces. Using your hands, roll each piece into a smooth ball. Grab your towel and cover the balls again to rise on the counter until they're nice and puffy, 15 minutes or so.

(recipe continues)

After 15 minutes, shape your bagels: Gently press a hole into the middle of each ball going all the way through and work the dough around your finger so you get a nice-lookin' bagel, with a 1-inch or so hole in the middle. Lay the bagels flat on a lightly floured surface again and cover with the towel for another 15 minutes for a second rise, until they're puffy again.

Meanwhile, preheat your oven to 350°F. Fill a large pot about halfway with water. Bring to a boil over medium-high; you want your water to boil before doing anything with the bagels. Line your baking sheet with parchment paper and keep it near your pot.

Once you see a consistent boil in the pot and the second rise is done, place 1 bagel in the boiling pot of water. (Depending on the width of your pot, you may be able to add 2 in at a time, but you don't want your bagels touching.) Boil the bagel until it has formed very small crevices and has a slightly bumpy surface, 2 minutes or so for each side; use your slotted spoon or a spatula to turn the bagel. (It may sink at first, but will eventually rise to the top.) After each side has had a chance to boil, fish the bagel out with your spoon and hold it over the pot to let any excess water drip off for a couple seconds, then put the bagel on the baking sheet. Repeat with the other bagels.

In a small bowl, beat together **1 large egg** and **1 tablespoon water** until completely smooth. Brush the egg wash over the tops of the bagels on the baking sheet, then very lightly sprinkle with some fine sea salt. If your heart desires, sprinkle on your jalapeno slices and a **handful of cheese,** too.

Bake the bagels until golden brown, 25 to 30 minutes. Move them over to a wire rack and let cool until they're just warm. Enjoy right away with some **cream cheese—**you've never had a bagel this fresh!

These bagels are best right away, but if you can't eat them all, freeze them on a baking sheet and then they will keep in a plastic bag for a couple months. Heat 'em up in the oven!

Flaky & Fluffy Croissants

GETS YOU 16 CROISSANTS ❖ TAKES AT LEAST 7 HOURS, PLUS TIME TO COOL

You can make these, I swear. If I can make a croissant, you absolutely can, too. I constantly have people telling me they could never successfully make them until they tried my recipe. I did everything in my power to make it simple—that's the name of the game with these. You still get those flaky, buttery, delicious layers as if it took you however many days, but you'll have these in way less time and without having to leave home. Now, your kitchen can be a French bakery, too, my friend.

❖ *Gather Up*

- 1 cup (227 grams to be exact) whole milk
- 4 tablespoons (50 grams) sugar
- 1 (¼-ounce) packet instant or active dry yeast (2¼ teaspoons)
- 3½ cups (420 grams) all-purpose flour, plus more for rolling
- 1 teaspoon fine sea salt
- 1½ cups (3 sticks/ 340 grams) cold salted butter, homemade if you want (see page 34)
- 1 large egg

❖ *Let's Get These Layers Going*

In a small pot over low heat, or in a small bowl in the microwave, heat **1 cup (227 grams) whole milk** and ½ **cup (114 grams) water** to a little warmer than body temperature (100° to 110°F). Add **1 tablespoon sugar** and **1 (¼-ounce) packet instant or active dry yeast (2¼ teaspoons).** Stir and set it aside to let the yeast do its thing (foam and froth) for 5 to 10 minutes.

In a large bowl, add **3½ cups (420 grams) all-purpose flour,** the other **3 tablespoons sugar,** and **1 teaspoon fine sea salt,** and then pour in the yeast mixture. Mix everything together with your hands and then knead until a smooth dough forms, 5 to 7 minutes. Cover the bowl with a kitchen towel and set aside for a few minutes to hang out. In the meantime, we're about to have some fun.

Grab a foot or so of parchment paper and **1½ cups (3 sticks/ 340 grams) salted butter,** and make sure it's *cold.* Unwrap your butter and place the sticks side by side on top of the parchment paper. Then grab another sheet of parchment paper (same length) and place it on top of the butter.

Get a rolling pin or other hard object and start whacking that butter. You want to pound it until it's an evenly flattened block of butter that's about 8 inches by 10 inches and ¼ inch thick. Once you've successfully let all your anger out onto those butter sticks, wrap them up in parchment and put the flattened butter and large bowl with the dough in the fridge for 1 hour to chill.

Grab the dough and take off the towel. Lightly flour your counter and roll out the dough. It might be a little sticky, and that's what we want. Using a rolling pin, roll out the dough into a large rectangle that's 12 inches by 15 inches or so, and ⅛ inch thick. Try to expand the dough as much as possible without getting it so thin that it rips.

(recipe continues)

Next, grab your flattened butter block. Take off the parchment paper and place the butter in the center of the dough rectangle. Take one side of your dough and fold it onto the butter, so half of the butter's completely covered. Repeat with the other side, then stretch the dough to meet in the middle, press together, and fold over the shorter edges so you've still got a nice and even rectangle and the butter is completely enclosed. Roll the dough out again into a rectangle that's ½ inch thick and fold it over itself, like you're folding a business letter. Wrap the dough in parchment paper and place it back in the fridge for 30 minutes.

Lightly flour your counter again. Unwrap the dough and roll it out to a ½ inch thick rectangle again. Fold it the same way again and roll out again. Your dough should now look like a condensed, folded brick. Wrap it in the same parchment paper and put it back in the fridge to let the butter firm up again, 1 hour or so.

Now, you're going to roll the dough out one more time to a rectangle that's 8 inches by 20 inches or so and ½ inch thick. Using a sharp knife, cut the rectangle in half lengthwise, so you have two long rectangles. Then make 3 perpendicular cuts so you have 8 rectangles. Cut each rectangle in half diagonally to make 16 triangles.

Line a baking sheet with parchment paper. Starting from the wide end and rolling toward the point of the triangle, roll each piece tightly into a croissant. Place the croissants on the baking sheet seam side down with 1 inch or so between them. Cover the baking sheet with a kitchen towel and let them rise until they double in size, 1 hour or so.

Move the croissants to the fridge to chill the butter for at least 1 hour and up to overnight. (You could also freeze them on the baking sheet, and when they're solid, put them in a bag and store for up to 3 months. Then bake them straight from frozen and add another 5 minutes or so of baking time.)

Preheat your oven to 375°F. In a small bowl, whisk **1 large egg** and **1 tablespoon water** until smooth.

When ready to bake, brush the tops with the egg wash. Bake until golden brown and puffy, 20 minutes or so. Put the croissants on a wire rack to cool until warm, then tear into those flaky layers you worked so hard to make.

Note: *I like to keep my croissants plain, but if you want to stuff them with a little square of chocolate, or some ham and cheese, or whatever your imagination dreams up, add it near the wide end of your dough triangles before you roll them into the croissant shape. Any meat or eggs should be fully cooked first before rolling up into your croissants.*

Homemade Sandwich Bread

GETS YOU 1 LOAF ❖ TAKES ABOUT 3 HOURS, PLUS TIME TO COOL

This is my summer bread. We're not heavy bread eaters, so I tend to make this sandwich loaf when we spend a lot of time out on the boat or being outdoors, and it's so easy to pack a cooler of sandwiches and go. Though now that I think about it, I bake it a lot in the winter, since we have grilled cheeses to go with our soups. And really all year-round so James can have his beloved French toast (see page 97) . . . Well, ignore what I just said; I guess this is my go-to loaf.

If you take one thing from this book, it should be that sandwich bread from the grocery store is freaky. It doesn't get moldy for two, three weeks. Think about how many preservatives it takes to keep bread good for that long! Make this loaf instead.

❖ *Gather Up*

- 1 cup (227 grams to be exact) warm whole milk, plus more if you need
- 1 (¼-ounce) packet instant or active dry yeast (2¼ teaspoons)
- 1 tablespoon sugar
- 3 cups (360 grams) all-purpose flour, plus more if you need
- 1 teaspoon fine sea salt
- 3 tablespoons salted butter, homemade if you want (see page 34), room temperature, plus more for the pan
- 1 large egg

❖ *Let's Knead Some Sandwich Bread*

In a small bowl, mix **1 cup (227 grams to be exact) warm whole milk** (a little warmer than body temperature, 100° to 110°F), **1 (¼-ounce) packet of instant or active dry yeast (2¼ teaspoons),** and **1 tablespoon sugar.** Set it aside to let the yeast do its thing (foam and froth) for 5 to 10 minutes.

In a large bowl, stir together **3 cups (360 grams) all-purpose flour** and **1 teaspoon fine sea salt.** Add **3 tablespoons softened salted butter** to the bowl, breaking up the butter into smaller chunks with your fingers and pressing it into the other ingredients. Keep going until there aren't any patches of dry flour, and your mixture looks like coarse crumbs (sort of like when you're making biscuits).

Grab the milk mixture in the small bowl and pour it into the large bowl. Break **1 large egg** into the large bowl, too; no need to beat it. Mix everything together with your hands until the mixture comes together in a sticky dough. Don't be afraid to get dirty! If it's too dry and there's a lot of dry flour, add one splash of milk at a time until you get a sticky dough.

Lightly flour your counter. Turn out the dough and continue to knead until the dough is smooth and no longer sticks to your hands, 5 to 10 minutes, adding a sprinkle of flour if it's too wet. Shape the dough into a ball and put it back into the large bowl. Cover the dough with the damp towel and let it rise until doubled in size, about 1 hour here in Georgia (it may be longer if it's colder where you are).

Generously butter your 9 × 5-inch loaf pan (an 8 × 4-inch pan will work, too).

Place the dough on your floured surface to roll out with a rolling pin until it's 2 finger-widths thick. Fold in every side to make a 9-inch square (or 8-inch for smaller pan). Starting from any side, roll your square into a log.

Place the log in the buttered loaf pan, seam side down, and let sit until it's puffed up and springs back when you poke it, another 30 minutes to 1 hour.

Preheat your oven to 350°F.

Bake until the loaf is well-browned and cooked through (either a thermometer reads 195° to 200°F or it sounds hollow when you tap it), 30 to 35 minutes. Put the pan on a wire rack and let cool for 10 minutes. Flip the pan upside down to let the loaf fall out, and put it right side up on the rack. Allow the loaf to completely cool (this is important!) before slicing, 30 minutes or so more. Enjoy your sandwiches, y'all!

Store any leftover bread on the counter in a plastic bag for a few days, or slice it and freeze the slices in a sealed plastic bag.

My Favorite Sourdough Loaf

GETS YOU 1 LOAF ❖

TAKES AT LEAST 24 HOURS, PLUS TIME TO COOL (AND A DAY TO MAKE THE STARTER)

My whole cooking journey started with bread. I was using a loaf of store-bought bread to make sandwiches, and I realized this week- or two-week-old bread looked exactly the same as when I bought it. That ain't right. So, I started with my sandwich loaf on page 222. I began with plain yeasted breads because they're easier, but I've really gotten into the long process of sourdough baking. It's a twofer: fresh baked bread, of course; and then I put the nutritious starter into every other dough I make until I run out. Our bodies are much happier since I've been doing that. I'm a few years into my sourdough journey, and it truly is a journey! It's not easy, and it takes a lot of practice, but believe me, if you start now, soon yours will look as good as it tastes. And until then, even if your loaves are lopsided or wonky, you'll be eating well. As I always say, "It ain't pretty, but it's homemade."

❖ Gather Up

- 1⅔ cups (400 grams to be exact) filtered water, room temperature, plus more if you need it

- 2 tablespoons (20 grams) Start Me Up Lazy Sourdough Starter (page 37), fed or unfed is fine

- 4 cups plus 2 tablespoons (500 grams) all-purpose flour, plus more for dusting

- 1½ teaspoons fine sea salt

❖ Let's Get Our Rise On

In a large bowl, combine **1⅔ cups (400 grams to be exact) room-temperature filtered water** and **2 tablespoons (20 grams) sourdough starter.** Use clean hands to dissolve the starter in the water until the mixture is smooth. Add **4 cups plus 2 tablespoons (500 grams) all-purpose flour** and **1½ teaspoons fine sea salt.** Mix everything together by hand, pinching the dough to mix in all that loose flour and scraping the bowl as you go in case there are any pockets of dry flour. The dough will be very shaggy. If it feels really dry, add another tablespoon filtered water, and keep pinching and mixing until no dry patches of flour remain. Cover the bowl with a clean towel, and let the dough rest for 1 hour.

After 1 hour, wet your hands and lift up one side of dough. Stretch it gently upward, then lay it over the ball of dough. Continue lifting the sides of the dough, rotating the bowl a quarter turn after each lift, until you've worked your way around the entire ball of dough. Use your hand to scoop up the dough ball, and flip it over. Cover with the towel, and let rest for another hour.

Repeat the stretch-and-fold process all the way around the dough twice more (for a total of 3 times and 3 hours resting), then flip the dough over. Cover with a reusable bowl cover or beeswax wrap and let it rise in the fridge for a minimum of overnight and up to 48 hours, if you like.

The next day, flour a proofing basket really good or line a medium bowl with a clean kitchen towel and flour the towel. Flour your counter, too. Scrape out the dough onto the surface and fold all 4 sides of the dough into the middle, so they're overlapping. Flip it over and let it rest on your floured counter for 10 minutes.

Now for the final shape. Flour your counter again. Flip the dough over and bring the sides in toward the center. To shape it into a ball, roll it up like a jelly roll, then bring the ends together underneath to form a ball. For more surface tension (and a better final shape), gently drag the dough toward you with your hands cupped on the sides, which makes the top of the dough taut. Pinch the bottom seams shut, and place the bread seam side up (this is very important!) in the proofing basket. Add a sprinkle of flour to the top, and cover with a kitchen towel. Let the dough rise until it's puffy and jiggy, 3 hours or so—but don't fret if it doesn't get much bigger; that's okay.

Preheat your oven to 500°F. Put a large Dutch oven with its lid on in the oven to preheat, too.

When your dough has risen, turn it out onto a square of parchment paper with the dough's seam side down. Slash or score the top with a sharp knife. The slash can be decorative, or a simple straight line down the center, around ½ inch deep.

Carefully, using oven mitts, take the *rippin' hot* Dutch oven out of the oven and take off the lid. Lift the corners of the parchment paper with the dough on it and gently place in the hot pot. Cover with the lid, and bake for 30 minutes. Take off the lid, and return the pot to the oven. Bake until the crust is dark brown, even mahogany in some spots, and the dough sounds hollow when tapped, 25 to 35 minutes more.

Put the baked loaf on a wire rack to cool completely (be patient; it'll be worth it!), 1 to 2 hours. When it's completely cool, you can finally slice into it.

Store any leftover bread on the counter in a plastic bag for a few days, or slice it and freeze the slices in a sealed plastic bag.

Dutch Oven Bread

GETS YOU 1 LOAF ❖ TAKES 4 HOURS, PLUS TIME TO COOL

Baking bread is my therapy. When I'm having a crappy day, I'll get to making a loaf of bread and ask James to make me some spaghetti. By the time the bread comes out of the oven, I'll have forgotten whatever it was that got me into the kitchen in the first place.

What I love about bread is that you have to pay attention. What works in my environment may not work in yours, and the most amazing thing about baking bread is you'll figure out what *your* flour, *your* yeast, and *your* air is telling you. You gotta listen. You have to get your hands dirty and all up in that dough to figure out if it's saying it's thirsty or if it's hungry for more flour. You gotta keep baking because I'm not gonna lie to you: Your first loaf won't be perfect. Your tenth loaf won't be, either, but keep going and you'll keep learning. You also have to try this loaf in particular—because who on earth wouldn't want garlic, herbs, and cheese in their bread??

❖ *Gather Up*

- 3 cups (360 grams to be exact) all-purpose flour, plus more for rolling

- 2 teaspoons fine sea salt

- 1 (¼-ounce) packet instant or active dry yeast (2¼ teaspoons; see my Note on page 215)

- 1½ cups (340 grams) warm water

- 2 garlic cloves

- A couple fresh rosemary sprigs

- ⅓ cup (1 ounce/28 grams) grated Parmesan cheese

- Ground black pepper

❖ *Let's Get Our Hands Messy*

In a large bowl, stir together **3 cups (360 grams to be exact) all-purpose flour, 2 teaspoons fine sea salt,** and **1 (¼-ounce) packet instant or active dry yeast (2¼ teaspoons).** Add **1½ cups (340 grams) warm water** (a little warmer than body temperature, 100° to 110°F). Stir everything together until a shaggy dough forms; use a wooden spoon or your hands, your choice. Cover the bowl with a clean kitchen towel and let it rest in a warm place until the dough has doubled in size, which takes 2 to 3 hours in my kitchen.

While the dough rises, chop up **2 garlic cloves** nice and small. Strip the leaves from **a couple of fresh rosemary sprigs** and chop them small too, so you get 2 tablespoons.

Preheat your oven to 450°F. Place a large Dutch oven with a lid on in the oven while it's preheating.

Lightly flour your counter. Turn out your dough and sprinkle the garlic, rosemary, **⅓ cup (1 ounce/28 grams) grated Parmesan cheese,** and **a couple pinches of ground black pepper** on top. Knead to get those ingredients evenly mixed throughout the dough, 2 to 3 minutes. Flour your hands so the dough doesn't stick to you, and shape the dough into a round that will fit in your Dutch oven. Place the dough on a square of parchment paper.

Time to get crafty! Use a sharp knife to carve a little slit along one side of the top to help it get some height in the oven and give it the nice crevices that you can see in that photo on the opposite page.

Once the oven is preheated, carefully, using oven mitts, take the *rippin' hot* Dutch oven out and uncover it. Gently drop the parchment paper with the dough into the Dutch oven. Put the lid back on and bake for 30 minutes. After 30 minutes, take off the lid and continue baking until the bread is golden brown and sounds hollow when you tap it, another 10 to 15 minutes.

Carefully take the bread out of the Dutch oven using the parchment paper on the bottom as a handle. Allow the bread to cool completely on a wire rack before slicing and serving, 1 to 2 hours. I know it's hard, but the bread will be so much better because you waited.

Store any leftover bread on the counter in a plastic bag for a few days, or slice it and freeze the slices in a sealed plastic bag.

DRINKS

———◆———

You need a special beverage
for every occasion—
boozy or not.

Homebrewed Blueberry Wine

GETS YOU ABOUT 18 CUPS ❖ TAKES AT LEAST 3 MONTHS

When me and James were little, all the older folks made their own wine at home, but the practice has died out. So this is our little pet project—bringing it back. It started when a woman who follows me sent me some wine. I'm not much of a wine drinker, but I liked her stuff. It was sweet and fruity and delicious. And you know me; once I like something, my next thought is *I could make this.* We dove right in, doing barely any research, and let me tell you, we got *a lot* of feedback from people as we posted the videos. We learned, and this is our tried-and-true (and updated) recipe right here.

There's something about the yeast and the sugar content of blueberries that I think makes it a lot harder to mess up than any other fruit wine, so it's a great place to start. Don't be intimidated by all the stuff you need! One trip to a homebrew store will have you covered on many of the ingredients and all the equipment, and a few months later you'll have bottles and bottles of your very own wine to sip on.

❖ Gather Up

- 2 pounds (907 grams to be exact) fresh or thawed frozen blueberries (6 to 8 cups)
- 1 gallon (3.78 kilograms) filtered water
- 3¾ cups (795 grams) sugar
- 1½ teaspoons acid blend
- ½ teaspoon pectic enzyme
- ½ teaspoon yeast energizer
- 1 campden tablet
- 1 (0.176-ounce) packet of wine yeast
- 1 cup red grape concentrate
- ½ teaspoon stabilizer

❖ Let's Make Some Magic

Be sure to thoroughly wash and sterilize all equipment you're going to use at every step. It's very important that no outside bacteria mess with your fermentation! Wash your primary fermenter and spoon real good with dish soap and hot water. Let them air-dry.

Rinse and drain **2 pounds (907 grams to be exact) fresh or thawed frozen blueberries.** Put them in your nylon straining bag, then put the bag in a large bowl and mash up the blueberries with a spoon. Strain out the berry juice into the 1-gallon primary fermenter. Keep everything in the straining bag, tie the top to seal it, and put it in the fermenter. Now, add **1 gallon (3.78 kilograms) filtered water, 3¾ cups (795 grams) sugar, 1½ teaspoons acid blend, ½ teaspoon pectic enzyme, ½ teaspoon yeast energizer,** and crush up **1 campden tablet.** Stir it all together. Cover your fermenter and keep it in a cool, dark place for 24 hours.

After 24 hours, sprinkle **1 (0.176-ounce) packet of wine yeast** over the top of your mixture, but do not stir. Cover again for another 24 hours in the same dark spot.

After 24 hours, start doing this daily until you get a specific gravity (SG) level of 1.030: Stir the contents of the fermenter with a clean spoon, gently and lightly press the bag with the pulp, and using your specific gravity hydrometer, take a reading of the SG level. This is important to make sure you've reached the proper fermentation. You'll feel like a mad scientist while you're doing it! It should take you 5 to 8 days to reach it. When your brew hits an SG level of 1.030, squeeze the last bit of juice from the bag, then you're done with it.

1 (1-gallon) primary fermenter

A nylon straining bag

A specific gravity ABV tester (hydrometer)

An auto siphon

1 or 2 (1-gallon) glass secondary fermenters

1 airlock

Now, use an auto siphon to move the wine into a 1-gallon glass secondary fermenter, leaving any sediment behind in the primary fermenter. Attach an airlock and let it sit in that dry, dark place for 4 weeks or so, or until the SG level has dropped to 1.000. When this happens, you can siphon the wine into another 1-gallon glass secondary container (you also can clean out the one you used earlier), leaving any sediment behind. Add in **1 cup red grape concentrate** and ½ **teaspoon stabilizer.** Stir everything together with a clean spoon and reattach the airlock. Put back into that dark spot.

Let sit for 2 months, then taste the wine. If it tastes like wine you want to drink, it's ready. If it doesn't, let it sit for another 2 weeks and check again. Then, the wine is good to serve! Drink a glass—you deserve it! Bottle it up in any type of bottle with a screw top, hinge top, or just stuff a cork in there, and it should be good for months stored in a dark, cool spot.

Strawberry Sip 'n' Spritz

My best creations come from necessity—in this case, using up an excess of alcohol in the house. It's another summer thirst quencher, more interesting than beer and inspired by fruit and some random bottles we had. It may not be child friendly, but you and yours can sit and sip this spritz after the kids go to bed all summer long.

❖ *Gather Up*

2 cups frozen strawberries

1 (750 ml) bottle pink Moscato sparkling wine

1 (16-ounce) bottle lemon-lime sparkling water

3 ounces (6 tablespoons) gin

Ice, for serving

A few fresh mint leaves, or any other garnishes you like

❖ *Don't Forget*

Your blender

❖ *Let's Make a Spritz*

Blend **1½ cups frozen strawberries** until smooth. Pour the strawberries into a pitcher and stir in **1 (750 ml) bottle of pink Moscato sparkling wine, 1 (16-ounce) bottle of lemon-lime sparkling water,** and **3 ounces (6 tablespoons) gin** and stir.

Fill 6 to 8 pretty glasses with **ice** and pour the spritz mix over. Divide the last ½ **cup frozen strawberries** among them for garnish, then top each glass with **a few fresh mint leaves** ('cause we fancy) or whatever garnishes your heart desires. Put your feet up and enjoy!

Bushwacker

For James's 19th birthday, his sister Heidi took him to the Virgin Islands, where he had his first Bushwacker. His initiation to legal drinking came in the form of this creamy, chocolaty rum cocktail that was invented right there in the Virgin Islands. He followed that first one with another one, then another one, then another one, and he's pretty sure he ended up on a beach in his underwear a few hours later. So, now when he's got a craving for rum and reminiscing about his wild days, I'll make us a batch of these.

❖ *Gather Up*

1½ cups ice

1½ cups vanilla ice cream

2 ounces (¼ cup) Kahlúa coffee liqueur

2 ounces (¼ cup) coconut cream rum or RumChata

A few maraschino cherries, plus 1 tablespoon of the juice

Chocolate sauce

Ground cinnamon

Whipped cream, for serving

❖ *Don't Forget*

Your blender

❖ *Let's Go Bushwacking*

In a blender, combine **1½ cups ice, 1½ cups vanilla ice cream, 2 ounces (¼ cup) Kahlúa, 2 ounces (¼ cup) coconut cream rum, 1 tablespoon maraschino cherry juice** (from a jar of cherries), **a squeeze of chocolate sauce,** and **a pinch of ground cinnamon.** Blend until smooth. Taste and add more chocolate or cinnamon, if you like.

Drizzle the inside of 2 nice glasses with some chocolate sauce and divide the drink between them. Top with the **whipped cream, another pinch of cinnamon,** and **a few maraschino cherries.** Get up to something good while you enjoy, my friend.

Sweetie's Sweet Iced Tea

Sweet tea is Southern hospitality in a glass. If you've never had it, it probably just means you've never been to a Southern home, because it's what anyone will offer you when you step inside. Luzianne makes the strongest tea, and is miles better than Lipton. Accept no substitutes. I brew it every week, and just as sure as the sun rises and sets, you know I'm making sweet tea when you smell smoke and hear the alarm going off—I *always* walk away and forget about it so it boils over.

❖ *Gather Up*

12 cups (3 quarts) water

1¼ cups sugar

4 Luzianne tea bags

Ice, for serving

❖ *Let's Get a Pot of Sweet Tea Going*

In a large pot, bring **12 cups (3 quarts) water** and 1¼ **cups sugar** to a boil over high heat, stirring a few times to help dissolve the sugar. Once it's boiling, add **4 Luzianne tea bags** and take the pot off the heat. Let the tea steep for 2 hours minimum before you toss the tea bags. The longer you let it steep, the stronger it is, but move it to the fridge after 3 or 4 hours; I wouldn't go any longer than 6 hours.

Add **a couple handfuls of ice** to a pitcher. Pour the tea over the ice and stir to dilute it some. Put some ice in glasses and enjoy right away, or stick it in the fridge and hope you got some company comin' over in the next few days.

Twang, Tang & Tart Lemonade

GETS YOU 7 CUPS ❖ TAKES 15 MINUTES

Any time I can add a little extra flavor to anything I'm making, I'm going to. We love lemons in this house, and while another flavoring like strawberry or raspberry is welcome sometimes, what we really want is that extra zip that makes your tongue stick to the roof of your mouth. This lemonade gets all the mileage it can by adding a whole lemon to the simple syrup while it's cooking.

❖ *Gather Up*

5 cups water

1 cup sugar

About 12 lemons

Ice, for serving

❖ *When Life Gives You Lemons . . . You Know What To Do*

In a medium pot, combine **2 cups water** and **1 cup sugar.** Cut **1 lemon** in half and add the whole thing to the pot. Bring to a boil over medium-high and cook, stirring to dissolve the sugar, 5 to 7 minutes.

Meanwhile, squeeze the other **11 lemons** to get you 2 cups of fresh lemon juice, then pour it into a pitcher.

Once the syrup comes to a boil, move the pot off the heat, discard the lemon, and add the syrup to the fresh-squeezed lemon juice. Pour in the other **3 cups water,** stir to combine, and serve cold over **ice.** Don't you feel refreshed now?

Fizzy Cranberry Punch

Did y'all know it gets hot and steamy in Georgia? Ha! By the time spring rolls around and we're already sweating all day, every day, I start making big batches of punch. We get tired of drinking plain water all the time, and I love to get creative with my punch, throwing in whatever I got to make it delicious and hydrating. The coconut water means we're all quenching our thirst, and the cranberries—well, I just love 'em. There's something about a tart and sweet drink on a hot day that is always exactly what you need. If you love cranberries as much as me, then you could make this when the weather cools down and you can get your hands on some fresh ones.

❖ Gather Up

- 4 **cups coconut water**
- 4 **cups organic sweetened cranberry juice**
- 2 **cups lemon sparkling water**
- 1 **cup frozen cranberries**
- **Ice**
- 1 **orange**
- **Fresh mint leaves**

❖ Let's Make Some Punch

In a pitcher, mix together **4 cups coconut water, 4 cups organic sweetened cranberry juice, 2 cups lemon sparkling water,** and **1 cup frozen cranberries.** Mix in a good amount of **ice** and stir again to chill it.

Slice up **1 orange** into half-moons. Serve the punch over more **ice,** garnished with **fresh mint leaves** ('cause we fancy) and the orange slices.

Hannah's Famous Hot Chocolate

After we've been sweating it out all summer and the temperature finally drops enough that I want to light up a fire, that's when I know it's hot chocolate season. During those months, any time someone comes over, they're asking for my famous hot chocolate. Then they're asking me for seconds of my famous hot chocolate. Have you ever even had seconds of hot chocolate—who can drink two cups?? Everyone who tries my recipe, that's who. Do not change a thing; this recipe is golden.

❖ *Gather Up*

1 cup whole milk

1 cup heavy whipping cream

Powdered sugar, as much as you like

⅓ cup granulated sugar

2 to 4 tablespoons unsweetened cocoa powder, up to you

Ground cinnamon

Vanilla extract, homemade if you want (see page 33)

Ground nutmeg

Cayenne pepper

Fine sea salt

❖ *Don't Forget*

Your stand mixer with the whisk attachment, or handheld mixer

❖ *Time to Cozy Up to Some Hot Chocolate*

In a small pot, combine **1 cup whole milk** and ½ **cup heavy whipping cream.** Heat it over medium, stirring regularly, until the milk starts to steam but does not boil, 5 minutes or so.

While you're waiting, make the whipped cream. In the bowl of a stand mixer fitted with the whisk attachment (or a medium bowl if you're using a handheld mixer), whip the other ½ **cup heavy whipping cream** on low speed until it forms soft peaks (meaning when you stop whipping, the cream can hold a shape but it droops), 2 to 3 minutes. Beat in **a spoonful of powdered sugar** (add another if you like—I do) and taste to make sure it's sweet enough for you. Continue to whip on low speed until stiff peaks form (meaning the cream holds its shape), 1 minute or so more. Set aside for a second.

When the milk is heated and steaming, whisk in ⅓ **cup granulated sugar, 2 to 4 tablespoons unsweetened cocoa powder** (depending on how chocolaty you like your cocoa), **a couple pinches of ground cinnamon, a splash of vanilla extract** (2, if you're sexy), and **a pinch each of ground nutmeg, cayenne pepper,** and **fine sea salt.** Whisk until everything is dissolved and smells heavenly. Taste it and see if it needs any more spices (add some extra cayenne if you're feeling spicy) or cocoa. You got to be happy with your hot chocolate!

Pour the hot chocolate into 2 mugs and add a dollop of whipped cream to each. I suggest sprinkling some **ground cinnamon** and **powdered sugar** on top for extra sweetness. Ooooooh, that first sip is going to be so good.

DESSERTS

————◆————

Now you *know* I saved
the best for last.

Classic Peanut Brittle

GETS YOU 8 CUPS OR SO BRITTLE PIECES ❖ TAKES 2 HOURS

When we were growing up, peanut brittle was one of the candies both James's parents and mine would always let us have. It didn't have any artificial food coloring, and that was good enough for them. This is my Granny Mary's recipe, passed down to me, with no changes. Don't skip that cayenne—that's what makes this better than any other brittle you've had. I make it during the holidays as a special treat to munch on and hand out. We have two pecan trees growing in the backyard and sometimes we'll make a pecan brittle, too.

❖ *Gather Up*

- 2 **cups sugar**
- 1 **cup light corn syrup**
- 2 **cups salted roasted peanuts**
- 4 **tablespoons (½ stick) salted butter, homemade if you want (see page 34)**
- 1 **tablespoon baking soda**

  Vanilla extract, homemade if you want (see page 33)

  Cayenne pepper

❖ *Don't Forget*

  Your thermometer

❖ *Let's Make Some Candy*

Go ahead and line a baking sheet with parchment paper and forget about it for now.

Get your medium pot and add **2 cups sugar** and **½ cup water.** Put it over medium heat to come to a boil, stirring well and often until the sugar is dissolved. Once you see it come to a low boil, add **1 cup light corn syrup.** Stir it so it dissolves in the water and get out your thermometer. Keep stirring until the mixture reaches 250°F. When it gets there, add **2 cups salted roasted peanuts** and keep stirring until the temperature hits 300°F. (Don't stop even if your arm is tired; it could take up to 10 minutes.)

Move your pan off the heat and immediately stir in **4 tablespoons (½ stick) salted butter, 1 tablespoon baking soda, a splash of vanilla extract (**call it 1 tablespoon), and **a couple pinches of cayenne pepper (**I like about 1 teaspoon). It will foam up and change texture immediately, but keep stirring until it's all mixed up and the butter is melted.

Pour the candy onto your lined baking sheet and use a butter knife to spread the mixture out smooth and even; the caramel should be about ⅛ inch thick. Allow it to cool completely, which should take between 1 and 2 hours.

Then, break it apart into bite-size pieces and eat the whole batch! If you manage to *not* eat the whole batch, it'll keep in a sealed bag out on the counter 'til it's gone.

Divinity "Kiss Me" Candy

GETS YOU ABOUT 24 CANDIES ❖ TAKES 1 HOUR

I don't think I've ever been to a gathering in the South and *not s*een a tray of divinity candy set out. Which is a little strange since they're actually pretty hard to make! Whipping up egg whites to the perfect consistency will depend on a lot of factors, like your syrup being the right temperature, no fat getting into the whites, and even the humidity. If yours don't whip up nice and fluffy the first time, don't panic. Keep making them, and you'll get it down, I promise. I call mine "Kiss Me" because the shape is kind of like a Hershey's Kiss—and after you eat one you're going to want to kiss me, and you're welcome to go right ahead.

❖ *Gather Up*

¾ **cup toasted pecans**

Heaping ¼ cup fresh or thawed frozen sweet cherries, or maraschino cherries

2 **cups sugar**

½ **cup light corn syrup**

2 **large egg whites, room temperature**

Vanilla extract, homemade if you want (see page 33)

❖ *Don't Forget*

Your thermometer

Your stand mixer with the whisk attachment, or handheld mixer

❖ *Let's Make These Heavenly Treats*

Go ahead and line a baking sheet with parchment paper and then forget about it for now.

Chop up ¾ **cup toasted pecans** nice and small so you get ½ cup. Get some paper towels and make sure your **heaping ¼ cup cherries** are good and dry, then chop them up nice and small, too, so you get ¼ cup. (If you're using fresh, don't forget to pit them first.)

In a small pot over medium heat, combine **2 cups sugar, ½ cup light corn syrup,** and ½ **cup water.** Bring to a boil, stirring every so often. When it starts to boil, get out your thermometer. You're looking to get the mixture to 260°F, stirring regularly, which will take 5 minutes or so.

Meanwhile, place **2 large egg whites** in your mixer bowl and whip them until they form stiff peaks. Once the thermometer hits 260°F, with your mixer running on high speed, start adding the sugar syrup to the egg whites, pouring it in very slowly right onto the egg, not the bowl, while whipping. Mix for 3 to 5 minutes, until the mixture holds its shape (if that's not happening for you and you get thick ribbons of egg white coming off the whisk, that's okay, too).

Add your pecans, cherries, and **a splash of vanilla extract** to the bowl and mix until completely combined, just a few seconds. Taste it and see if it needs more vanilla for you.

Get 2 spoons. Take a spoonful (a tablespoon or so) of the mixture and place it on your lined baking sheet, scraping the first spoon with the second spoon (this prevents your fingers from getting sticky). It will be in a cute little mound that looks like a Hershey's Kiss. Keep going, making more mounds and placing them on the sheet without touching. You want to work quickly so the mix doesn't sit in the bowl too long.

Let the candies sit on the parchment paper for 10 to 20 minutes until they're set and stiff, then enjoy. I'd tell you how to store any leftovers, but I've never had them, so you're going to have to tell me.

Mama's Oatmeal Raisin Cookies

As a kid, whenever I picked up a buttery, cinnamony whiff coming from the kitchen, I knew my Mama was doing something nice for herself. Baking oatmeal raisin cookies was an act of self-care—because she sure as hell wasn't making those cookies for us kids. We'd eat them, of course, after all the other sweets in the house had been decimated and these were all that was left. Usually by then she'd have had her fill of them, so she didn't mind my brother and I sneaking a few. I can appreciate these cookies a lot more now that I'm grown. Plus, having a bite of one takes me right back to my Mama's kitchen.

❖ Gather Up

- 1 cup (2 sticks/226 grams to be exact) salted butter, homemade if you want (see page 34), room temperature
- 1 cup (190 grams; don't pack it) light brown sugar
- ½ cup (100 grams) granulated sugar
- 2 large eggs, room temperature
- 1 tablespoon vanilla extract, homemade if you want (see page 33)
- 1½ cups (180 grams) all-purpose flour
- 1 tablespoon baking powder
- 1 teaspoon fine sea salt, plus more for sprinkling
- Ground cinnamon
- Ground nutmeg
- 2 cups (180 grams) old-fashioned rolled oats
- 1½ cups (224 grams) raisins

❖ Don't Forget

- Your stand mixer with the paddle attachment, or handheld mixer

❖ Let's Bake Some Cookies

Grab your stand mixer (or a large bowl if you're using a handheld mixer), and put on the paddle attachment. In the bowl, beat **1 cup (2 sticks/226 grams to be exact) softened salted butter** on medium speed until light and fluffy, 3 minutes or so. Add **1 cup (190 grams) light brown sugar** and ½ **cup (100 grams) granulated sugar** and beat on medium-high speed until well combined, 1 to 2 minutes. Keep the machine running and beat in **2 room-temperature large eggs** and **1 tablespoon vanilla extract** until smooth, 1 minute or so. Add in 1½ **cups (180 grams) all-purpose flour, 1 tablespoon baking powder,** and **1 teaspoon fine sea salt, a couple pinches** (I like about 1 tablespoon, you do you) **ground cinnamon, and a couple pinches of ground nutmeg.** Mix on low speed until everything is evenly mixed, 1 minute or so. Make sure there's no pockets of flour or butter hiding on the bottom; stop the machine and scrape the sides of the bowl, if you need to.

Add **2 cups (180 grams) old-fashioned rolled oats** and 1½ **cups (224 grams) raisins.** Mix on low speed until it's all evenly mixed, just a minute or two. Cover the bowl with beeswax wrap or a reusable bowl cover and refrigerate the dough for at least 2 hours and up to 48 hours (you *can* skip this, but the cookies are so much better if you don't!).

Preheat your oven to 350°F. Go ahead and line a baking sheet with parchment paper.

Scoop up a palm-size piece of dough (call it 2 tablespoons) and roll it into a ball with your hands. Put it on the baking sheet and leave it as a ball—do *not* squish it! Repeat with more of the dough, spacing the balls 2 inches apart, until you've filled up the baking sheet.

Bake until slightly golden on top, 10 to 12 minutes. Take them out of the oven and sprinkle the tops with some fine sea salt. Let the cookies sit on the hot baking sheet for 5 minutes, then move them over to a wire rack to cool. Continue shaping and baking the rest of the dough and cooling the cookies. Then enjoy, my friend. Store any extras in a cookie jar on the counter for a few days.

Chocolate Date Caramel Brownies

GETS YOU 9 BROWNIES ❖ ABOUT 1¼ HOURS

I love sweets and sugar, and I don't believe anyone should feel any shame whatsoever about food. But even I can admit that maybe eating sugar all the time isn't the best for me. That's how I got to experimenting with dates in my baking. This is a new version of me that's trying to be healthy, and I am discovering that I *love* dates. It's a miracle that this flavor somehow just grows on trees! These brownies are my best date recipe yet, and their amazing flavor really comes through in the date caramel I make to stir into my brownie batter. I wanted to make something that my kids would eat that uses dates, and that I would gladly keep around to snack on every day. Here you go.

❖ *Gather Up*

Nonstick cooking spray

About 2 cups (10 ounces/ 283 grams to be exact) pitted dates

½ **cup (77 grams) coconut sugar**

¼ **cup (60 grams) coconut milk**

¼ **cup (78 grams) maple syrup**

1 **large egg**

1 **tablespoon vanilla extract, homemade if you want (see page 33)**

1¼ **cups (115 grams) oat flour**

¼ **cup (21 grams) unsweetened cocoa powder**

1 **teaspoon baking powder**

1 **teaspoon ground cinnamon**

1 **teaspoon fine sea salt, plus more for sprinkling**

Cayenne pepper

Flaky sea salt, if you want

❖ *Don't Forget*

Your blender

❖ *Let's Make These Brownies*

Preheat your oven to 350°F. Spray an 8-inch square baking dish with **nonstick cooking spray** so nothing sticks to it. Boil a kettle of water now, too.

Put **about 2 cups (10 ounces/283 grams to be exact) pitted dates** in a large heatproof bowl and cover with boiling water. Let soak for 10 minutes, then drain all but about ¼ cup of the liquid. Put the dates in a blender and blend until creamy and smooth, adding the water 1 tablespoon at a time until it's as thick as apple butter. You just made nature's caramel!

In a large bowl, combine ½ **cup (77 grams) coconut sugar**, ¼ **cup (60 grams) coconut milk**, ¼ **cup (78 grams) maple syrup**, **1 large egg,** and **1 tablespoon vanilla extract.** Whisk everything together real well, until the egg is blended in, then add 1¼ **cups (115 grams) oat flour**, ¼ **cup (21 grams) unsweetened cocoa powder, 1 teaspoon baking powder, 1 teaspoon ground cinnamon, 1 teaspoon fine sea salt,** and **a pinch** (I like about 1 teaspoon, you do you) **of cayenne pepper** and stir together until everything is combined and smooth.

Stir in half the date caramel to the brownie bowl, mixing it in to get all that good date flavor in every bite. Pour your batter into the greased pan and spread it out smooth. Bake until a toothpick poked into the middle comes out clean, 15 to 20 minutes.

Put the baking pan on a cooling rack and let those brownies cool to room temperature, or just slightly warmer if you're getting impatient, 45 minutes or so. Once the brownies are cool, add the rest of your date caramel to the top, spreading it out into a nice even layer. Sprinkle the top with **a little more fine** or **flaky sea salt** and take that first bite—ain't that amazing how good it tastes? Store any extra brownies in a closed container on the counter for a few days.

Apple Cinnamon Bread Pudding

I love my chickens so much. Whenever I have some stale bread, I walk out to the chicken coop and bond with the ladies as I feed them the butts of my loaves. But I can feed them only so much bread; I need something to make when the chickens have had their fill, and I'm thinking, *Well, what the hell am I supposed to do with all this bread?* So, I make bread pudding. This is *easy,* y'all. You just throw it in a pan, pour over some milk and eggs, and you're giving your old bread a honey-and-cinnamon makeover.

❖ *Gather Up*

- 1 tablespoon salted butter, homemade if you want (see page 34), plus more for greasing
- 1 loaf stale or fresh French bread (10 ounces/ 283 grams or so)
- 1 large tart apple (I like Honeycrisp)
- ¾ cup (79 grams to be exact) pecans
- 2 cups (454 grams) whole milk or buttermilk, homemade if you want (see page 34)
- 4 large eggs
- ½ cup (168 grams) honey, plus more for serving
- 1 tablespoon vanilla extract, homemade if you want (see page 33)
- Ground cinnamon
- Cayenne pepper
- Ground nutmeg

❖ *Let's Make Some Bread Pudding*

Grease an 8-inch square baking pan with some butter. Chop **1 loaf stale or fresh French bread** into bite-size pieces—I usually get about 6 cups. Chop **1 large tart apple** so you have 1½ cups. Chop **¾ cup (79 grams to be exact) pecans** so you have ½ cup.

Spread the bread in the baking dish. In a medium bowl, mix together **2 cups (454 grams) whole milk, 4 large eggs, ½ cup (168 grams) honey, 1 tablespoon vanilla extract, 1 palmful ground cinnamon** and **a couple pinches each** (I like about 1 teaspoon, you do you) **of cayenne pepper** and **ground nutmeg** until completely smooth. Pour the mixture on top of the bread and press down so the bread is all covered.

Sprinkle the apples and pecans over the top and press them down a little into the bread. Now, sprinkle with more cinnamon ('cause we fancy) and pinch **1 tablespoon salted butter** into small pieces to dot the surface. Cover the pan with beeswax wrap or foil and let rest in the fridge for at least 1 hour and up to overnight.

Preheat your oven to 350°F.

Bake uncovered until the pudding is browned on top, 35 to 45 minutes. Let cool for 10 minutes before eating the whole pan. You can even drizzle more honey over the top ('cause we really fancy)!

Midnight's Blackberry Dumplings

FEEDS 6 ❖ TAKES 1 HOUR

Midnight is my favorite cat. He loves human foods, his favorite being these dumplings.

❖ *Gather Up*

For the Blackberry Sauce

2 tablespoons salted butter, homemade if you want (see page 34)

3 pints (about 1 pound) fresh blackberries

1 cup sugar

½ lemon

Ground cinnamon

Vanilla extract, homemade if you want (see page 33)

For the Dumplings

2 cups (240 grams to be exact) all-purpose flour

¼ cup (50 grams) sugar

1 tablespoon baking powder

1 teaspoon ground cinnamon

1 teaspoon fine sea salt

8 tablespoons (1 stick/ 113 grams) salted butter, room temperature

½ cup (114 grams) buttermilk, homemade if you want (see page 34)

1 tablespoon vanilla extract

❖ *Don't Forget*

Your stand mixer with the paddle attachment, or handheld mixer

❖ *Let's Simmer Some Dumplings*

Start with your blackberry sauce: Over medium, heat up your 12-inch cast-iron skillet with **2 tablespoons salted butter.** When the butter is melted, add **3 pints fresh blackberries, 1 cup sugar,** and **½ cup water.** Squeeze in the juice from ½ **lemon,** add **a couple pinches of ground cinnamon,** and **a splash of vanilla extract.** Stir it all together and bring it up to a boil. Reduce the heat to medium so the sauce simmers and let it do its thing, stirring every so often and getting the blackberries nice and juicy but not fallin' apart, while you take 5 minutes or so to make the dumplings.

Now, let's make the dumplings: Grab your stand mixer (or a large bowl, if you're using a handheld mixer), and put on the paddle attachment. In the bowl, combine **2 cups (240 grams to be exact) all-purpose flour,** ¼ **cup (50 grams) sugar, 1 tablespoon baking powder, 1 teaspoon ground cinnamon,** and **1 teaspoon fine sea salt** and mix on low speed just to combine it. Now, add **8 tablespoons (1 stick/113 grams) softened salted butter,** ½ **cup (114 grams) buttermilk,** and **1 tablespoon vanilla extract** and mix on medium speed until you have a nice and shaggy dough, 1 to 2 minutes.

Back to the blackberries: Taste a bite and make sure you're happy with the seasonings. Scoop some of your dough—a heaping spoonful—and place it on top of the simmering blackberry mixture. Keep scooping until it's all out of the bowl and in the sauce; make sure you allow a little room between the dumplings so they don't touch. Cover the pan, reduce the heat to low, and let simmer until the dough is cooked through and the blackberries are very soft, 15 minutes or so.

Allow it to cool for 10 minutes then enjoy, my friend.

Sexy 'n' Spicy Peach Pecan Cobbler

FEEDS 6 TO 8 ❖ TAKES 1 HOUR

Like many dear-to-me recipes, my cobbler was inspired by Granny Mary. She was known for a handful of dishes, and cobbler was one of her best. I've messed around with her recipe, and this version right here has become my signature: Georgia peaches mixed with a generous amount of bourbon and pecans. The bourbon idea came from one night when me and James were imbibing and feeling a little (a lot) sexy and spicy, and a good amount of the bottle ended up in our cooking. The pecans are from the two trees on our property.

I did an event a while back where I made this cobbler while some of y'all cooked it along with me. I asked for pictures to see how it turned out in your own kitchens, and they're right here, in my very first cookbook! I am so blessed to be able to inspire people to get into the kitchen, and you keep inspiring me right back with your willingness to try something new while you feel your best, most confident selves. And look how good all these cobblers look! Well, I'm blubbering like a baby now.

❖ *Gather Up*

Butter, bacon grease, or the fat of your choice, for the pan

For the Filling

3 **cups frozen sliced peaches**

2 **tablespoons salted butter, homemade if you want (see page 34)**

½ **cup (no need to pack it) brown sugar**

1 **ounce (2 tablespoons) bourbon, or more, up to you**

Ground cinnamon

Cayenne pepper, if you want

1 **cup pecans**

Vanilla extract, homemade if you want (see page 33)

❖ *Now It's Your Turn to Bake This Cobbler!*

Preheat your oven to 375°F. Go ahead and generously grease your 10-inch cast-iron skillet however you like (I prefer butter). Put the skillet in the oven while it preheats. You can just leave it in there as long as you don't smell any burning.

Start with the filling: Grab your medium pot and add **3 cups frozen sliced peaches** and 2 tablespoons salted butter. Put the pot over medium-low and let the butter melt and get those peaches simmering, stirring every so often. Add **½ cup brown sugar, 1 ounce (2 tablespoons) bourbon** (add an extra splash if you're feeling sexy), and **a couple pinches of ground cinnamon** and **a pinch of cayenne pepper** (if you want). Stir it all to coat the peaches. While that's happening, chop up **1 cup pecans** to get ¾ cup. If you've got extra, that's great—save them for sprinkling on top.

Reduce the heat to low and let those peaches soak up all that sugary bourbon, stirring every once in a while, until everything starts coming together, 2 to 3 minutes (this is usually when I start drooling from the smell!). Take the peaches off the heat, stir in **2 big splashes of vanilla extract,** and set aside, letting 'em rest so the sauce thickens slightly. When it's cooled off a bit, take a taste and make sure you're happy with the seasoning.

(recipe and ingredients continue)

2 tablespoons
all-purpose flour

For the Topping

8 tablespoons (1 stick/
113 grams to be exact)
salted butter

1 cup (120 grams)
all-purpose flour

1 cup (227 grams) whole milk

½ cup (100 grams)
granulated sugar

¼ cup (50 grams; no need
to pack it) brown sugar

1 ounce (2 tablespoons)
bourbon, if you want

1 tablespoon baking powder

1 tablespoon vanilla extract

1 teaspoon ground cinnamon

1 teaspoon fine sea salt

Now, make the topping: In a small pot over low heat, or in a small bowl in the microwave, melt **8 tablespoons (1 stick/113 grams to be exact) salted butter.** Take your skillet out of your oven (even if the oven ain't done preheating) and rest it on your countertop. You'll use it later.

Grab your medium bowl and add **1 cup (120 grams) all-purpose flour, 1 cup (227 grams) whole milk, ½ cup (100 grams) granulated sugar, ¼ cup (50 grams) brown sugar, 1 ounce (2 tablespoons) bourbon** (if you want), **1 tablespoon baking powder, 1 tablespoon vanilla extract, 1 teaspoon ground cinnamon,** and **1 teaspoon fine sea salt.** Pour the melted butter into the bowl. Mix everything together using your whisk until you get a smooth batter. Set aside.

Now, go back to your peaches: Add **2 tablespoons all-purpose flour** to the peaches and stir again so they thicken up a bit. Lastly, throw in the chopped pecans and stir again so the bourbon glaze gets all over the nuts. Put the peaches in the skillet and make a nice, even layer. Grab your topping and pour it all over the peaches. If you have extra chopped pecans, finish off with a sprinkle or two of them nuts.

Bake until lightly browned on top, 35 to 40 minutes. Let it cool for 5 minutes, then take that first spicy, boozy bite. I'm so glad you made this recipe!

Lily's Poppy Stems

GETS YOU 24 CAKE POPS ❖ TAKES ABOUT 3 HOURS

My oldest is obsessed with cake pops. I make them for her on special occasions and she goes crazy for all of them: chocolate, strawberry, vanilla. As long as it's a little mini cake on a stick, she's happy. I have been known to enjoy my own fair share, since mixing the cake right up with the frosting means they're always moist and fudgy in the way I love.

My biggest pet peeve, maybe in the whole world, is a dry cake. I make mine extra moist and, sorry to brag, but they're always the first ones gone at the barbecue. Lily has inherited my taste for cake, and I'm happy to indulge her with these "poppy" cakes. I usually serve them like a flower arrangement for her. To make them extra pretty, stir in a natural food coloring, like a tablespoon or so of beet powder.

❖ Gather Up

Butter or vegetable oil, for the pan

For the Cake

1 cup (200 grams to be exact) granulated sugar

8 tablespoons (1 stick/ 113 grams) salted butter, homemade if you want (see page 34), room temperature

2 large eggs, room temperature

1 cup (227 grams) whole milk or buttermilk, homemade if you want (see page 34), room temperature

1 tablespoon vanilla extract, homemade if you want (see page 33)

2 cups (240 grams) all-purpose flour

1 tablespoon baking powder

1 teaspoon fine sea salt

❖ Roll Up Your Sleeves and Get Baking

Preheat your oven to 350°F. Go ahead and grease an 8- or 9-inch cake pan with butter so nothing will stick.

Start with the cake: Grab your stand mixer (or a large bowl, if you're using a handheld mixer), and put on the paddle attachment. In the bowl, combine **1 cup (200 grams to be exact) granulated sugar** and **8 tablespoons (1 stick/113 grams) softened salted butter,** and cream them together on medium-high speed until they're light and fluffy, 2 to 3 minutes. Stop the mixer, add **2 room-temperature large eggs,** and beat on medium-high speed until they're good and mixed, 1 to 2 minutes. Now, add in **1 cup (227 grams) room-temperature whole milk** and **1 tablespoon vanilla extract** and mix on low speed just until it's all coming together, 1 minute. Finally, add **2 cups (240 grams) all-purpose flour, 1 tablespoon baking powder,** and **1 teaspoon fine sea salt** and mix on low speed until you don't see any dry flour anywhere, just a few seconds. Scrape down the sides of the bowl and make sure there's no flour hiding anywhere.

Add your cake batter to the buttered pan and gently spread it into an even layer. Bake until a toothpick poked into the middle comes out clean, 30 minutes or so. Set it aside to cool completely in the pan, about 1 hour.

Now, on to the buttercream: Clean the bowl and paddle attachment you used to make the cake. In the bowl, beat **8 tablespoons (1 stick) softened salted butter** on medium speed until it's light and fluffy, 2 to 3 minutes. Add **2½ cups powdered sugar, a splash of vanilla extract,** and **a splash of whole milk.** Mix on low speed until everything is

(recipe and ingredients continue)

For the Buttercream Frosting

8 tablespoons (1 stick) salted butter, room temperature

2½ cups powdered sugar

Vanilla extract

Whole milk or heavy whipping cream

For the Pops

3½ cups (20 ounces/ 567 grams) white chocolate melting wafers

Pretty sprinkles, for sprinkling of course

❖ *Don't Forget*

Your stand mixer with the paddle attachment, or handheld mixer

24 candy sticks or cake sticks

Some uncooked rice, for holding the pops up as they set

smooth and blended together, 1 minute or so. If it's too thick, add another splash of milk. Increase the speed to medium-high and beat until the buttercream is light and fluffy, another 2 to 3 minutes.

Combine the cake and frosting: When the cake is cooled, get your hands in there and break it up into tiny pieces in a large bowl, then add half your buttercream frosting. Stir it together with a spatula until it's good and mixed; you want the mixture to hold together if you squeeze it in your hand. If it crumbles, it will not hold together and you will need to add more buttercream. Keep adding buttercream until you can shape it. (You might have some leftover buttercream; you can keep it for a few days or freeze it.)

Line a baking sheet with parchment paper. Using a dough scooper or your hands, grab a piece of the cake mixture that's 2 tablespoons or so and roll it into a ball, then place it on the baking sheet. Repeat until you've rolled all the cake mix. Freeze the balls for 30 minutes so they're set.

Form the pops: Right before you're ready to take the balls out of the freezer, you're gonna melt the chocolate. Put **3½ cups (20 ounces/567 grams) white chocolate melting wafers** in a heatproof medium bowl and melt the wafers in the microwave or on the stovetop. If you're doing it in the microwave, nuke it in short, 15-second bursts, stirring after each one until the chocolate is mostly melted (the rest will melt soon after). If you're doing it on the stove, put about 1 inch of water in a medium pot and put the bowl on top, making sure the bottom of the bowl doesn't touch the water. Heat the water over medium-low, and keep stirring the chocolate until it's melted, just a few minutes, then immediately move it off the heat.

Fill a deep container (like a wide-mouth mason jar) with rice so you can stick the pops in it and they'll stand upright after you dip them in the white chocolate. Put the **sprinkles** in a small bowl and keep it nearby.

Working with one ball at a time, dip one end of your candy stick into the melted white chocolate to help the cake stay put, and then push that end of the stick into the middle of the cake ball. Now, dip your cake pop in the melted white chocolate, turning and totally coating it, then gently tapping off any excess. Quickly—before it hardens— shower some sprinkles onto the pop so they stick. Quickly stick the pop in the rice jar so it can dry upright; it takes just a few minutes. Keep going with the rest of the cake balls, coating them, sprinkling, then positioning them in the rice to dry, and moving them over to a plate after the chocolate sets so you always got room in your jar.

Enjoy those perfect and beautiful cakes! Any extras can be stored in a container in the fridge for a few days.

Blue Ridge S'more Cupcakes

GETS YOU 24 CUPCAKES ❖ TAKES 2 HOURS

We have car-camped many a day on the Blue Ridge Parkway that runs from North Carolina into Virginia. And when you're out in those woods, you can't help but build a fire and roast some s'mores. I got my technique down: I like a slow-roasted, no-char, light to medium brown marshmallow that's heated all the way through and practically falling off the stick. When I'm missing those family nights out in the woods, I make these cupcakes. Making your own marshmallow fluff is so easy, I swear, and if you do have a kitchen torch (or a blowtorch!), you can get that perfectly toasted texture on these cupcakes, too.

❖ Gather Up

For the Cake

- 2 cups (240 grams) all-purpose flour
- ½ cup (42 grams) unsweetened cocoa powder
- 1 tablespoon baking powder
- 1 teaspoon baking soda
- 1 teaspoon fine sea salt
- 2 cups (400 grams) sugar
- ½ cup (99 grams) oil of your choosing (like vegetable oil or avocado oil)
- 2 large eggs
- 2 tablespoons vanilla extract, homemade if you want (see page 33)
- 1½ cups (340 grams) whole milk or buttermilk, homemade if you want (see page 34)
- ½ cup (114 grams) boiling water

For the Fluffy Marshmallow

- 3 large eggs whites, room temperature
- 1 teaspoon cream of tartar

❖ Get Ready to Be Transported Right to a Campfire

Preheat your oven to 350°F. Go ahead and line a muffin tin with cupcake holders.

Let's make this cake: In a medium bowl, combine **2 cups (240 grams) all-purpose flour, ½ cup (42 grams) unsweetened cocoa powder, 1 tablespoon baking powder, 1 teaspoon baking soda,** and **1 teaspoon fine sea salt** and whisk until just combined. In a large bowl, combine **2 cups (400 grams) sugar, ½ cup (99 grams) oil, 2 large eggs,** and **2 tablespoons vanilla extract** and whisk until smooth. Now, whisk in **1½ cups (340 grams) whole milk** until incorporated. Stir the dry mix into the wet mix until just combined. Finally, add ½ cup **(114 grams) boiling water** while whisking until it's all mixed in.

Pour the batter into the muffin cups, filling them no more than two-thirds of the way (learned that the hard way). If using only one tin, you'll bake these in 2 batches. Bake the cupcakes until a toothpick poked into the middle of one comes out clean, 18 to 20 minutes. Let them cool in the pan completely before putting on a rack to rest while you bake the other batch. They need to be totally cool before frosting, 1 hour or so.

While the cupcakes are baking, get to the marshmallow: Grab your stand mixer (or large bowl, if you're using a handheld mixer), and put on the whisk attachment. In the bowl, combine **3 room-temperature large egg whites** and 1 **teaspoon cream of tartar.** Start mixing on medium speed and slowly pick up the speed to high until you have soft peaks (that means when you pull the whisk out, the tip of the whites droop over), 3 to 5 minutes. Turn off the mixer but leave the whisk attached.

In a medium pot, combine ¾ **cup sugar,** ¾ **cup light corn syrup,** and ⅓ **cup water** and mix to combine. Put it over medium-high and do not stir while it's heating. Get out your thermometer. You want it to get to 240°F, which takes 5 minutes or so.

¾ cup sugar

¾ cup light corn syrup

1 tablespoon vanilla extract

Fine sea salt

For Decorating

Crushed graham crackers

24 Hershey's Kisses

❖ *Don't Forget*

1 or 2 (12-cup) muffin tins and cupcake holders (or whatever those things are called)

Your stand mixer with the whisk attachment, or handheld mixer

Your thermometer

When the sugar syrup hits 240°F, move the pan off the heat and over to the mixer. Set the mixer to low speed and start pouring the sugar syrup into the bowl very, very slowly. Once it's all in, raise the speed to medium. Continue to mix until the mixture is very thick and fluffy, 6 to 8 minutes. Add in **1 tablespoon vanilla extract** and **a big pinch of fine sea salt** and whip until the fluff is cool, another 2 to 3 minutes.

Get creative with the decoration: Frost the cupcakes with as much of the fluff as you like. (If you are going to torch them, do that now, before adding the toppings.) Then, sprinkle them with **crushed graham crackers** and top each with **a Hershey's Kiss.** Pretend like you're sitting in the woods under the stars and enjoy these with a friend. Store any extras in a container in the fridge for a few days.

Pineapple Upside-Down Cake

FEEDS 6 TO 8 ❖ TAKES ABOUT 2 HOURS

I'd rather have a cake made in a Bundt pan than in anything else. It's "Bundt or bust" in my kitchen. All the extra surface area means the cake cooks faster and stays moister, and that's the secret for a cake that will have people asking for seconds. If you don't have a Bundt pan, you *could* make this in a regular round cake pan, but just make sure it's not one of those springform cheesecake pans where you can remove the sides. A girlfriend baked my recipe in one of those springform pans and the juice ran out all over the place. She had to scrub the bottom of her oven for hours, and even worse, we all had to eat dry cake.

❖ *Gather Up*

For the Cake

- 12 tablespoons (1½ sticks/ 170 grams) salted butter, homemade if you want (see page 34), room temperature
- ½ cup (100 grams) granulated sugar
- ¼ cup (57 grams) whole milk
- ¼ cup (70 grams) fresh pineapple juice
- ¼ cup (57 grams) sour cream
- 2 large eggs, room temperature
- 1 tablespoon vanilla extract, homemade if you want (see page 33)
- 1½ cups (180 grams) all-purpose flour
- 1½ teaspoons baking powder
- 1 teaspoon fine sea salt

For the Topping

- 1 little fresh pineapple
- ¼ cup fresh cherries
- ½ cup (don't pack it) brown sugar

❖ *Put on Some Good Music (Maybe Prince) and Let's Get Baking*

Preheat your oven to 350°F.

Let's make this cake: In a small saucepan over low heat, or in a small bowl in the microwave, melt **4 tablespoons (½ stick/57 grams) of the softened salted butter.** Generously grease your standard 12-cup Bundt pan with it, getting it into all those nooks and crannies good! Make sure nothing will stick, and let the extra butter pool in the bottom.

Grab your stand mixer (or a large bowl, if you're using a handheld mixer), and put on the paddle attachment. In the bowl, combine the other **8 tablespoons (1 stick/113 grams) softened salted butter** and ½ **cup (100 grams) granulated sugar.** Cream them together on low speed until they're smooth and creamy with no lumps, 2 to 3 minutes. Stop the mixer and add ¼ **cup (57 grams) whole milk,** ¼ **cup (70 grams) fresh pineapple juice,** ¼ **cup (57 grams) sour cream, 2 room-temperature large eggs,** and **1 tablespoon vanilla extract.** Mix on low speed until they're all good and mixed together, 1 minute or so. Now, add **1½ cups (180 grams) all-purpose flour, 1½ teaspoons baking powder,** and **1 teaspoon fine sea salt** and mix just until you don't see any dry flour anywhere, a few seconds.

Let the batter sit while you prepare the topping: Trim the top and bottom from **1 little fresh pineapple,** then cut it into quarters from the top to the bottom, and cut out the tough core. Cut the pineapple into slices about ½ inch thick, in whatever direction you want so that you can cover the bottom of your cake pan nicely. Pit ¼ **cup fresh cherries.**

Sprinkle ½ **cup brown sugar** in the bottom of the Bundt pan to mix with the butter. Then add your pineapple slices and cherries. Make it pretty so you can show off a little. I like to cover the whole bottom of the pan with the pineapple slices touching, then fit the cherries in the spaces between them. Keep going until you've made whatever

(recipe continues)

**Your stand mixer with
the paddle attachment,
or handheld mixer**

design you like, and save any leftover pineapple as a snack. Pour the batter over the pineapple and cherries and carefully spread it into a smooth layer.

Bake until a toothpick poked into the thickest part comes out clean, 30 to 35 minutes. Put the cake pan on a rack and let it cool completely before messing with it. When ready, run a knife around the edges of the pan to loosen the cake, taking your time; you don't want this beauty to stick to the pan and you got only one shot at this, so make sure you separate those edges. Now, put a cake plate over the Bundt pan and flip it in one confident motion. If you don't feel that pretty thing pop out, tap the bottom of the pan with your hand until it does. If you used plenty of butter, it'll happen eventually. And if the cake breaks a little, well, that's okay, too.

Look how pretty she is! Slice and enjoy. Good job, friend—I'm proud of you! If there's any left, store it covered in the fridge for a few days.

Citrus Pound Cake

FEEDS 6 TO 8 ❖ TAKES 2 HOURS

My Mama and Granny were known for their lemon pound cake, my Mama especially. Any time there was a get-together, that's what she was bringing. So, I kept up the tradition and I added some orange in there, too, because more citrus is always better in my mind. I get in all the sweet and tangy flavor I can pack into this cake by drizzling on a citrus soak after baking. With all that flavor, this is one cake that don't need any frosting; add a little glaze before serving, and it's really all you need.

❖ *Gather Up*

Butter, for the pan (see my Note)

For the Cake

2 **oranges**

2 **cups (400 grams to be exact) granulated sugar**

12 **tablespoons (1½ sticks/170 grams) salted butter, homemade if you want (see page 34), room temperature**

4 **large eggs, room temperature**

1 **tablespoon vanilla extract, homemade if you want (see page 33)**

½ **cup (114 grams) buttermilk, homemade if you want (see page 34)**

3 **cups (360 grams) all-purpose flour**

1 **tablespoon baking powder**

1 **teaspoon fine sea salt**

For the Orange and Lemon Soak

1 **lemon**

1 **orange**

¼ **cup granulated sugar**

2 **tablespoons salted butter**

❖ *Ooooh This Cake Is Good, You're Gonna Flip*

Preheat your oven to 350°F. Grease up your standard 12-cup Bundt pan with **butter,** getting it good! Make sure nothing will stick.

Start with the cake: Squeeze **2 oranges** so you get ½ cup of juice. Grab your stand mixer (or a large bowl if you're using a handheld mixer), and put on the paddle attachment. In the bowl, combine **2 cups (400 grams to be exact) granulated sugar** and **12 tablespoons (1½ sticks/170 grams) softened salted butter** and mix on medium-high speed until it's light and fluffy, 3 to 5 minutes. Add **4 room-temperature large eggs** and **1 tablespoon vanilla extract** and beat on medium speed until well combined, 1 to 2 minutes. Now, add ½ **cup (114 grams) buttermilk** and the orange juice and mix on low speed until it's smooth, 1 minute or so.

Add **3 cups (360 grams) all-purpose flour, 1 tablespoon baking powder,** and **1 teaspoon fine sea salt** and mix on low speed until you don't see any dry flour anywhere, just 30 seconds. Scrape down the sides if you need to, to get all the flour.

Scrape the batter into the pan and spread it in an even layer. Bake until a toothpick poked into the thickest part comes out clean, 45 to 60 minutes. Allow the cake to cool in the pan completely.

While you wait, make that soak: Cut **1 lemon** in half and squeeze out 2 tablespoons juice. Juice **1 orange** so you get ¼ cup of juice. In a small pot over medium heat, bring the lemon juice, orange juice, and ¼ **cup granulated sugar** to a boil, stirring without stopping now since this takes only a few minutes. Once it is at a boil and the sugar is completely melted, take the pan off the heat and add **2 tablespoons salted butter.** Keep stirring until the butter is melted. Set aside.

(recipe and ingredients continue)

For the Glaze

1 orange

1 or 2 lemons

2½ cups powdered sugar

Fine sea salt

❖ *Don't Forget*

Your stand mixer with the paddle attachment, or handheld mixer

And that glaze: First, zest and juice **1 orange** so you got 1 tablespoon zest and 2 tablespoons juice and put the juice in a medium bowl (save the zest for later). Zest **1 or 2 lemons** until you get 1 tablespoon, then cut them in half and squeeze out 2 tablespoons juice; add the juice to the bowl and save the zest. Now, add **2½ cups powdered sugar** and **a pinch of fine sea salt** to the bowl and mix until that baby is smooth and there ain't no lumps of sugar. Set aside.

When your cake has cooled, run a knife around the edges to loosen them, place a plate on top, and invert the mold onto a cooling rack.

Make sure you got something under the rack, like a plate, then pour your soak over it nice and slow so it sinks in, or brush it on the cake all over. Then drizzle your glaze over the top and make it look nice and pretty. Sprinkle with the orange and lemon zests for that final nice touch.

Now, get some coffee, slice up the cake, and make sure you got someone to share it with. Keep any extra in the fridge, covered, for a few days.

Note: *My secret to a good pound cake is to butter the hell out of the pan. You gotta get into all those corners with your hand, and if you need to use half a stick of butter to do it, well, that's just what's going to have to happen. After baking, let the cake cool all the way in the pan before you turn it over, and it should slide right out.*

Georgia Peach Cheesecake

FEEDS 8 TO 10 ✧ TAKES 3 HOURS

I think a peach cheesecake is real unique; I've never seen one other than Gigi's recipe right here. And you know I had to get a few recipes that use sweet Georgia peaches in my repertoire. Gigi, my spiritual mother, is the cheesecake maker in our family. She is so freakin' good at it—her cheesecakes look so professional, like you'd buy them in a store. She makes some interesting flavors, like pistachio, and white chocolate and macadamia nut, but this one to me is the most special. She bakes the peaches into the middle, not just on top, so you get some real nice jammy bits in every bite. It's a taste of Georgia that's almost as fine as me.

✧ Gather Up

Ice water

2 fresh peaches

For the Crust

8 tablespoons (1 stick/ 113 grams to be exact) salted butter, homemade if you want (see page 34)

2 cups (200 grams) graham cracker crumbs (or crush 16 crackers)

¼ cup (50 grams) granulated sugar

For the Filling

3 (8-ounce) packages cream cheese, room temperature

1 cup granulated sugar

¾ cup sour cream, room temperature

6 large eggs, room temperature

1 tablespoon vanilla extract, homemade if you want (see page 33)

1 teaspoon plus 2 tablespoons ground cinnamon

✧ This Cheesecake Will Make You "Peachless"

Preheat your oven to 325°F. Go ahead and line a 10-inch springform pan with parchment paper on the bottom.

Start by bringing a medium pot of water to a boil. Fill up a medium bowl with **ice water.** Cut a shallow "x" in the bottom of **2 fresh peaches.** Drop the peaches into the boiling water and let them cook until you start to see the skin peeling back by the cut, 30 seconds or so. Fish them out with a slotted spoon or spider strainer and drop into the ice water. When they're cold, a minute or so later, remove the peaches and peel off the skin starting at the cut. Set them aside for now.

Now, let's get to that crust: In a small saucepan over low heat, or in a small bowl in the microwave, melt **8 tablespoons (1 stick/ 113 grams to be exact) salted butter.** In a medium bowl, mix together **2 cups (200 grams) graham cracker crumbs** and ¼ **cup (50 grams) granulated sugar,** then add the melted butter and stir until everything is evenly combined and the butter is distributed. Pack the mixture to line the bottom and halfway up the sides of your pan.

Bake the crust until it's firm and just a little browned on the edges, 12 to 15 minutes, then set aside to cool. Don't you turn that oven off yet; we're not done.

Make the filling: Grab your stand mixer (or a large bowl, if you're using a handheld mixer), and put on the whisk attachment. In the bowl, blend together **3 (8-ounce) packages room-temperature cream cheese, 1 cup granulated sugar,** and ¾ **cup room-temperature sour cream** on medium-high speed until light and fluffy, 2 to 3 minutes. Add **6 room-temperature large eggs, 1 tablespoon vanilla extract,**

(recipe and ingredients continue)

2 tablespoons
all-purpose flour

2 tablespoons brown sugar

For the Topping

1 tablespoon granulated sugar

½ cup heavy whipping cream

1 tablespoon powdered sugar

Vanilla extract

Pretty flowers, if you want

❖ *Don't Forget*

Your stand mixer with
the whisk attachment,
or handheld mixer

and **1 teaspoon ground cinnamon** and beat on medium speed until smooth, 2 to 3 minutes. Finally, add **2 tablespoons all-purpose flour** and mix on low speed until just combined and there aren't any lumps, less than 1 minute.

Pit 1 of your peeled peaches and cut them into ½-inch-thick slices so you get 1 cup (if you got more than that, snack on the extra).

Now, take your springform pan and fill it with half the cream cheese mixture. Add your peaches and spread them across the surface and sprinkle with the last **2 tablespoons ground cinnamon** and **2 tablespoons brown sugar** over the top. Now, add the rest of your cream cheese mixture and spread the top into a smooth layer.

Bake until just the outer two inches of the cake is firm, and the center is still jiggly, 40 to 60 minutes, then turn off the oven and allow the cake to stay in there another 30 minutes without opening the door. After you wait, you can crack the door of the oven and let it cool another 15 minutes before removing the cheesecake. Allow the cheesecake to cool on the counter until it's room temperature, 1 to 2 hours. (Once it's cool, you can cover it with beeswax wrap and refrigerate it up to overnight.)

When you're ready to serve, make the topping: Pit your last peeled peach and cut it into ½-inch-thick slices, so you get about 1 cup. Put the slices in a medium bowl and toss the peaches with **1 tablespoon granulated sugar.**

Get your mixer and bowl back out. To the bowl, add ½ **cup heavy whipping cream, 1 tablespoon powdered sugar,** and **a splash of vanilla extract** and start whipping on medium speed, slowly bumping up to medium-high until you got stiff peaks, meaning those babies don't fall over when you stop the mixer and pull out the whisk, 2 to 3 minutes. Taste it and add more vanilla if you want, but don't mix it for more than a couple seconds or else you'll get butter.

Run a knife around the edges, then open and lift off the sides of your pan so you can see this pretty thing. Add the rest of your peaches to the center of your cake. You can arrange them however you want to get creative! Dollop the whipped cream around the peaches—have fun with this part! I freestyle it every time. Add some **flowers** if your heart desires. Now, cut you a slice and enjoy (if your flowers aren't edible, take them off after you get your *oohs* and *aahs*). Is that not the best cheesecake you have ever made? If there's any left, it'll keep in the fridge for a few days.

Indie Lou's Blueberry Cake

GETS YOU ONE 8-INCH LAYER CAKE ❖ TAKES 3 HOURS

Ever since I was a kid I've had a blueberry cake for my birthday. My two oldest, Lily and Buck, are chocolate-cake lovers through and through. I'd been hoping to have a kid I could share this tradition with, and you know how they say that third time's a charm? Well, my Indie Lou adores blueberries just as much as I do. This is a custardy blueberry cake with fluffy sweetened whipped cream between each and every layer. Lucky for us, we now get to eat it twice a year instead of just once. I've definitely already said it, but you can ignore me: *This* is my favorite recipe.

❖ *Gather Up*

Butter or baking spray, for the pan

For the Cake

3 cups (360 grams to be exact) all-purpose flour

1 tablespoon baking powder

1 teaspoon fine sea salt

2 cups (400 grams) granulated sugar

1 (8-ounce/228 gram) package cream cheese, room temperature

8 tablespoons (1 stick/ 113 grams) salted butter, homemade if you want (see page 34), room temperature

4 large eggs, room temperature

1 tablespoon vanilla extract, homemade if you want (see page 33)

1½ cups (340 grams) buttermilk, homemade if you want (see page 34), room temperature

½ cup (99 grams) vegetable oil

❖ *Get Ready to Celebrate*

Preheat your oven to 350°F. Go ahead and **butter** three 8-inch cake layer pans and then line the bottoms with parchment paper. Butter the paper too.

First, make the cake batter: In a medium bowl, stir together **3 cups (360 grams to be exact) all-purpose flour, 1 tablespoon baking powder,** and **1 teaspoon fine sea salt.**

Grab your stand mixer (or a large bowl if you're using a handheld mixer), and put on the paddle attachment. In the bowl, cream **2 cups (400 grams) granulated sugar, 8 ounces (228 grams) room-temperature cream cheese,** and **8 tablespoons (1 stick/113 grams) softened salted butter** on medium-high speed until light and fluffy, 5 minutes or so. Beat in **4 room-temperature large eggs** and **1 tablespoon vanilla extract** on low speed just until combined, 1 minute or so. With the mixer running on low speed, slowly add in the flour mixture, then pour in **1½ cups (340 grams) room-temperature buttermilk** and **½ cup (99 grams) vegetable oil.** Mix just until the batter is smooth. Use a spatula to fold in **1½ cups (233 grams) fresh blueberries.**

Divide the batter evenly among the 3 cake pans, and smooth out the tops. Bake until a toothpick poked into the middle comes out clean, rotating the cakes after 30 minutes, for 45 to 50 minutes total. Put the pans on a wire rack and let them cool completely, 1 to 2 hours, before you remove the cake from the pans.

(recipe and ingredients continue)

1½ cups (233 grams) fresh blueberries

For the Blueberry Sauce

2 cups fresh blueberries

½ cup granulated sugar

4 tablespoons (½ stick) salted butter

For the Whipped Cream Topping

4 tablespoons (½ stick) salted butter, room temperature

2 cups heavy whipping cream

2 to 4 cups powdered sugar, up to you

For Decoration

½ cup fresh blueberries

Powdered sugar

Pretty flowers, if you want

❖ *Don't Forget*

Your stand mixer with the paddle and whisk attachments, or handheld mixer

While the cakes cool, make the blueberry sauce: In a small pot, combine **2 cups fresh blueberries, ½ cup granulated sugar,** and **4 tablespoons (½ stick) salted butter.** Heat over medium-low, stirring from time to time, until the berries are nice and soft with lots of juices to make them all saucy, 10 to 15 minutes. Move the sauce to a medium bowl and put it in the fridge to cool completely, 30 minutes or so.

Now, make the whipped cream topping: Get your mixer and bowl back out, and use the whisk attachment this time. Beat **4 tablespoons (½ stick) softened salted butter** on medium speed until light and fluffy, 2 to 3 minutes. Add **2 cups heavy whipping cream** and beat on medium speed until soft peaks form (meaning when you stop the mixer, those peaks of cream fall right over); timing will depend on a lot of factors, could be 3 minutes, could be 5, so just look out for those soft peaks! Add **4 cups powdered sugar** (or just 2 cups if you like it less sweet) and mix on medium speed until everything is combined and you got stiff peaks now (those babies stay standing on the whisk), a couple minutes more. Put it in the fridge until you're ready to frost.

Assemble and decorate the cake: Once the cake layers are completely cool, it's time to put it all together. Get a cake plate and put one layer flat side down in the center. Add one-third of the whipped cream topping and spread it out, then top with one-third of the blueberry sauce and spread it out. Repeat with the other 2 layers, flat side up. Once you've added the last of the blueberry sauce, sprinkle the cake with the ½ **cup fresh blueberries** on top and dust with **powdered sugar.** If you're feeling it, decorate with **pretty flowers** (don't forget to remove them eventually if they're not edible).

I hope you got someone to sing happy birthday to! Slice it up and serve. Store any leftovers in the fridge for a couple days.

Acknowledgments

The past two years have been nothing short of extraordinary. I am truly at a loss for words to express my gratitude to each and every one of you who has supported me and shown unwavering love as we journeyed through all things LilyLouTay. There are a few special people I want to thank for making this all possible.

James: I honestly can't imagine life without you. Your support, wisdom, guidance, and brilliance mean more to me than words can express. You are my rock, and I'm so grateful to have created this book with you. You make life truly meaningful. Love you endlessly, my man.

Lily, Buck, and Indie: You are the greatest blessings in my life, and everything I do is for you. You hold my whole heart, and I am beyond grateful to have you with me on this journey. I love you more than words could ever express.

Nicole: Thank you for the countless phone calls and the energy it took to keep me grounded throughout this big adventure. You've taught me so much about the meaning of true friendship and love. You are truly extraordinary.

My incredible **LilyLouTay online family, friends, and fans:** Thank you, from the bottom of my heart. Your love and support have brought me to where I am today, and I will never take that for granted. Your kindness is a true light in this world, and I can't express how much your comments and messages mean to me. None of this would have been possible without you, and I will forever be grateful. I love you all more than words can say.

My wonderful publisher and everyone at **Clarkson Potter. Jenn Sit:** You're a breath of fresh air and comfort in a space that was very new to me. Thank you for believing in my cooking, recipes, and ability to take on this project. I am forever grateful for your support. **Elaine Hennig, Jan Derevjanik, Natalie Blachere, Jessica Heim, Carole Berglie, and the whole marketing and publishing teams:** This book could not have happened without each and every one of you.

Emily Stephenson: Thank you for helping me put into words my experiences, thoughts, feelings, sentiments, memories, and recipes. You bring so much life to this book, and I am so honored to have gotten to work with you and your genius pen.

Eliza Winograd, Rinne Allen, Tami Hardeman, Abby Gaskins, and Jo Nicol: Thank you all for helping me add some structure to my otherwise chaotic method of cooking. Your expertise is beyond incredible, and the way you worked through everything on our short timeline to produce beautiful work will never cease to amaze me.

My agents **Travis Eller, Andrew Graham, Rachel O'Brien, Sydney Shiffman, and Anthony Mattero:** None of this would be possible without you. I cannot tell you enough how much I love you. Thank you for believing in me and always advocating for me.

Index

Note: Page references in *italics*
indicate photographs.

A

All-Purpose Seasoning, 38
Apple Cider Vinegar, *40,* 41
Apple(s)
Cinnamon Bread Pudding, 256, *257*
Cinnamon Strudels, *106,* 107–8
Let's Get Saucy Cranberry
Applesauce, *60,* 61
Applesauce, Cranberry, Let's Get
Saucy, *60,* 61
Aunt Teisha's Cowboy Caviar, 114, *115*

B

Bacon
BBQ Pineapple Chicken Bake, 168,
169
Breakfast Hash Croissant
Sandwiches, 90, *91*
Collard Greens, Bebop's Sweet, 131
Hahira Breakfast Cups, *82,* 83–84
Honey Green Beans, Smokin', 132,
133
Loaded-Up Potato Skins, 122, *123*
Rookie's Cookies (Homemade Dog
Treats), 75
Scalloped Potatoes & Ham
Casserole, 176, *177*
Sunrise Quiche, 85–86, *87*
Sweet Meets Spicy Supreme
Omelet, 80, *81*
Bagels, Cheddar Jalapeño, *216,*
217–18
BBQ Pineapple Chicken Bake, 168,
169
BBQ Ribs, Slow Cooker, *160,* 161
Bean(s)
Aunt Teisha's Cowboy Caviar, 114,
115
First Night Chili, 193–94, *195*
Green, Smokin' Honey Bacon, 132,
133
Lima, Ham Hock Soup, Knock-Out,
182, 183

Slow Cooker Brunswick Stew,
198–99, *200–201*
Bebop's Sweet Bacon Collard Greens,
131
Beef
Bone Broth, 53, *55*
Chicken Fried Steak with Gravy,
156, 157
First Night Chili, 193–94, *195*
James's Smash Burgers, *164,* 165
Lover's Lasagna, 178–79, *180–81*
Luke the Duke's Corn Dogs, 72, *73*
Mary's Meatloaf, 158, *159*
My Go-To Pot Roast, 162, *163*
Sloppy James, 150, *151*
Slow Cooker Brunswick Stew,
198–99, *200–201*
Beer
First Night Chili, 193–94, *195*
Berry(ies)
Bluegurt Ice Pops, *64,* 65
Buck's Poppin' Tarts, 66–67, *68–69*
Cranberry-Orange Cinnamon Rolls
with Lemon Glaze, 104–5, *105*
Fizzy Cranberry Punch, *242,* 243
Fruity Roll'em Ups, 62, *63*
Hoe Cakes with Cranberry Jam &
Powdered Sugar, *100,* 101
Homemade Blueberry Wine,
232–33, *233*
Indie Lou's Blueberry Cake, 277–78,
279
Let's Get Saucy Cranberry
Applesauce, *60,* 61
Midnight's Blackberry Dumplings,
258, 259
Mixed, Scones, 98, *99*
Strawberry Sip 'n' Spritz, 234, *235*
Biscuits
Cinnamon Raisin, 208–10, *211*
Classic, & Milk Sausage Gravy,
204–6, *207*
Bisque, Nice & Creamy Crab, 184, *185*
Blackberry(ies)
Dumplings, Midnight's, *258,* 259
Fruity Roll'em Ups, 62, *63*
Blueberry(ies)
Bluegurt Ice Pops, *64,* 65
Cake, Indie Lou's, 277–78, *279*

Fruity Roll'em Ups, 62, *63*
Wine, Homemade, 232–33, *233*
Blue Ridge S'more Cupcakes, 266–67,
267
Bone Broth
Beef, 53, *55*
Chicken, 54, *55*
Bourbon
Sexy 'n' Spicy Peach Pecan Cobbler,
260–62, *261*
Vanilla Extract, 33
Bread Pudding, Apple Cinnamon,
256, *257*
Breads
Butter My Rolls, 214–15, *215*
Cheddar Jalapeño Bagels, *216,*
217–18
Cheesy & Herby Dutch Oven,
228–29, *229*
Cinnamon Raisin Biscuits, 208–10,
211
Classic Biscuits & Milk Sausage
Gravy, 204–6, *207*
Cranberry-Orange Cinnamon Rolls
with Lemon Glaze, 104–5, *105*
flat, remedies for, 26
Mixed Berry Scones, 98, *99*
My Favorite Sourdough Loaf,
224–25, *226–27*
Sandwich, Homemade, 222–23, *223*
Soufflé French Toast Casserole, *96,*
97
Southern Sweet Cornbread with
Honey Butter, *212,* 213
Breakfast recipes
Apple Cinnamon Strudels, *106,*
107–8
Baked Cheesy Garlic Grits, *78,* 79
Breakfast Hash Croissant
Sandwiches, 90, *91*
Chicken & Waffles, *92,* 93–94
Cranberry-Orange Cinnamon Rolls
with Lemon Glaze, 104–5, *105*
Hahira Breakfast Cups, *82,* 83–84
Hoe Cakes with Cranberry Jam &
Powdered Sugar, *100,* 101
Mixed Berry Scones, 98, *99*
Soufflé French Toast Casserole, *96,*
97

Sour Cream Vanilla Coffee Cake,
102–3, *103*
Sunrise Quiche, 85–86, *87*
Sweet Meets Spicy Supreme
Omelet, 80, *81*
Whipped Chocolate Ganache
Donuts, 109–10, *111*
Brittle, Classic Peanut, 248, *249*
Broccoli
Chicken & Rice Casserole, *170,* 171
Mama's Chicken Pot Pie, *140,*
141–42
Brownies, Chocolate Date Caramel,
254, 255
Brunswick Stew, Slow Cooker, 198–99,
200–201
Buck's Poppin' Tarts, 66–67, *68–69*
Burgers, James's Smash, *164,* 165
Bushwacker, *236,* 237
Butter
& Buttermilk, B & B Twofer, 34–35, *35*
Honey, Southern Sweet Cornbread
with, *212,* 213
-Roasted Chicken, *144,* 145
Buttermilk
& Butter, B & B Twofer, 34, *35*
Instant, 34
Butter My Rolls, 214–15, *215*

C

Cakes
Blueberry, Indie Lou's, 277–78, *279*
Blue Ridge S'more Cupcakes,
266–67, *267*
Citrus Pound, 271–72, *273*
Lily's Poppy Stems, 263–65, *264*
mistakes and fixes, 25
Pineapple Upside-Down, *268,*
269–70
Sour Cream Vanilla Coffee, 102–3,
103
Candy
Classic Peanut Brittle, 248, *249*
Divinity "Kiss Me," *250,* 251
Carrots
My Go-To Pot Roast, 162, *163*
Cast-iron, seasoning, 21
Cereal Squares, Cinnamon Toasted,
58, *59*

Cheese
Baked Cheesy Garlic Grits, *78,* 79
Breakfast Hash Croissant
Sandwiches, 90, *91*
Cheddar Jalapeño Bagels, *216,*
217–18
Cheesy & Herby Dutch Oven Bread,
228–29, *229*
Chicken & Rice Casserole, *170,*
171
Crispy Creamy Mac 'n,' 172–73, *173*
Fry Me a River, Corny Fritters!, *120,*
121
Hahira Breakfast Cups, *82,* 83–84
Homemade Fresh, *48,* 49
James's Smash Burgers, *164,* 165
Loaded-Up Potato Skins, 122, *123*
Lover's Lasagna, 178–79, *180–81*
Mini Pizza Pies, *128,* 129–30
Sauced Up Shrimp Linguine, *174,*
175
Scalloped Potatoes & Ham
Casserole, 176, *177*
Sloppy James, 150, *151*
Spring Creek Boat Rolls, 126–27,
127
Sunrise Quiche, 85–86, *87*
Sweet Meets Spicy Supreme
Omelet, 80, *81*
Won't Make You Cry Onion Soup,
186, 187
You Butter Believe Butternut
Squash Casserole, *166,* 167
Cheesecake, Georgia Peach, *274,*
275–76
Cherries
Bushwacker, *236,* 237
Divinity "Kiss Me" Candy, *250,* 251
Fruity Roll'em Ups, 62, *63*
Pineapple Upside-Down Cake, *268,*
269–70
Chicken
Bake, BBQ Pineapple, 168, *169*
Bone Broth, 54, *55*
Butter-Roasted, *144,* 145
& Dumplings for My Dumplin', *190,*
191–92
Finger Lickin' Fried, 153–54, *155*
Gumbo, Damn Good, *196,* 197
Hot, Sweet & Sexy Wings, *124,* 125

Jazzy Jambalaya, *148,* 149
Lil's Chick Nuggs, *70,* 71
Pot Pie, Mama's, *140,* 141–42
& Rice Casserole, *170,* 171
Slow Cooker Brunswick Stew,
198–99, *200–201*
& Waffles, *92,* 93–94
Chicken Fried Steak with Gravy, *156,*
157
Chili, First Night, 193–94, *195*
Chocolate
Blue Ridge S'more Cupcakes,
266–67, *267*
Bushwacker, *236,* 237
Date Caramel Brownies, *254,* 255
Ganache, Whipped, Donuts, 109–10,
111
Hot, Hannah's Famous, *244,* 245
Lily's Poppy Stems, 263–65, *264*
Cinnamon
Apple Bread Pudding, 256, *257*
Apple Strudels, *106,* 107–8
Mama's Oatmeal Raisin Cookies,
252, *253*
Raisin Biscuits, 208–10, *211*
Rolls, Cranberry-Orange, with
Lemon Glaze, 104–5, *105*
Sour Cream Vanilla Coffee Cake,
102–3, *103*
Toasted Cereal Squares, 58, *59*
Citrus Pound Cake, 271–72, *273*
Cobblers
Midnight's Blackberry Dumplings,
258, 259
Peach Pecan, Sexy 'n' Spicy, 260–62,
261
Coffee Cake, Sour Cream Vanilla,
102–3, *103*
Coffee liqueur
Bushwacker, *236,* 237
Collard Greens, Bebop's Sweet
Bacon, 131
Cookies
Mama's Oatmeal Raisin, 252, *253*
Rookie's (Homemade Dog Treats),
75
Cooking
don't accept bland food, 19
equipment and tools, 21–22
following your taste buds, 18–19

cooking (*cont.*)
 making yourself happy, 18
 measurements as suggestions, 19
 mistakes and fixes, 25–26
 pantry ingredients, 22
 removing fear from, 18
Corn
 Aunt Teisha's Cowboy Caviar, 114,
  115
 First Night Chili, 193–94, *195*
 Fry Me a River, Corny Fritters!, *120,*
  121
 Slow Cooker Brunswick Stew,
  198–99, *200–201*
Cornbread, Southern Sweet, with
 Honey Butter, *212,* 213
Corn Dogs, Luke the Duke's, 72, *73*
Cornmeal
 Hoe Cakes with Cranberry Jam &
  Powdered Sugar, *100,* 101
 Luke the Duke's Corn Dogs, 72, *73*
 Southern Sweet Cornbread with
  Honey Butter, *212,* 213
Cowboy Caviar, Aunt Teisha's, 114, *115*
Crab Bisque, Nice & Creamy, 184, *185*
Cranberry
 Applesauce, Let's Get Saucy, *60,* 61
 Jam & Powdered Sugar, Hoe Cakes
  with, *100,* 101
 -Orange Cinnamon Rolls with
  Lemon Glaze, 104–5, *105*
 Punch, Fizzy, 242, *243*
Cream cheese
 Georgia Peach Cheesecake, *274,*
  275–76
 Indie Lou's Blueberry Cake, 277–78,
  279
 Mama's Chicken Pot Pie, *140,*
  141–42
 Smoked Salmon Dip, *116,* 117
 Spring Creek Boat Rolls, 126–27, *127*
Croissants, Flaky & Fluffy, 219–20, *221*
Croissant Sandwiches, Breakfast
 Hash, 90, *91*
Cucumbers
 Dill Me a Pickle Relish, 46, *47*
Cupcakes, Blue Ridge S'more, 266–67,
 267

D

Date Caramel Chocolate Brownies,
 254, 255
Desserts
 Apple Cinnamon Bread Pudding,
  256, *257*
 Blue Ridge S'more Cupcakes,
  266–67, *267*
 Chocolate Date Caramel Brownies,
  254, 255
 Citrus Pound Cake, 271–72, *273*
 Classic Peanut Brittle, 248, *249*
 Divinity "Kiss Me" Candy, *250,* 251
 Georgia Peach Cheesecake, *274,*
  275–76
 Indie Lou's Blueberry Cake, 277–78,
  279
 Lily's Poppy Stems, 263–65, *264*
 Mama's Oatmeal Raisin Cookies,
  252, *253*
 Midnight's Blackberry Dumplings,
  258, 259
 Pineapple Upside-Down Cake, *268,*
  269–70
 Sexy 'n' Spicy Peach Pecan Cobbler,
  260–62, *261*
Deviled Eggs, Mama's Classic Fried,
 118, *119*
Dill
 Dill Me a Pickle Relish, 46, *47*
 Smoked Salmon Dip, *116,* 117
Dips
 Aunt Teisha's Cowboy Caviar, 114, *115*
 Smoked Salmon, *116,* 117
Divinity "Kiss Me" Candy, *250,* 251
Dog Treats, Homemade (Rookie's
 Cookies), 75
Donuts, Whipped Chocolate
 Ganache, 109–10, *111*
Drinks
 Bushwacker, *236,* 237
 Fizzy Cranberry Punch, 242, *243*
 Hannah's Famous Hot Chocolate,
  244, 245
 Homebrewed Blueberry Wine,
  232–33, *233*
 Strawberry Sip 'n' Spritz, 234, *235*
 Sweetie's Sweet Iced Tea, 238, *239*
 Twang, Tang & Tart Lemonade,
  240, 241
Dumplings
 Blackberry, Midnight's, *258,* 259
 Chicken &, for My Dumplin', *190,*
  191–92

E

Eggs
 Breakfast Hash Croissant
  Sandwiches, 90, *91*
 Fried Deviled, Mama's Classic, 118,
  119
 Hahira Breakfast Cups, *82,* 83–84
 Sweet Meets Spicy Supreme
  Omelet, 80, *81*
Extract, Vanilla, 33

F

Fish
 Smoked Salmon Dip, *116,* 117
 Tacos, Good Ole, 146
Five-second rule, 26
Flavored Mayo, 42
French Toast Casserole, Soufflé, *96,*
 97
Fritters!, Corny, Fry Me a River, *120,*
 121
Fruit. *See* Berry(ies); *specific fruits*
Fruity Roll'em Ups, 62, *63*

G

Ganache, Whipped Chocolate,
 Donuts, 109–10, *111*
Garlic
 Butter-Roasted Chicken, *144,* 145
 Cheesy & Herby Dutch Oven Bread,
  228–29, *229*
 Flavored Mayo, 42
 Grits, Baked Cheesy, *78,* 79
Georgia Peach Cheesecake, *274,*
 275–76
Gin
 Strawberry Sip 'n' Spritz, 234, *235*
Graham crackers
 Blue Ridge S'more Cupcakes,
  266–67, *267*

Georgia Peach Cheesecake, *274,* 275–76

Gravy
Chicken Fried Steak with, *156,* 157
Milk Sausage, & Classic Biscuits, 204–6, *207*
mistakes and fixes, 26

Green Beans, Smokin' Honey Bacon, 132, *133*

Greens. *See* Collard Greens; Spinach

Grits, Baked Cheesy Garlic, *78,* 79

Gumbo, Damn Good Chicken, *196,* 197

H

Hahira Breakfast Cups, *82,* 83–84

Ham
Hock Lima Bean Soup, Knock-Out, *182, 183*
Mini Pizza Pies, *128,* 129–30
& Scalloped Potatoes Casserole, 176, *177*

Herbs. *See also* Dill
Butter-Roasted Chicken, *144,* 145
Cheesy & Herby Dutch Oven Bread, 228–29, *229*
My Go-To Pot Roast, 162, *163*

Hoe Cakes with Cranberry Jam & Powdered Sugar, *100,* 101

Honey
The Absolute Best Sweet Potatoes, *134,* 135
Bacon Green Beans, Smokin', 132, *133*
Butter, Southern Sweet Cornbread with, *212,* 213

Hot Chocolate, Hannah's Famous, *244,* 245

Hot dogs. *See* Corn Dogs

I

Ice cream
Bushwacker, *236,* 237

Iced Tea, Sweetie's Sweet, 238, *239*

Ice Pops, Bluegurt, *64,* 65

Indie Lou's Blueberry Cake, 277–78, *279*

J

Jambalaya, Jazzy, *148,* 149

James's Smash Burgers, *164,* 165

K

Kids & pups
Bluegurt Ice Pops, *64,* 65
Buck's Poppin' Tarts, 66–67, *68–69*
Cinnamon Toasted Cereal Squares, 58, *59*
Fruity Roll'em Ups, 62, *63*
Let's Get Saucy Cranberry Applesauce, *60,* 61
Lil's Chick Nuggs, *70,* 71
Luke the Duke's Corn Dogs, 72, *73*
Rookie's Cookies (Homemade Dog Treats), 75

Kitchen staples
All-Purpose Seasoning, 38
Apple Cider Vinegar, *40,* 41
B & B Twofer Butter & Buttermilk, 34–35, *35*
Beef Bone Broth, 53, *55*
Chicken Bone Broth, 54, *55*
Dill Me a Pickle Relish, 46, *47*
Homemade Fresh Cheese, *48,* 49
Never Go Back to Store-Bought Mayonnaise, 42, *43*
Pasta Dough & Noodles, 50–52, *51*
Start Me Up Lazy Sourdough Starter, *36,* 37
Vanilla Extract, 33
Zesty Mustard, *44,* 45

L

Lasagna, Lover's, 178–79, *180–81*

Lemonade, Twang, Tang & Tart, *240,* 241

Lemons
Citrus Pound Cake, 271–72, *273*
Flavored Mayo, 42
Twang, Tang & Tart Lemonade, *240,* 241

Lil's Chick Nuggs, *70,* 71

Lily's Poppy Stems, 263–65, *264*

Lover's Lasagna, 178–79, *180–81*

Luke the Duke's Corn Dogs, 72, *73*

M

Mac 'n' Cheese, Crispy Creamy, 172–73, *173*

Main recipes
BBQ Pineapple Chicken Bake, 168, *169*
Butter-Roasted Chicken, *144,* 145
Chicken & Dumplings for My Dumplin', *190,* 191–92
Chicken Fried Steak with Gravy, *156,* 157
Chicken & Rice Casserole, *170,* 171
Cream of Mushroom Soup, 188, *189*
Crispy Creamy Mac 'n' Cheese, 172–73, *173*
Damn Good Chicken Gumbo, *196,* 197
Finger Lickin' Fried Chicken, 153–54, *155*
First Night Chili, 193–94, *195*
Good Ole Fish Tacos, 146
James's Smash Burgers, *164,* 165
Jazzy Jambalaya, *148,* 149
Knock-Out Ham Hock Lima Bean Soup, *182,* 183
Lover's Lasagna, 178–79, *180–81*
Mama's Chicken Pot Pie, *140,* 141–42
Mary's Meatloaf, 158, *159*
My Go-To Pot Roast, 162, *163*
Nice & Creamy Crab Bisque, 184, *185*
Sauced Up Shrimp Linguine, *174,* 175
Scalloped Potatoes & Ham Casserole, 176, *177*
Sloppy James, 150, *151*
Slow Cooker BBQ Ribs, *160,* 161
Slow Cooker Brunswick Stew, 198–99, *200–201*
Won't Make You Cry Onion Soup, *186,* 187
You Butter Believe Butternut Squash Casserole, *166,* 167

Mama's Chicken Pot Pie, *140,* 141–42

Mama's Classic Fried Deviled Eggs, 118, *119*

Mama's Oatmeal Raisin Cookies, 252, *253*

Mary's Meatloaf, 158, *159*

Mayonnaise
  Flavored, 42
  Never Go Back to Store-Bought, 42, *43*
Meat. *See also* Beef; Pork
  overcooked, remedy for, 25
  Spring Creek Boat Rolls, 126–27, *127*
  undercooked, remedy for, 26
Meatloaf, Mary's, 158, *159*
Midnight's Blackberry Dumplings, *258,* 259
Milk Sausage Gravy & Classic Biscuits, 204–6, *207*
Mini Pizza Pies, *128,* 129–30
Mushroom(s)
  Soup, Cream of, 188, *189*
  Sunrise Quiche, 85–86, *87*
Mustard, Zesty, *44,* 45

N

Never Go Back to Store-Bought Mayonnaise, 42, *43*
Noodles & Pasta Dough, 50–52, *51*
Nuts. *See also* Pecan(s)
  Classic Peanut Brittle, 248, *249*

O

Oatmeal Raisin Cookies, Mama's, 252, *253*
Omelet, Supreme, Sweet Meets Spicy, 80, *81*
Onion Soup, Won't Make You Cry, *186,* 187
Orange(s)
  Citrus Pound Cake, 271–72, *273*
  -Cranberry Cinnamon Rolls with Lemon Glaze, 104–5, *105*

P

Pasta
  Crispy Creamy Mac 'n' Cheese, 172–73, *173*
  Dough & Noodles, 50–52, *51*
  Lover's Lasagna, 178–79, *180–81*
  Sauced Up Shrimp Linguine, *174,* 175

Peach
  Georgia, Cheesecake, *274,* 275–76
  Pecan Cobbler, Sexy 'n' Spicy, 260–62, *261*
Peanut Brittle, Classic, 248, *249*
Peanut butter
  Rookie's Cookies (Homemade Dog Treats), 75
Pecan(s)
  The Absolute Best Sweet Potatoes, *134,* 135
  Apple Cinnamon Bread Pudding, 256, *257*
  Divinity "Kiss Me" Candy, *250,* 251
  Pecan Cobbler, Sexy 'n' Spicy, 260–62, *261*
Pepperoni
  Mini Pizza Pies, *128,* 129–30
Peppers
  Aunt Teisha's Cowboy Caviar, 114, *115*
  Cheddar Jalapeño Bagels, *216,* 217–18
  Sloppy James, 150, *151*
  Sunrise Quiche, 85–86, *87*
Pickle Relish, Dill Me a, 46, *47*
Pie crust mistakes and fixes, 26
Pineapple
  Chicken Bake, BBQ, 168, *169*
  Upside-Down Cake, *268,* 269–70
Pizza Pies, Mini, *128,* 129–30
Poppin' Tarts, Buck's, 66–67, *68–69*
Poppy Stems, Lily's, 263–65, *264*
Pork. *See also* Bacon; Ham; Sausage
  Mary's Meatloaf, 158, *159*
  Slow Cooker BBQ Ribs, 160, 161
Potato(es)
  Breakfast Hash Croissant Sandwiches, 90, *91*
  Hahira Breakfast Cups, *82,* 83–84
  Mashed, Ultimate, 136, *137*
  My Go-To Pot Roast, 162, *163*
  Scalloped, & Ham Casserole, 176, *177*
  Skins, Loaded-Up, 122, *123*
  Slow Cooker Brunswick Stew, 198–99, *200–201*
  Sunrise Quiche, 85–86, *87*
  Sweet, The Absolute Best, *134,* 135
Pot Pie, Mama's Chicken, *140,* 141–42

Pound Cake, Citrus, 271–72, *273*
Pudding, Apple Cinnamon Bread, 256, *257*
Punch, Fizzy Cranberry, 242, *243*

Q

Quiche, Sunrise, 85–86, *87*

R

Raisin
  Cinnamon Biscuits, 208–10, *211*
  Oatmeal Cookies, Mama's, 252, *253*
Raspberries
  Fruity Roll'em Ups, 62, *63*
Relish, Dill Me a Pickle, 46, *47*
Rice
  & Chicken Casserole, *170,* 171
  Jazzy Jambalaya, *148,* 149
Roll'em Ups, Fruity, 62, *63*
Rolls
  Butter My, 214–15, *215*
  Cranberry-Orange Cinnamon, with Lemon Glaze, 104–5, *105*
  Spring Creek Boat, 126–27, *127*
Rookie's Cookies (Homemade Dog Treats), 75
Rum
  Bushwacker, *236,* 237

S

Salmon, Smoked, Dip, *116,* 117
Salt, 25
Sandwich Bread, Homemade, 222–23, *223*
Sandwiches
  Breakfast Hash Croissant, 90, *91*
  Sloppy James, 150, *151*
Sausage
  Breakfast Hash Croissant Sandwiches, 90, *91*
  Damn Good Chicken Gumbo, *196,* 197
  Hahira Breakfast Cups, *82,* 83–84
  Jazzy Jambalaya, *148,* 149
  Milk Gravy & Classic Biscuits, 204–6, *207*
  Mini Pizza Pies, *128,* 129–30
  Sunrise Quiche, 85–86, *87*

Sweet Meets Spicy Supreme Omelet, 80, *81*
Scalloped Potatoes & Ham Casserole, 176, *177*
Scones, Mixed Berry, 98, *99*
Seafood
    Damn Good Chicken Gumbo, *196,* 197
    Good Ole Fish Tacos, 146
    Nice & Creamy Crab Bisque, 184, *185*
    Sauced Up Shrimp Linguine, *174,* 175
    Smoked Salmon Dip, *116,* 117
Seasoning, All-Purpose, 38
Shrimp
    Damn Good Chicken Gumbo, *196,* 197
    Linguine, Sauced Up, *174,* 175
Sloppy James, 150, *151*
Slow Cooker BBQ Ribs, *160,* 161
Smash Burgers, James's, *164,* 165
Smoked Salmon Dip, *116,* 117
S'more Cupcakes, Blue Ridge, 266–67, *267*
Snacks, apps & sides
    The Absolute Best Sweet Potatoes, *134,* 135
    Aunt Teisha's Cowboy Caviar, 114, *115*
    Bebop's Sweet Bacon Collard Greens, 131
    Fry Me a River, Corny Fritters!, *120,* 121
    Hot, Sweet & Sexy Wings, *124,* 125
    Loaded-Up Potato Skins, 122, *123*
    Mama's Classic Fried Deviled Eggs, 118, *119*
    Mini Pizza Pies, *128,* 129–30
    Smoked Salmon Dip, *116,* 117
    Smokin' Honey Bacon Green Beans, 132, *133*
    Spring Creek Boat Rolls, 126–27, *127*
    Ultimate Mashed Potatoes, 136, *137*
Soufflé French Toast Casserole, *96,* 97
Soups
    burnt bits on bottom, fix for, 25
    Cream of Mushroom, 188, *189*

Ham Hock Lima Bean, Knock-Out, *182,* 183
    Nice & Creamy Crab Bisque, 184, *185*
    Onion, Won't Make You Cry, *186,* 187
    Sour Cream Vanilla Coffee Cake, 102–3, *103*
    Sourdough Loaf, My Favorite, 224–25, *226–27*
    Sourdough Starter, Start Me Up Lazy, *36,* 37
Spiciness, 25
Spinach
    Spring Creek Boat Rolls, 126–27, *127*
    Sweet Meets Spicy Supreme Omelet, 80, *81*
Spring Creek Boat Rolls, 126–27, *127*
Squash, Butternut, Casserole, You Butter Believe, *166,* 167
Stews
    Brunswick, Slow Cooker, 198–99, *200–201*
    burnt bits on bottom, fix for, 25
    Chicken & Dumplings for My Dumplin', *190,* 191–92
    Damn Good Chicken Gumbo, *196,* 197
Strawberry(ies)
    Buck's Poppin' Tarts, 66–67, *68–69*
    Fruity Roll'em Ups, 62, *63*
    Sip 'n' Spritz, 234, *235*
    Strudels, Apple Cinnamon, *106,* 107–8
Sweet Potatoes
    The Absolute Best, *134,* 135
    Sunrise Quiche, 85–86, *87*

T
Tacos, Good Ole Fish, 146
Tea, Sweetie's Sweet Iced, 238, *239*
Tomatoes
    Aunt Teisha's Cowboy Caviar, 114, *115*
    First Night Chili, 193–94, *195*
    Jazzy Jambalaya, *148,* 149
    Lover's Lasagna, 178–79, *180–81*

Mini Pizza Pies, *128,* 129–30
Sauced Up Shrimp Linguine, *174,* 175

U
Upside-Down Cake, Pineapple, *268,* 269–70

V
Vanilla
    Extract, 33
    Sour Cream Coffee Cake, 102–3, *103*
Vegetables. *See also specific vegetables*
    Mama's Chicken Pot Pie, *140,* 141–42
Vinegar, Apple Cider, *40,* 41

W
Waffles & Chicken, *92,* 93–94
Whipped Chocolate Ganache Donuts, 109–10, *111*
White chocolate
    Lily's Poppy Stems, 263–65, *264*
Wine
    Blueberry, Homemade, 232–33, *233*
    Strawberry Sip 'n' Spritz, 234, *235*

Y
Yogurt
    Bluegurt Ice Pops, *64,* 65

CLARKSON POTTER/PUBLISHERS
An imprint of the Crown Publishing Group
A division of Penguin Random House LLC
1745 Broadway
New York, NY 10019
clarksonpotter.com
penguinrandomhouse.com

Penguin Random House collects and processes your
personal information. See our Notice at Collection and
Privacy Policy at prh.com/notice.

Additional lifestyle photos © LilyLouTay, LLC on pages 1, 8,
11, 12, 20, 24, 27, 74, 84, 88, 95, 143, and 288

Library of Congress Cataloging-in-Publication Data
Names: Taylor, Hannah (Social media influencer), author.
  Title: Measure with your heart / Hannah Taylor;
  photographs by Rinne Allen. Identifiers: LCCN 2024047283
  (print) | LCCN 2024047284 (ebook) | ISBN 9780593800645
  (hardcover) | ISBN 9780593800652 (ebook) Subjects:
  LCSH: Cooking, American—Southern style. | LCGFT:
  Cookbooks.
Classification: LCC TX715.2.S68 T3896 2025 (print) | LCC
  TX715.2.S68 (ebook) | DDC 641.5975—dc23/eng/20241205
LC record available at https://lccn.loc.gov/2024047283
LC ebook record available at https://lccn.loc.gov/2024047284

ISBN 978-0-593-80064-5
Signed edition ISBN 979-8-217-03521-2
Ebook ISBN 978-0-593-80065-2

Editor: Jennifer Sit
Editorial assistant: Elaine Hennig
Designer: Jan Derevjanik
Design manager: Mia Johnson
Art director: Stephanie Huntwork
Production editor: Natalie Blachere
Production: Jessica Heim
Prepress color manager: Kelli Tokos
Production designer: Christina Self
Compositors: Merri Ann Morrell and Nick Patton
Food stylist: Tami Hardeman
Food stylist assistant: Abby Gaskins
Baker: Jo Nicol
Prop stylist: Rinne Allen
Recipe tester: Eliza Winograd
Copy editor: Carole Berglie
Proofreaders: Rachel Holzman, Patricia Dailey,
  Mike Richards, and Miriam Taveras
Indexer: Elizabeth Parson
Publicists: Kate Tyler and Jana Branson
Marketer: Stephanie Davis

Manufactured in China

10 9 8 7 6 5 4 3 2 1

First Edition

The authorized representative in the EU for product
safety and compliance is Penguin Random House Ireland,
Morrison Chambers, 32 Nassau Street, Dublin D02 YH68,
Ireland, https://eu-contact.penguin.ie.